D1316563

Capitalism Vs. Capitalism

Capitalism Vs. Capitalism

How America's Obsession
with Individual Achievement
and Short-term Profit
Has Led It to the Brink of Collapse

MICHEL ALBERT

Introduction by
Felix G. Rohatyn

Translated by
Paul Haviland

Four Wall Eight Windows
New York

© Introduction 1993 Michel Albert
© Foreword 1993 Felix G. Rohatyn
A revised edition of the book originally published as
Capitalism Against Capitalism , © 1993, by
Whurr Publishers Ltd., London, England.

Published in the United States by:
Four Walls Eight Windows
39 West 14th Street
New York, N.Y., 10011

First printing October 1993.

Library of Congress Cataloging-in-Publication Data:
Albert, Michel.
[Capitalisme contre capitalisme. English]
Capitalism versus Capitalism: how America's obsession with
individual achievement and short-term profit has led it to the
brink of collapse/ by Michel Albert; foreword by Felix G.
Rohatyn; translated by Paul Haviland.
p.   cm.
(cloth) ISBN: 1-56858-004-5
(paper) ISBN: 1-56858-005-3
1. Economic history—1990- 2. Capitalism. 3. United
States—Economic Conditions. I. Title. II. Title: Capitalism
vs. capitalism.
HC59.15.A4313   1993
          330.973—dc20
93-4542
                                          CIP

Printed in the United States

Contents

Preface
to the American Edition

This book was completed in August 1991. Strong as my convictions were, I would, at that point, never have dared predict that the ideas I suggested with some temerity would be more current—and thus easier to accept—two years later. It is unusual to be so well served by the always unpredictable course of events. Without indulging in some misguided self-satisfaction, I will say only that in this day and age, an economic analysis that can thus survive the vagaries of current events probably deserves at least to be debated. That was my primary concern in writing this book.

In 1992, the debate between "the two capitalisms" which this book modestly sought to launch had not yet really begun in political circles or in the media. At that point, the only capitalist model known, identified, and taught around the world was the Anglo-Saxon model, modified by what was called "the conservative revolution," of Margaret Thatcher in Great Britain and Ronald Reagan in the United States. Moreover, the U.S. had just given a dazzling demonstration of its superiority during the Gulf War, and the world business community's pleased astonishment still lingered.

On a cultural level, the model I then called "neo-American" was based on values which seemed to be gaining ground everywhere: the individualism which held that each person should take responsibility for him or herself, and the critique of the "welfare cycle" blamed by Republicans for encouraging laziness, irresponsibility, unemployment, etc. In 1991, moreover, though Communism appeared to have been laid to rest once and for all (especially after the failed military coup in Moscow that August), social democracy was still holding on. In Great Britain, for example, a Labour victory was predicted for the spring 1992 elections, and the sober *Financial Times* itself had endorsed Labour. In Europe, social democracy could still pass as a credible alternative to capitalism. Besides that, certain capitalists continued to feel they still had enemies; they were not eager to open the door to a kind of "family quarrel." By postulating that, on the contrary, capitalism now has no competition—except within itself—I ran the risk of being misunderstood, or of shocking my readers. Particularly in the Anglo-Saxon countries.

The fate of the various editions of this book that have appeared around the world clearly reflect these problems of immediate comprehension. In France, the book irritated the new school of liberal—or ultra-liberal—universities whose influence has grown over the last dozen years. However, the business schools of continental Europe took an interest in this relatively new description of the Rhine model and in the expression "Rhine model" itself which they now use regularly and teach. In Japan, where the first translation of the book appeared, *Capitalism Vs. Capitalism* rapidly became a bestseller. In 1993, I had the opportunity to meet with 140 of the most prominent Japanese leaders who attended a lecture I was invited to give by the Keidanren, the Japanese entrepreneurs' association. In the Latin countries (Italy, Portugal, Spain, and Latin America) the work was quite well received. This was also the case in the countries of Eastern Europe which, though for a time overwhelmed and fascinated by the "American model," rapidly became interested in the Rhine model when their transformation to a market economy posed much more serious difficulties than had been foreseen. In the Anglo-Saxon countries, the book's publication was slower and more difficult. Only a handful of intellectuals and businessmen and -women were interested in it from the beginning.

Where do we stand two years later? One might say that most of the political and economic givens have radically changed. Social democracy was the first victim of the death of communism, and no one thinks of it as competition for capitalism any longer. Almost everywhere in Europe, conservatives are in power. The left has been defeated in France and came very close to being defeated in Spain. Capitalism's "solitary"—and dangerous—monopoly, which my analysis took as its point of departure, is now spectacularly confirmed.

In the United States, the way to Bill Clinton's success was paved by a lengthy critical reflection on the neo-American model of the Reagan years, a reflection which is largely in agreement with certain of my own remarks concerning, for example, the dramatic social drawbacks of a "dual society," the economic disadvantages linked to an excess of deregulation, the administrative difficulties within corporations arising from the exaggerated pre-eminence of ever more unstable and demanding shareholders. In a word, the neo-American model I criticized was itself displaying its own limits, and certain economists within the United States were quick to become alarmed.

In the fall of 1992, Edward Luttwak, former adviser to Reagan, published a provocative article on the question "When Will the United States Become a Third World Country?" His answer: between 2020 and 2035. Around the same time, *The Economist* of London denounced—as I myself had—the metastasizing, within the United States, of a costly, paralyzing, and parasitic economy, particularly insofar as the sway of lawyers over the business world is concerned.

Moreover, in my book I cite the work of Lester Thurow, dean of M.I.T.'s Sloan School of Management. His book, *Head to Head*, published in 1992, is particularly concerned with the Japanese model, but nevertheless explodes certain of the American model's taboos and incongruities. For example, he noted that in 1990 an American C.E.O. earned 119 times the average worker's salary, while the average Japanese C.E.O., whose performance is often superior, earned only 18 times the worker's salary. In his criticism of this disparity, Lester Thurow deliberately went against the Reagan-Thatcher philosophy.

Today, Lester Thurow is one of President Clinton's advisers. Clinton has chosen to surround himself with people who are particularly attuned to this kind of critique, such as Laura Tyson, head of the Council of Economic Advisors, and the President's old friend Robert Reich, the Secretary of Labor. In his book *Work of Nations*, Reich wrote that the objective of Washington's industrial politics should be to augment the value that American workers can add to the American economy and not to augment the profitability of the stock of rudderless American companies.

Naturally, I feel quite close to this kind of observation. Ronald Reagan and his advisers reasoned, it seems to me, in the instinctive manner of consumer society: everything and right now. Bill Clinton appears to be more concerned about the long term, more convinced of the necessity of preparing for the future. He also seems prepared to propose bold measures as unpopular as that of raising the price of gasoline in a country where the electorate is viscerally attached to its "right" to waste energy. It is clearly on the basis of an analogous philosophy that he has entrusted Hillary Rodham Clinton with the task of revising the American health care system in an attempt to make it beneficial to all citizens and no longer to only a privileged minority.

In this respect, two things particularly struck me. During the 1988 campaign, George Bush's "miracle invention" for rising in the polls was televised to the entire world: "Read my lips: No new taxes." It was the antithesis of Kennedy's message. In 1992, Bill Clinton conducted his campaign by indicating he would follow the opposite course of action and announcing that he would increase taxes on the wealthiest citizens and on foreign companies doing business in America.

Moreover, during his campaign, Bill Clinton spoke out on behalf of the public school system, and his daughter Chelsea attended public school in Little Rock. Her parents tried to send her to public school in Washington, but unfortunately they found no suitable school in the federal capital and had to place Chelsea in a private day school costing $10,000 a year. It would be difficult to make the President agree that Washington is "more advanced" than Arkansas.

These are, of course, only anecdotes. Nevertheless, since 1992 it would seem that the pendulum is swinging away from the American model. For a dozen years, the United States was involved in a veritable love affair with the market. The private sector was the angel; the public sector became something like the devil. Now the balance has shifted the other way, and deregulation—the market given over to it itself—is unhesitatingly blamed for the savings and loan crisis and the airline mess. In the same way, a medical profession more and more thirsty for profit is held partially responsible for the huge growth in health care costs.

It is also clear that the role of shareholders has again been opened to debate. The American press is continually evoking the new "corporate governance" and claiming that pension funds, given their great size, are certain to become stable shareholders—which is viewed positively.

But we must, nevertheless, arm ourselves in advance against an excess of optimism. If the Reagan model I criticize in this book is receding in the United States, particularly since Clinton's election, I would still hesitate to conclude from this that the United States is purely and simply rallying around the Rhine model. Bill Clinton, for example, was forced to relinquish the gist of his proposal to give free vaccines against a number of diseases to all American children. The fundamental philosophy of the United States has not changed: the principle that health care costs are the individual's responsibility and that the government should intervene as little as possible remains firmly in place.

I would like to add another word on the subject of the country I took, in this book, as a "counter model:" Germany. Certainly, I made it clear in 1991 that this model was not ideal and was undergoing serious difficulties. Those difficulties, as everyone knows, have grown worse, primarily because the Germans have not wanted to pay for the enormous cost of reunification out of their pockets. Refusing to agree to that effort, they forced the Bundesbank to raise its interest rates to the detriment of neighboring countries. And even that wasn't enough... In short, as former Chancellor Helmut Schmidt said: "Since reunification, Germany has been copying the bad example of the Reagan economy and its budgetary deficit." The German unions have compounded this by their irresponsibility in demanding and receiving reckless increases in salary at a time when sacrifices were clearly necessary.

Though delighted to see certain of the analyses in this book corroborated by recent events, I am nevertheless only moderately optimistic regarding capitalism's capacity to reform itself, to change, to become better, now that it no longer has any serious rival. In Europe, for example, an "every man for himself" attitude is developing; Europeans are losing sight of the fundamental harmony that exists between social solidarity and economic efficiency. This attitude appears to be a kind of epidemic which is spreading once again among the developed countries across the globe; it can even be found at the heart of the objections that have been made to the idea of European unity since 1992.

What should Europe be? Just a large market, or a political federation as well? This debate goes to the very heart of the dilemma of *Capitalism Vs. Capitalism*. It also encloses, in large measure, Reagan's and Clinton's two very different visions, and it lies within the scope of the new questioning of themselves that the Japanese call the quest for a "symbiosis."

MICHEL ALBERT
Paris, July 1993
Translated by Esther Allen

Foreword

Michel Albert's thesis in his book *Capitalism Vs. Capitalism* is absolutely correct. The ideological arguments about how best to organize an advanced industrial democracy at the end of the Twentieth Century will be about what type of capitalism is appropriate. The bankruptcy of communism, as a viable economic system, will also eliminate socialism as a viable alternative. This is partly due to a general rejection of government control over large parts of the economy and partly due to the fact that communist countries, over the last decades, always referred to themselves as "Socialist." Even though socialism, as practiced in Western Europe, was probably the strongest enemy of communism, the apparent relationships between socialism and communism, as economic systems, will mark the end of socialism as a serious alternative to capitalism.

This, then, leaves the question, as Michel Albert puts it: "What kind of capitalism?" The choices really consist of the free-market capitalism as practiced at this time in the U.S. and the U.K. (i.e., politically conservative), and the capitalism of Northern Europe which is essentially social-democratic in its true political and economic sense. A third model could be the Japanese model, which I will come back to, but which may be so uniquely applicable that it cannot be used as an option for Western countries.

The arguments about the most effective forms of capitalism are much more than interesting theological arguments. They are completely relevant to the present efforts of the Eastern European as well as the former Soviet Republics to make the transition from communist systems to market systems and democracy.

The main differences between the present Anglo-Saxon market systems and what I will refer to as the Social-Democratic systems are in two main categories: 1) The role of government in the economy, and 2) the social safety net.

In the U.S., there has been an ongoing and deep-seated political and philosophical struggle on these issues, with cycles going from the Jazz Age of the 1920s, to the New Deal of the Depression, to the Great Society of L.B.J. and finally to Reaganism and the Casino Society of the 1980s. The objectives of our system are individual freedom, equality of opportunity and "The pursuit of happiness." That translates itself in the United States into freedom, fairness, and wealth.

For the democracies of the West, the last ten years of this century will witness the continuous trade-offs and strains between freedom, fairness and wealth. In the United States, conservatives have consistently focussed on freedom and wealth; liberals, on freedom and fairness. We have yet to build a political bridge, however, that gives all three their due weight; unless we are able to do so, we will face greater and greater difficulties.

Freedom is not an absolute; it must be tempered by justice. In a world of finite resources, this requires political leadership of a high order, more interested in leading than in lasting. Only rarely will correct long-term decisions turn out to be popular.

Fairness and wealth have to go hand in hand. The "Zero-Sum Society" can be neither free nor fair. Without the capacity to create wealth, it is impossible to deal with the issue of fairness. The disparities in our society, between classes and races, between sunbelt and frostbelt, are deep and getting deeper. Only with sustained economic growth, a strong free market and an active government willing to intervene when needed, will these disparities be reduced.

Fairness is also not an absolute. But even the most hardened conservatives must find conditions in the inner-city ghettos a blight on our society, and an indictment of the status quo. At the same time, realistic liberals have to recognize that government has not solved, and cannot solve, all the problems of race and poverty. Only a growing private-sector economy can do that, provided government is not afraid of directing some of that growth. This obviously is not what is happening today.

For the U.S., the 1980s marked the end of the post-World War II cycles of economic growth. The growth of the 1980s was artificial. It was driven by government and private borrowing on a fantastic scale in order to finance private consumption and military-spending. It was not invested wisely and the results are now apparent. Economic growth has stopped; the demands for social services (i.e., health care, education, drug prevention, homelessness, unemployment and housing benefits, etc.) are growing; the need for government action to stimulate the economy is evident, but the government has little room left for effective action.

The resulting social tensions and political pressures are the direct result of the inadequate social safety net in our system (as compared to Social-Democratic systems) as well as the difficulty for any democratic form of government to allocate sacrifice. A growing economy allows government to allocate benefits to everyone; the fairness of the allocation is secondary to the benefit itself. It is impossible, politically, to explain that sacrifice, in any amount, is allocated fairly.

This problem is even greater with our system of government than with a parliamentary system. We have a federal system; a divided government (executive and legislative); significant division of powers and responsibilities between the federal government and the states and the cities (many of which have divided government themselves). The result is political paralysis for practically any program which requires one constituency to give up a benefit to subsidize another. This is not the case with a parliamentary system, where the party in power commands a majority to implement a program.

One must also remember that the excesses of the 1980s followed the great expansion of the New Deal programs by L.B.J.'s "Great Society," which significantly expanded on the safety net concepts of the New Deal and created a welfare state.

The New Deal and the Great Society were the great liberal economic watersheds of this century. They were fundamentally different in their aims and results. The New Deal sought to put people to work and curb the excesses of the 1920s; it also saved the capitalistic system in America. The R.F.C., C.C.C., R.E.A., and T.V.A. all aimed at stimulating production and employment. They succeeded. The S.E.G., Social Security, the Federal Reserve Board, the F.D.I.C., antitrust laws aimed at regulating excesses and protecting the public, succeeded. The Great Society, on the other hand, aimed at cradle-to-grave security, income transfer, elimination of poverty, pervasive regulation; to the extent it failed, it did so largely because America could not afford it. By attempting to reduce the element of risk it succeeded in eliminating many of the incentives to create wealth.

The conservatism of Reagan and Thatcher was the reaction to those trends. Reagan reduced the social safety net by lower tax rates and by asking state and local governments to assume responsibilities for national problems. Thatcher reduced government's involvement in the economy by starting a movement to privatize government-owned industries which is now sweeping the Third World and influencing Eastern Europe and the Soviet Union.

In the Anglo-Saxon democracies, especially in the U.S., we have chosen a social and economic policy of low taxes, greater risk and limited security for those in need. That policy was debated strenuously in the 1992 Presidential election as a result of the social and racial tension generated by a slow-growth economy.

In the Social Democracies of Northern Europe, however, the issues of immigration, taxation and the allocation of benefits are also being debated. In Germany, France, Holland, and Italy ugly racial and social tensions are apparent and the role of the Government in the economy is put in question.

The answers to this debate are important not only for the Western democracies, but for the Eastern European countries, and the new republics of the former Soviet Union. These new democracies are all looking for models to provide a bridge from communism to democracy and a market system.

The Japanese model is a unique system of one-party government with immense business involvement, a disciplined population willing to forego present benefits in exchange for national economic power, as well as the ability to be protected geographically from the tensions and problems connected with immigration. It cannot serve as a model for the new democracies.

For Eastern Europe as well as for the more European Russian republics, a system combining the Social Democracy of Northern Europe with the present French model (significant government ownership within a competitive pricing and capital system) would seem to be the most logical approach. The big leap to an immediate free market seems to me fraught with political danger as the present evolution of Poland would seem to indicate.

For the Western democracies, the debate will continue. The voters of Western democracies seem more and more willing to experiment ideologically in order to find satisfactory economic performance. The danger in such experimentation is their possible willingness to turn to extremes if they believe all else has failed. If the current economic program fails, with its underlying conservative and nearly radical social philosophy, there will be only two alternatives. Either a middle-of-the-road philosophy, halfway between deficit-spending liberalism of the 1960s and the current conservatism, will evolve and prevail, or we may try and extreme. Whether the extreme is right-wing or left-wing is irrelevant; hemlock is as lethal served from the left as from the right.

As a nation, we clearly have the resources—financial, technical, and intellectual—to solve our problems. Whether we have the political will and the commitment is another question. Questions of fairness and wealth must be answered by today's politicians. The answers will determine whether, in a world of limited resources, Western democracy can make the trade-offs, and simultaneously maintain freedom.

There are no permanent solutions to ever-changing problems. We do not need to plan for one hundred years, but we need a government which is pragmatic and flexible, willing to intervene when necessary.

It is doubtful that today's conservatism will provide all the answers. Liberalism's hour may come again. To meet the test, however, liberalism will have to come out of the political boudoir and get back to the inner-city streets, to the factory floor and to the defense of our vital interests. Because that is where reality lies.

FELIX G. ROHATYN
New York, July 1993

Chapter 1
Introduction

As the year 2000 approaches, the great ideological debate of this turbulent century has been settled once and for all. For the first time in history, capitalism has triumphed on every front.

The first battle in capitalism's stunning global victory had to be won at home, in Britain and America. Margaret Thatcher and Ronald Reagan joined forces to lead the first 'conservative revolution' against the too-powerful state and its poisonous interventionism. With their rallying cry 'Less government is better government', the shopkeeper's daughter and the Hollywood actor unleashed their most powerful weapon: tax cuts for the rich. If, they reasoned, the wealthy capitalists paid fewer taxes, the economy could grow faster and everyone would benefit. In 1981, when Reagan entered the White House, the federal income tax on top earnings was 75 per cent; by the time of his departure in 1989, the top rate had fallen to 33 per cent. In the UK, the change was even more dramatic: under Labour governments, the highest tax band (on capital earnings) had reached 98 per cent; Mrs. Thatcher brought it down to 40 per cent. This fiscal reform was to prove wildly popular and soon spread to dozens of other countries, changing the very nature of the relationship between the state and its citizens. Two centuries of a steadily increasing tax burden, notably in the industrialized nations, were reversed almost at a stroke: today's watchword is tax relief – and not just in the developed world. More than just a reform, this has been a genuine revolution.

Capitalism's second great victory is even more impressive, given that it was more or less delivered on a plate after half a century of all-out, no-holds-barred confrontation. In the 100 years of rivalry between communism and capitalism, the last 50 have seen the bitter contest between the USA and the USSR dominate every aspect of international relations. But on 9 November 1989, everything changed. The young East Germans who dared to breach the Berlin Wall were to herald the revolt of 300 million disillusioned souls trapped within the communist bloc and starved of freedom – but starved, too, of consumer goods and supermarkets. In other words, hungry for capitalism.

A third battle, lasting only 100 hours, recently took place on the southern borders of Iraq. In narrow terms it was a victory of American might in the service of international law, backed by 28 nations (including eight Muslim countries) and even gaining support in the UN from the Soviet Union and communist China. But it was also, in the broader sense, a victory for capitalism. The Gulf War dashed the messianic dreams of whole populations long cheated of economic opportunity by oppressive dictatorial regimes. It is a safe bet that, sooner or later, the masses who fell prey to Saddam Hussein's brutal masquerade will choose the same path as those who have been swindled by communism: the capitalist road.

The triumph of capitalism sheds an entirely new light on the economic history of the world, while at the same time profoundly altering its economic geography. Now that the 'Siberian night' of communism is over, we can at last see more clearly into the reality of our past, which shows up as two starkly contrasting movements:

1. Before capitalism, the nations and civilizations of our planet, including the mightiest and most brilliant, resembled what we call today the Third World or the developing countries. Into this world men and women were born 'naturally' and lived out their biological lives in less than 30 years, on average; death came equally naturally, in cycles of famine and disease, driven by malnutrition and the oppressive power of the sacred – another name for the authorities. It is worth reminding ourselves that France, which we are accustomed to visualize as a horn of agricultural plenty, was regularly stricken with genuine famines well into the last century. The pre-capitalist world was one of chronic want, of divinely ordained penury and deprivation. In economic terms, it is the prehistoric age.

2. Three centuries of capitalism constitute the age of humankind's first credible onslaught, and real success, against the unholy trinity of poverty, famine and sacrificial slaughter. Taking root in the Western

nations of Judaeo-Christian tradition, the capitalist revolution has, within the last 100 years, spread to the Far East, where it has been further refined and speeded up. Yet, wherever it is to be found, the same three principles form the cornerstones of the new social and institutional system: namely, capitalism – which I define for brevity's sake as the free determination of prices in the market place and the private ownership of the means of production; human rights – of which the first must surely be freedom of conscience; and finally, the continuous development of the democratic process and the separation of powers.

The human economic prehistory of permanent want lasted thousands of years. The history of development has only just begun, and the map of its dominions is only now becoming clear. The triple victory of capitalism is a lens through which we can finally see two distinct regions being formed.

Capitalism's recent successes mean that one particular sword of Damocles no longer hangs over our heads: the oil supply – the oxygen of our economic life – has been physically secured for some time to come. The question is no longer *whether* there will be enough oil but rather how much it will cost, in both financial and ecological terms; nor will the race to find new oil reserves exercise our minds quite so much as the search for alternative energy sources and better tools for fighting pollution.

On a more fundamental level, the new economic geography means that the expression 'Third World' suddenly seems wholly illogical. While the Cold War raged and communism fought capitalism on the common battlefield of economic performance, it was still possible to retain (and pretend to believe in) the notion of a tripartite division of the world into capitalist, communist and developing or Third World countries. It was not so long ago that Khrushchev could claim, in his famous speech at the United Nations, that the Soviet economy would have caught up with America by the year 2000… and be taken seriously, not least by thousands of astonishingly blinkered 'experts' in Western universities. Now that the scales have fallen from everyone's eyes, it is plain that the communist economies should actually have been classified under the same heading as the developing countries. In other words, the world is divided into two, not three parts: on the one hand, the developed (and the rapidly developing) countries, all of which are capitalist; on the other, the developing, i.e. poor, countries. 'Third World' no longer makes sense; the term is henceforth a solecism.

Capitalism is, of course, not a magic wand that will transform any economy overnight into a modern industrial state; the state itself must be relatively efficient, free of corruption and able to enforce the law. Nor can it banish poverty; in some of the most advanced capitalist economies, the number of poor is actually on the rise – especially in the USA. (It is curious to note that one of America's health problems, obesity, is an affliction of the poor.)

The atlas of developed, or rapidly developing, capitalist countries can be divided as follows:

- North America, including Mexico, and Chile (these last two are in a phase of vigorous growth).
- Virtually all the western European countries, whether members of the European Community as such, or of EFTA (the European Free Trade Association), now closely linked to the EC.
- Japan and the newly industrialized countries of Asia: Thailand, South Korea, Taiwan, Hong Kong and Singapore.

And that is all.

A number of objections may be levelled at this list, including the following:

- Why not include Saudi Arabia and the Emirates? They are, after all, extraordinarily rich. But their wealth is not generated on the market, it is pumped out of the ground – which is why, incidentally, they have so far been able to resist the move towards democracy and the separation of powers.
- Why Mexico and Chile, but not the rest of Latin America? Because both have taken steps to open their economies to foreign trade and the free play of market forces, with Mexico going so far as to sign a free trade agreement with the USA. In the rest of Latin America, a great many fortunes are made entirely outside the basic capitalist framework of open competition in the free market. Not merely aberrations, these powerful forces actually hinder development, and their economies are racked by inflation as a result.
- Why does South Africa not make the list, now that apartheid is on

the way out? But the crumbling of social segregation has made even more visible the other apartheid, which is economic. What is not so well known (while we are on the subject of Africa) is that there is one country on that unhappy continent which has been making a sustained effort to bridge the gap between North Africa and southern Europe: I am referring to Morocco.

The new economic geography is disarmingly simple. It would seem to fly in the face of the widespread perception that the world is daily becoming more complex. Can things really be so black and white, so crisply contrasted, so polarised? More disturbingly, can capitalism adjust to its new status as the unchallenged leader, the holder of a world monopoly? Nothing could go more against the grain, because capitalism is by nature a market system, and in such a system there must be competitors. Yet capitalism has virtually wiped out the competition on the path to total victory.

Having no challengers, capitalism now has no mirror in which to examine itself, no alter ego against which to measure its performance. Democracy, liberalism and capitalism are by definition unqualified to exercise any sort of monopoly. What they all do especially well – their trademark, as it were – is to sort out conflicting claims through the free exercise of choice. How will they manage now that there is, literally, no contest?

Before attempting an answer, it may prove instructive to look at some concrete illustrations of the capitalist approach to a number of specific issues. What interests me, in the examples I have chosen (arbitrarily, perhaps), is the variety of *opposing* responses which capitalism is capable of bringing to the same problem. There is little doubt that capitalism is no monolithic structure, but an aggregate of tendencies out of which, in each case, two diverging currents, two broad 'schools' emerge … and challenge one another for supremacy. Hence, *Capitalism Vs. Capitalism*.

Immigration

Immigration could well turn out to be *the* subject of political debate in most of the developed nations in the twenty-first century. Its interest for the capitalist lies principally in the fact that imported labor will nearly always provide a given output of work at a lower cost than domestic labor. This probably explains why the USA has dramatically relaxed its once stringent immigration policies, notably to the advantage of Latin Americans. In 1986, a broad amnesty allowed up to 3 million clandestine immigrants to obtain their papers; another law, passed in 1990, ensures that legal immigration will increase to 700 000 newcomers a year (from 470 000) by 1995. This is in spite of the fact that the famous melting pot is showing signs of cracking. Today we hear talk of the 'New Tribalism' of America's multifarious ethnic groups, who are more concerned with affirming their separate cultural identities than with becoming 'typical Americans'.

Looking towards Japan – a genuine capitalist country – the contrast could hardly be more striking. Japan is an ethnically closed country; that it is also very densely populated may be one, but not the only, explanation. What is certain is that the treatment meted out to Korean or Filipino immigrants in Japan would not be tolerated in the USA; the Japanese find equally unimaginable the idea that General Colin Powell, the Chairman of the Armed Forces Joint Chiefs of Staff – who happens to be Black – would have been a hugely popular choice as George Bush's running mate in 1992, according to opinion polls.

Turning to Europe, Britain – like America – has traditionally shown great latitude in granting citizenship to it immigrants, whether from the West Indies, Africa or Asia; Germany, on the contrary, applies the criterion of blood descent in determining its citizenship and immigration policies. This means that there is room in the country, and in the culture, to embrace newcomers of German ancestry from around the world, but no room (at least in the culture) to absorb the country's Turkish immigrants. The pattern reveals an Anglo-American model of immigration on the one hand, and a German–Japanese model on the other.

Poverty

The question of poverty (frequently linked to that of immigration) provokes deeply divergent approaches from the various capitalist countries, both in the way it is asked and in the way the response is organized in practice. First of all, what does it mean to be poor? In most human societies down through the ages, the poor man (or woman) has been viewed as a pathetic character, a hopeless case, a failure, a shiftless good-for-nothing: suspect, if not actually guilty.

Even today, it is doubtful that there is anywhere a society where the privilege of being employed does not also entail at least a hint of scorn for those who are not so privileged. In the two most powerful capitalist economies, the USA and Japan, it is more than a hint: there, the unemployed are at best weaklings who lack the drive and determination to adapt to the requirements of the labor market, at worst incorrigible shirkers.

Neither country, as a result of this deeply rooted attitude, has any intention of setting up the kind of social protection system that European countries set up to tackle chronic poverty and unemployment – which they did nearly 50 years ago, when the average European income was just a fraction of what the average American or Japanese earns today.

The contrast, once again, is stark. Part of the explanation may lie in the traditional European view that the poor are more sinned against than sinning – victims, not culprits. There is more scope, more room for nuances in the European perception, which sees links between poverty and ignorance and more readily takes account of personal tragedy or social disadvantage.

Europe is nevertheless faced with the problem of actually paying for its welfare systems, knowing as it does that its two great industrial rivals are troubled by no such fiscal burden. France, in particular, is in urgent need of a solution to this very problem.

How does social security affect economic development?

This question actually precedes that of society's attitude towards poverty, and is every bit as controversial. For the Reagan–Thatcher school of capitalists, the welfare state is a hindrance to development: they would argue that social security inevitably creates a dependency syndrome which rewards laziness and encourages irresponsibility. (Yet it is a curious footnote to the Thatcher era that, in more than a decade of radical reform, the NHS remained largely intact.) As for the Japanese, social security is not considered a matter for the state; rather, it is up to businesses to provide some form of social safety net, insofar as they can afford to do so – and many small firms cannot. Japanese capitalists are here in agreement with the new Anglo-American conservatism, even though their companies help fund a variety of optional social insurance schemes.

A different view prevails in much of Europe. From the Alps to the Benelux countries and in Scandinavia, social security enjoys broad support: it has traditionally been seen as the rightful outcome of economic progress, and there are many who would argue that it positively promotes development by preventing the creation of a permanent 'underclass' of the poor who, beyond a certain point, cannot be salvaged. This is the reasoning behind policies of guaranteed income support, as applied in all the highly developed European nations (Germany, France, Holland, Denmark, and. . . yes, Britain too).

Not coincidentally, this traditional view is most loudly trumpeted at election time. Nevertheless, there is evidence of a shift in the European political debate over social security, whose fiscal burden on the economy (and its consequent effect on international competitiveness) is increasingly open to question. Even in Stockholm, the famous 'Swedish model' is for this reason under attack from the Social Democratic government itself.

Conversely, the lack of adequate social security provision in the USA is judged intolerable by a growing section of American public opinion – but not yet by the majority. Clearly, the issue of social protection is, today more than ever, one which the capitalist logic cannot avoid.

The income spread

The use of wage differentials and salary scales to motivate workers is a fundamental part of the capitalist logic. Individuals are to be paid individually, according to output – end of argument. Policies on hiring and firing form a subset within this same implacable arithmetic.

There is a large American insurance company whose pay policy has made it famous throughout the industry. Every year, it publishes its 'Christmas list' of staff performance: the company calculates how much each employee costs the firm, and how much each one brings in; salaries (and careers) are then adjusted accordingly. In America, at least, this offends nobody.

In the days when social welfare and state interventionism were thought to be signs of progress, the gap between top and bottom incomes was gradually narrowing in all the major industrialized countries. Then came the conservative revolution of the 1980s, and now the gap has started to widen again in the USA, Britain and a number of other camp-followers of the Anglo-American model. In France, for example, the majority view now seems to be that the demands of economic competitiveness justify a broader spread of incomes than is presently the case.

But there are other capitalist countries where the private sector deliberately endeavors to keep the income spread within certain well-defined limits. Japan provides the most striking example of collective, consensual pay bargaining, in which the added factor of strong company loyalty proves to be a greater incentive than mere money. The income gap is similarly held in check in the 'Alpine economies' (I will explain this term later) of Switzerland, Austria and Germany. Yet in all of these countries, traditional attitudes are once again being challenged. There are impatient voices within the ranks of the professions, business and industry who are calling for greater recognition – and rewards – for their talents from an ageing senior management still clinging to yesterday's prerogatives.

Should taxation promote savings or borrowing?

In France, public opinion is still largely in favor of the former, although the level of savings is steadily dropping. In Germany and Japan, thrift is an almost patriotic virtue, and the tax structure is designed to encourage it.

At the other end of the scale is the USA, where prodigality rules: personal success is measured in terms of external signs of opulence – 'conspicuous consumption' – notably since the Reagan revolution. The tax structure is designed to encourage borrowing, given that the higher one's level of indebtedness, the less the taxman can take. In which case, why pass up the opportunity to consume conspicuously... on credit? The 1980s produced a spectacular turnaround in this department in both the USA and the UK: in the space of 10 years American household savings, as a proportion of disposable income, fell from over 13 per cent to 5 per cent, while British savings plummeted from 7 per cent to less than 3 per cent.

The pattern is again that of Germany and Japan in one camp, America and the UK in the other. It should come as no surprise that the former have, for some time now, been financing the latter. The reason is plain: over the last decade, German and Japanese households have been saving at about twice the rate of their British and American counterparts.

Capitalist nations cannot do without a healthy level of personal savings, and the gap that now separates the two camps is untenable in the longer term. Anglo-American capitalism now faces the urgent task of persuading its electorate to rediscover the virtues of thrift, as once practised in Puritan (or Victorian) times. It is likely to be an uphill struggle, not least because the 'savings gap', as we shall see, is like a magnifying glass which reveals in fine detail both the causes and the consequences of the conflict between the two strains of capitalism.

Which is the better strategy: More state regulation (and hence more civil servants in charge of enforcement) or less regulation (hence more lawyers to deal with the increase in litigation)?

In all places and at all times, capitalists have objected to official regulation, and never more so than when they are prosperous. For some 50 years, their pleas were ignored; government interventionism was the flavor of the century. In Britain, successive Labour governments relied so heavily on state regulation of the economy that the Thatcherite backlash, when it came, was both ruthless and popular. Ever since then, deregulation has been the First Commandment of the neo-conservative gospel.

Today, the debate has moved on somewhat, and two contrasting movements can be discerned:

1. In the USA (and, to some extent, in the UK), it is increasingly obvious that the major 'winners' in the drive to deregulate the economy have been the lawyers, for whom chaos in the airlines industry and bankruptcy among the savings and loans associations have been an unqualified boon. The practice of law in today's America is no longer a liberal profession in the European tradition; it is a commercial venture, having expanded beyond all recognition with the boom in the consumer litigation 'industry'. The USA now has more lawyers than farmers.

2. The Japanese have not been tempted down this road: for them, bringing a lawsuit is as shameful as consulting a psychiatrist. The

Germans, too, with their notorious sense of discipline, prefer their system to be based on precise rules and regulations. But the European Commission, and EC law in general, have been strongly influenced by the philosophy of deregulation, and national parliaments are beginning to worry about the loss of their own regulatory powers. The debate, it seems, has only just started to hot up.

Bankers or brokers?

Liberal economic theory teaches that the optimal distribution of the financial resources needed for businesses to develop and expand can be obtained if, and only if, there is free movement of capital in an openly competitive environment. For many, this means that the banks' grip on credit needs to be reduced, in the interest of greater efficiency. In 1970, the US intermediation rate (i.e. the proportion of company financing provided by banks) was 80 per cent; by 1990, it had fallen to 20 per cent. This spectacular drop in bank financing has been matched by an equally spectacular growth in the market for debt and securities – or, to put it in the simplest possible terms, the stockbrokers have taken over from the bankers. The 'neo-American model' of capitalism, as will soon become clear, is predicated on an almost visceral preference for the stock exchange; it also happens that the British EC Vice-President (and Commissioner responsible for financial institutions and competition policy), Sir Leon Brittan, shares this preference.

In the 'Alpine model' of finance – which, for our purposes, must include Japan – the bankers still have the upper hand. France has yet to make a clear-cut choice between the two models: the young, upwardly mobile decision-makers and the older financiers generally support the Anglo-American approach, while senior management is on record as favoring the Alpine model (as reported by the Institut de l'Entreprise, an independent think-tank connected to the French employers' federation).

The question is, in any case, of vital importance to all genuine capitalists, for whom there are only two admissible methods of making a fortune: by competing successfully in production or in speculation. Economies that favor the banks over the brokers provide fewer opportunities to make fortunes *quickly*. Only those capitalists who are immune to the charms of pure speculation – i.e. the prospect of becoming rich overnight – can afford to stand back from the debate.

Bankers or brokers? It is a question which the USA, in particular, will have to air fully and with candour in the coming years. When the Bush administration brought forward its proposals for rescuing the nation's archaic banking system from the brink of insolvency, the reform package was clearly inspired by European, and specifically Alpine, examples. The plan, however, would mean reducing the number of banks from 12 500 to about a 1000, and creating some 200 000 redundancies spread throughout the 50 states. And that is just the beginning.

How should power be distributed within companies?

This question, closely linked to the preceding one, basically comes down to the division of powers between owners, on the one hand, and management and employees, on the other. From my own experience, I know that it can transform boardrooms into battlefields. There are companies in which shareholders 'grill' their Chief Executive Officer, who must always face them alone (however, they may bring a secretary); others where shareholders and managers always meet in exactly equal numbers; and still others in which it is the management who choose the shareholders instead of vice versa.

In short, the debate is open. The map of the different realms of power and authority within the modern capitalist company is still being drawn, and on it depends the nature of the capitalist enterprise itself. Are companies to be bought and sold by their owners (the shareholders) like any other commodity or merchandise? That is the Anglo-American view; but according to others the company is in fact a community, a complex organism in which the prerogatives of the shareholders must be balanced with those of management – who in turn are more or less co-opted by the banks and (implicitly, at least) by employees. This power-sharing model – held together with the glue of consensus – is characteristic of the German and Japanese approach to company organization.

What part should business and industry play in education and training?

The Anglo-American answer is, briefly, as little as possible. Two reasons can be given: first, training has to be paid for on the spot, but its profitability works out only in the long term – and who has time to think about the long term? Management in Britain and America are far too busy trying to get immediate results, and the bigger the profits the better. Second, investing in training is too risky: a mobile workforce means that once you have trained them, you lose them to your competitors – which is only to be expected if the 'labor market' is functioning properly.

Again, the Germans and the Japanese adopt an entirely different strategy. They apply what might be called 'career management through forward planning' – in other words, professional advancement for all employees is based on long-term considerations of both individual performance and community (i.e. company) interests. In this scenario, the danger is that talented individuals may become frustrated and impatient within the confines of a traditional hierarchy. But the danger of the Anglo-American approach is that training and experience gained in one company can so easily be lost to another, higher 'bidder' in the labor market.

Behind the debate over training lurks the larger question of the ultimate role and purpose of the company in a capitalist economy. In the Anglo-American tradition, its sole function is to generate profits; continental Europe and Japan tend to look beyond the bottom line and see the company as fulfilling a variety of needs which range from job creation to the enhancement of national competitiveness.

Insurance

The insurance business, it seems to me, can stand as a paradigm of the conflicting tendencies within modern capitalism. As I am myself an insurer, I may be open to the charge of subjectivity and personal preference in making this assertion, but I would argue that the development and refinement of insurance is an indispensable part of the capitalist process and has a direct bearing on factors such as innovation or competitiveness. Moreover, the most striking aspect of the 'capitalism vs capitalism' debate is the relative importance which each model attaches to the present and to the future. There can be no field in which these dimensions are of greater concern than in the insurance business, because the insurer's job is to add value to present resources by transferring them to the future.

The debate within insurance is increasingly polarised between the Anglo-American stance (insurance is a market commodity like any other – a view much in vogue at EC headquarters in Brussels) and the Alpine position, which emphasizes the institutional nature of insurance as a guarantor of security for firms and individuals alike. Anyone who thinks this debate is arcane or irrelevant is taking a bit too much for granted, for who can be sure that the future holds no car accident, no old-age infirmity requiring home care?

The opposing tendencies of modern insurance go back to ancient beginnings; today, these differences show up as a stark contrast between, on the one hand, a gamble based on the calculation of individual risk and, on the other, a collective endeavor to provide a secure basis on which to explore the future.

Insurance, then, will serve as an exemplary portrayal of the two models of capitalism which I propose to examine. Some readers may (understandably) object that this amounts to a caricature of what is, after all, an exceedingly complex question. My only defense is that, in the age of the identikit and the three-minute news analysis, it is pointless to be coy about the advantages of simplification: caricature need not be synonymous with exaggeration.

The ten preceding examples of capitalism in action are of interest for two reasons. First, they contradict the outward impression that, having obtained an ideological monopoly which is against its very nature, capitalism is as much a monolithic, impermeable bloc as was Soviet communism: a new determinism to replace a discredited dialectical Marxism. Seen from the inside, however, the picture is very different. In the real life of capitalism as lived by different nations and cultures, no one best way, no single unambiguous answer to the great social questions is apparent. Just the opposite: capitalism is a versatile, complex aggregate of energies and movements. It is a practice, not a theory.

The other point of interest is provided by the tendency of these diverse practices and approaches to coalesce into two great streams of comparable size, two opposing models of capitalism locked in a conflict whose outcome is far from certain.

The claim may appear outrageous, and that is why I began with a few concrete examples of observable facts. Certainly my hypothesis has

against it the full weight of Anglo-American liberal economic theory –
and its weight in today's world is considerable (if not totally dominant),
from the canteen to the boardroom, from the classroom to the economic think-tank. According to this school of thought, the market economy
can never have more than one pure, efficient rationale. Any deviation
from price rationality, any taint of political or social or institutional
perrogatives are automatically rejected as an unwarranted muddying of
the waters.

For the theorists of this school, the USA is the one true reference,
the proving ground on which the theory must stand or fall. It is the
New Jerusalem of the New Conservatism.

In practice, things are – fortunately – not so simple. The main purpose of this book is to demonstrate the existence of a second model of
capitalism, one which can match and even out-perform the American
model, whether measured by the yardstick of economic efficiency or by
that of social justice.

Before going any further, there is the matter of nomenclature. Each
model needs a name, a handy 'label'.

'Anglo-Saxon' vs 'German–Japanese' model

At first glance, the temptation is to set an 'Anglo-Saxon' or 'English-
speaking' model against a 'German–Japanese' model.

The former terms probably go too far: it does not seem right for Aus-
tralia and New Zealand, with their strong Labour tradition, to be brack-
eted with the Britain of Mrs. Thatcher and her successors. And Canada's French-speaking province of Québec would look even more out
place, especially as it owes much of its exceptional growth of the last 15
years or so to financial institutions (such as the Caisse de Dépôts or the
Groupe Desjardins) whose strategies are diametrically opposite to those
characteristic of the 'Anglo-Saxon' model over the last decade.

But the main objection lies in the uncomfortable pairing of the
USA and the UK, which overlooks a fundamental difference, mentioned above, in the realm of social welfare. The disparity here is enormous: not between two different systems, but between a long-established, comprehensive system (inspired by Bismarck, no less) that even
Mrs. Thatcher could not undo, and the complete absence of any system
of protection at all.

As for the latter term, 'German–Japanese', there are points in its favor beyond the recognition that, for over 100 years, the Japanese have been routinely described as 'the Germans of Asia', or the fact that today the major German and Japanese corporations are teaming up to form industrial alliances of unparalleled potential (e.g. Mitsubishi and Daimler Benz, Toyota and Volkswagen, Matsushita and Siemens). There are precisely analogous traits which bring the two naturally together, such as their methods of corporate financing or the social role of the company. The principal resemblance in economic terms is, beyond question, the emphasis on export-led growth. Yet there are a number of striking differences: there is no German equivalent of the huge Japanese business firms, nor is German industry so radically polarised, as it is in Japan, between large corporations and small sub-contractors. The French research center CEPII (which has been studying the question for at least 20 years) has even found that, in the matter of industrial specialization, there could not be two more opposite cases than those of Germany – with its stable base of traditional expertise in mechanical engineering, chemicals and transport equipment – and Japan, where the breakneck pace of industrial change has seen textiles vanish, shipyards being reconverted, and new specializations (such as cars and consumer electronics) popping up virtually overnight. On closer inspection, then, these terms are not entirely satisfactory.

The American model or, more accurately, the 'neo-American model'

Given that the UK, for all Mrs. Thatcher's efforts to import Reaganism, is destined to draw nearer to Europe while distancing itself somewhat from America, the inescapable conclusion must be that the USA constitutes an economic model in and of itself.

Since 1980, America's singularity has been even more pronounced. The election of Ronald Reagan put an abrupt end to the tendency, apparent since the Depression, of US capitalism to take on some of the characteristics of European capitalism (e.g. greater state intervention in the economy). This movement had much to do with the need for trans-Atlantic solidarity in the confrontation with communism.

Nowhere in continental Europe has there been anything remotely like the 'Reagan revolution' in the USA. A new economic model was forged (and baptized Reaganomics, already in every dictionary); its fame was to spread far beyond the boundaries of America, even as its shortcomings have started to become apparent at home. It is an extraordinary phenomenon, and part of its complexity stems from psychological factors which seem to outweigh real economic performance. The American model has been transformed by Reaganism into something new, which I will henceforth refer to as the *neo-American model*.

Can one therefore speak of a 'European model' as such?

Everything would seem to point in that direction: the European Community has been under construction for over 30 years; it takes the form of an essentially economic union, regardless of the current debate over political, social, diplomatic or military ties; it is a concrete reality with its own dynamics. And yet there is no single, consistent European economic model. The British pattern more closely resembles that of America than of Germany; the Italian version (dominated by 'family capitalism' and characterised by an almost non-existent state, an astronomical public-sector deficit and an amazing vitality among small and medium-sized businesses) resembles no other, with the possible exception of the Chinese diaspora.

France and Spain are unusual cases as well – all the more so as, contrary to appearances, they have a great deal in common. Both have long experience of protectionism, state interventionism and inflationary corporatism, and both have been actively engaged in throwing off these obsolete accoutrements in a frenzy of modernisation. Finally, they are both torn between competing tendencies. Against the pull of institutional traditions which, if rejuvenated, would take them in the 'Alpine' direction, there are strong 'Americanizing' forces in the growth of new businesses, increased speculative activity and a plethora of social tensions typical of polarized economies; furthermore, there is even an 'Italian tendency' at work, with the rise of great personal and family fortunes.

Decidedly, it would be unwise to speak of a 'European model'.

'Core' model of classic European economy

There does exist, nevertheless, a kind of 'core' model of the classic European economy. It has two complementary sides to its nature:

1. The *Alpine* aspect, i.e. the 'Deutschmark zone' of influence which includes Switzerland and Austria, but not the Netherlands. Seen from a monetary and financial angle, the Alpine model embodies all the principal features that run directly counter to the neo-American model. In particular, no currency has been managed more differently from the dollar in the last quarter-century than the German mark.
2. The *Rhine* aspect, i.e. the social component of the economic policies and practices of the new Germany, which took shape in Bonn (on the Rhine River) and not in Berlin, capital of Prussia.

It was on the banks of the Rhine, in the spa town of Bad Godesberg, that the German Social Democratic Party decided, during its historic 1959 conference, to commit itself to capitalism. It seemed a surprising choice at the time. Yet there could be no mistake: the new SPD program explicitly insisted on 'the need to protect and promote private ownership of the means of production' and gave full approval to 'open competition and free enterprise'. Every socialist party in Europe cried treason, of course. . . and every one of them has come to accept the same principles (if not always so explicitly, then at least in terms of pragmatic behaviour).

Today, Helmut Kohl continues in the tradition of Adenauer, Erhard, and even Brandt and Schmidt, at the helm of an economy which exemplifies what I call the *Rhine model* of capitalism. It includes not only the Rhine countries in the narrow geographical sense – Switzerland, Germany and the Netherlands – but also, to some extent, Scandinavia and (with allowances for the inevitable cultural differences) Japan as well.

Now that the actors are in position, the show can begin.

With the collapse of communism, it is as if a veil has been suddenly lifted from our eyes. Capitalism, we can now see, has two faces, two personalities. The neo-American model is based on individual success and short-term financial gain; the Rhine model, of German pedigree but with strong Japanese connections, emphasizes collective success, consensus and long-term concerns. In the last decade or so, it is this Rhine model – unheralded, unsung and lacking even nominal identity papers – that has shown itself to be the more efficient of the two, as well as the more equitable.

As the year 1990 drew to a close, Helmut Kohl was triumphantly returned as German Chancellor, while Margaret Thatcher was unceremoniously removed from power. These events cannot be explained solely in terms of domestic politics. With a little hindsight, it will be apparent that they represent the first skirmish in the coming ideological battle. But this time it will not be socialism or communism against capitalism; this time, the combat will pit neo-American capitalism against Rhine capitalism.

The confrontation we are about to witness will be cruel and implacable, of course, but it will take place largely under the surface of things, insidiously, and with more than a hint of hypocrisy. Such is the nature of family feuds and internecine quarrels, where the adversaries share a common origin. Each of these models belongs to the liberal, capitalist family by right, yet each carries an inner logic which contradicts the other. The battle may ultimately come down to a confrontation between whole value-systems, and on its outcome will be decided the answers to such issues as the individual's place within the company, the function of the market place in society, and the role of law and authority in international economic affairs.

Those who were quick to proclaim the end of ideology, if not the demise of history itself, are sure to be disappointed.

Chapter 2
America is back

The yellow ribbons tied round the columns of the White House porch to honor George Bush in his hour of glory – the successful conclusion of the Gulf War – almost made one forget that it was Ronald Reagan who first adopted 'America is back!' as his slogan and election platform. Yet it is Reagan's America, already a decade old, which continues to spread its influence across the globe.

In the southern hemisphere, Reagan's brand of triumphant capitalism still fascinates decision-makers and intellectuals alike as they seek a cure for the twin economic ills of massive debt and oppressive state intervention. The veneration of Reaganism has been growing steadily since the mid-1980s. From Brasilia to Lagos, it is today the very embodiment of the ideals of success, prosperity and vitality.

Meanwhile, as the former communist bloc crumbled in 1989–90, whole populations seemed to join in the chorus of praise: Ronald Reagan (and Mrs. Thatcher) have achieved the status of exalted, almost mythical, heroes behind the old Iron Curtain. The new Hungarian parties, whether they call themselves Forum for Democracy or Democratic Alliance, all swear by the market economy – preferably in its purest, most radical form – while the Polish 'liberal clubs' which have sprung up from Gdansk to Cracow are so many chapels dedicated to the worship of Reagan and Thatcher. Poland's relatively successful economic reform program, the Balcerowicz Plan (named after the youthful Finance Minister) openly takes its inspiration from Reaganite principles. And in the unexpectedly large vote garnered by Stanislaw Tyminski in the first round of Poland's presidential elections in November 1990, that influence is apparent yet again: Tyminski's simplistic message (basically, 'Follow my example and get rich!') was meant to sound like pure Reaganese. Even in this exaggerated version, popular acclaim for the Reagan doctrine is not surprising in societies where everyone now believes communism to have been the incarnation of absolute evil, and a total failure. Who can blame them for jumping to the conclusion that, in order to aspire to absolute good, what is needed is unalloyed, absolute capitalism?

One of the foremost British observers of the East European scene, Timothy Garton Ash, who chronicled each step of the '1989 revolution' for *The New York Review of Books*, wrote in his latest book (*We the People*) that 'it seems as if the free market has become the latest Central European utopia'.

Perhaps it is a utopia that the 500 or 600 Muscovites who queue for hours on Pushkin Square in front of McDonald's Restaurant (established 1990) hope to find once they enter the fast-food sanctuary, or 'Lenin's new tomb' as local wags have christened it. Utopia, or simply a miracle? And a continent away, in China (yes, even in China), the man on the Beijing omnibus not only knows who Ronald Reagan is, but will freely admit to admiring him.

If these examples of popular appeal seem laughably naïve or exotic, it is worth turning to western Europe to confirm Reaganism's continuing prestige abroad, even as America begins to have doubts. Deregulation, tax cuts, profit for profit's sake, 'meeting the challenge' and 'less government is better government': these buzz words and expressions are still very much in vogue. The new European credo is aggressively ultra-liberal, not only on the Right (which, in the late 1980s, tended to be more Reaganite than Reagan) but on the Left as well, still reeling from the discovery of the virtues of profit and free enterprise now that the dream of a 'natural' socialist majority has evaporated.

The 12 states of the European Community have consecrated the final victory of Reagan and Thatcher. In spite of the latter's apparent fall from grace at the hands of her own party, in a dispute over the future direction of the EC, she has left a lasting legacy in the form of the Single Market, due to be completed by the end of 1992. Margaret Thatcher insisted on, and obtained, a Europe of thrusting business and beefed-up trade at the expense of Jacques Delors' vision, shared by the European Parliament, of a political and social Community. A market, then, and little else: a supermarket of impressive dimensions, undeniably, yet never before in history has such close integration of markets been accompanied by so little political control. Not even in America itself.

The values espoused by Reagan seem to have taken up permanent residence on the Old Continent, regardless of their intrinsic merit. Insidiously, spontaneously, they have been absorbed almost as if they had been released into the air we breathe. Yesterday's Europessimism has given way to a rugged, if limited, version of liberalism. In the new Europe, winners are lionized and losers ignored, production and performance are revered while social welfare is relegated to the back-burner. Europe in the early 1990s is the final vindication of the 1980s White House, its cowboy hero and his Star Wars scenario.

It is a triumph founded on a grave misunderstanding, however, because just as western Europe drastically over-estimated the strength of Soviet economic power a decade ago, it is similarly mistaken with regard to America today, failing to see the economic and social fault lines beneath the surface of US military might. In the case of the former USSR, such short-sightedness may be excusable, given the Kremlin's secrecy, its double-think and double-speak, its phony statistics and trumped-up achievements. No such excuse is available for our inability to see clearly into the heart of the world's premier democracy, an open society whose dirty linen is regularly washed in the full glare of the spotlights. Apparently, those spotlights have blinded more than one observer.

The birth of the universe, Reagan-style

For the light of the Reagan revolution to go on illuminating (with all its attendant distortions) the furthest reaches of the globe, its origin must have been a particularly powerful Big Bang. Seen from afar, the birth of Reaganism at the beginning of the 1980s makes a fascinating study. What happened, and why just at that time? As with any sudden explosion, there must be a chain of events and causes that can be elucidated.

Campaigning for the Presidency in 1980, Ronald Reagan launched his rallying-cry: 'America is back!' In other words, America was about to shrug off its torpor, banish the 'Vietnam syndrome' once and for all, and regain its pioneer spirit. No one could argue that a revival was unnecessary at that point: bogged down in a tangle of domestic woes, humiliated abroad by Khomeini's Iran and the hostage crisis, feeling threatened by Soviet military might and already looking economically vulnerable in the face of growing competition from Europe, and especially from Japan, the USA was still the world's greatest superpower (not least in military terms), but the future looked bleak indeed.

What ill wind had blown the proud Ship of State into such troubled waters? More importantly, what undercurrents in the national psyche, what eddies of doubt and confusion drove its passengers and crew to entrust their fate to this unlikely captain? How did an ex-actor with strong convictions of no particular subtlety, a celluloid cowboy preaching old-fashioned morality and a vaguely archaic set of beliefs, come to lead the 'conservative revolution' (as it was promptly dubbed) that was to sweep the nation? Was this the same ultramodern, permissive society which only a few years before had been entranced by George McGovern and his team of ardent reformers, the society which always looked westward, to California and the 'New Age'? Why this sudden desire for power, this thirst for revenge?

These questions remain highly relevant; it is in fact urgent to find answers to them if we are to understand today's America, the America of George Bush, glorious in battle but riddled by debt. A full understanding of American capitalism must include the long-term transformations taking place at the deepest levels of society and culture, and which are often the hardest to spot. Such changes stem from a number of basic features, each of which contributes both to America's strength and to its vulnerability.

Too many humiliations, not enough certainties

Ronald Reagan came to power at a time when the nation felt deeply troubled over its recent past, marked by a series of humiliations abroad and a lack of self-assurance at home. In the decade leading up to the 1980 election America had suffered one setback after another on the world scene, and not just minor ones. It was as if the fiascos of Vietnam and Cambodia had set in motion an unstoppable decline in American power and prestige overseas. In Africa, the USSR and Cuba were scoring what seemed to be the deciding goals in Ethiopia, Angola, Guinea-Bissau and Mozambique; in the Middle East, America lost her trusted ally, the Shah of Iran, who had policed the Persian Gulf on her behalf; in the Levant, Lebanon remained a no-go area for US diplomacy as Syria stoked the fires of the civil war which had begun in 1975 – the same year Henry Kissinger had to work so hard to achieve Israel's disengagement from the Sinai. On its own doorstep, in Central America, the fall of the Somoza regime in Nicaragua and the Sandinista victory seemed to sound the death-knell of the venerable Monroe Doctrine, according to which Latin America was one vast zone of privileged, and unchallengeable, US influence.

On every continent, America seemed to be in retreat, powerless to stop Soviet expansionism. Scenes from the developing countries of the Stars and Stripes going up in flames, of crowds chanting their defiance and hatred of Uncle Sam, were part of the daily television diet of audiences from Atlanta to Albuquerque. Humiliation, fatigue and a dollop of impotent rage: all the ingredients needed to brew up a dark potion of nostalgia for the past, when America was great and powerful. If Ronald Reagan had not existed – with his easy-to-grasp ideas couched in the vocabulary of John Wayne – they would assuredly have had to invent him. The new sheriff rides into town: America is back!

Even more painful to bear, perhaps, than this avalanche of humiliations was the vague, hollow feeling throughout American society that the old certainties had gone. The 1970s had been sombre years in this department too, as confidence waned and was replaced by doubt. The American Dream had become the American Disease, as Michel Crozier entitled the account of his return to Harvard, where he had taught 10 years before: 'Everything was the same, yet different; nothing meant the same as before. The dream was gone – only words and empty rhetoric remained' (Le Mal Américain: Fayard, 1980).

But this American disease was more than a passing, vague depression of the sort that nations occasionally give in to. It had begun to affect the country's great institutions, and most noticeably the rule of law. In a land founded on the Bible and the Constitution, the law is every US citizen's true birthright. With Watergate, the cover-up and Nixon's unseemly departure, public confidence in the bedrock of the law began to slip – to such a degree that Jimmy Carter inherited a weakened, discredited executive. Yet Congress was never able to provide a credible alternative: the disease had spread to the legislative branch as well. How was the world's number one superpower to govern itself when the system of checks and balances, inspired by Montesquieu, had literally paralysed the executive? Henry Kissinger has revealed in his memoirs how the State Department constantly strove to outmanoeuvre the rest of the government in order to preserve the secrecy necessary to conduct foreign policy.

Given the climate of suspicion and doubt, the traditional apathy of the American voter (election turnout is seldom above 50 per cent) was quickly turning to disgust. By the end of the 1970s, the public had largely given up on politics. Yet, in some confused, inarticulate corner of the national psyche, the people awaited a saviour.

There were other, more insidious, ills gnawing away at the fabric of the American way of life. At the other extreme of the rule of law, for example, could be seen the orgy of litigation which grew out of the legal system's transformation into a kind of fetishistic religion. It is worth remarking that the fashionable view that was beginning to take hold in Europe at that time held that the American justice system, founded on a continuously updated and refined jurisprudence, was superior to continental European systems. The reality was quite different: the national binge of litigation was causing the judicial machinery of the state to seize up, and the more frantically it tried to cope, the more incomprehensible it all became. . . except, perhaps, to the lawyers, who were cheerfully making their fortunes. Anything and everything could be the pretext for a lawsuit, and lawyers grew ingenious at turning any legal molehill into a mountain. In one notorious example, IBM had to rent an entire office block in Washington DC, merely to house its team of legal experts fighting a case – a single trial – against the government.

Thus the law, America's cornerstone and final arbiter of the social contract, had become an impenetrable jungle in which the body of jurisprudence as well as the volumes of local, state and federal regulations were growing exponentially.

Elsewhere, another cornerstone of American society was showing signs of fatigue. De Tocqueville had praised what we now call the voluntary sector: those innumerable associations, clubs, groups and movements dedicated to all manner of causes and activities, frivolous or not, from charity to politics, from business to sport. What the European observer could see was that society was the better for them, for their energy, for their role in imparting a civic sense and embodying the notion of the common good. Now, however, America was falling prey to an attitude which had never been part of her traditional value-system: scheming cynicism.

It particularly saddened the famous 'Silent Majority' of Americans to realize that the social fabric, and the political system as well, were wearing out. They were growing frightened too, as the pace of change became incremental and the siren-song of 'permissiveness', California-style, beckoned. A disoriented majority naturally longed for a return to traditional values; they craved certainties, simple ones, even archaic ones. Ronald Reagan's plain, forceful talk was exactly what the people were waiting to hear. He was also ideally poised to make full use of a favorable economic wind which would blow right through the bloated bureaucracy of an interfering government. The intellectual climate was right, too. And best of all, the international situation would provide the stage from which the Reagan message could be proclaimed, and amplified a hundredfold: America is back!

The new American challenge

Election Day, November 4, 1980: the Republican Party candidate, Ronald Reagan, triumphs over Jimmy Carter with a majority of 9 million votes. Reagan wins in 45 states, Carter in only 5 (plus the District of Columbia), failing even to hold New York and the other industrial states of the north, traditional heartland of the Democratic Party. Four years later, Reagan's victory over Walter Mondale is even more impressive, winning in 49 states with a 17 million overall majority.

The pundits had not expected Reagan to do so well, coming as he did from the far right of the Republican Party and fighting on a platform of a few broad principles steeped in the mythology of the Founding Fathers and the pioneers. But Reagan was able to defend his program with the consummate skill of a seasoned performer and master of televisual communication.

The first plank in Reagan's winning platform was to revive America's leadership in world affairs. No more humiliations, no more defeats, never again the frightful images that had seared the American psyche during the previous decade: Army helicopters carrying out the last-minute evacuation of Saigon from the US Embassy rooftops; the charred bodies of GIs in the Iranian desert after the failed mission, in April 1980, to rescue the embassy hostages in Teheran. Never again would the USA abandon its allies, or capitulate to the 'forces of evil'. America was the world's greatest military power and no one, least of all Brezhnev and the Soviet expansionism he represented, would be left in any doubt about it. And it was to the Soviets that he issued his most spectacular challenge, the Strategic Defense Initiative (SDI), or 'Star Wars'.

On 23 March 1983, Reagan unveiled his grand design before the American public in a televised address. With his characteristic blend of sincerity and stage-management, he explained that SDI would eliminate the threat of nuclear war, thanks to a protective shield, in permanent orbit around the Earth, which would detect and intercept Soviet missiles. The system would incorporate existing technologies (electronic detection, killer satellites) and create new ones (lasers, electron-beam guns). SDI would make American soil impregnable from Soviet aggression – forever.

As a practical undertaking, Star Wars did not quite add up. The experts were sharply divided over its feasibility, but all agreed that some aspects of the project would require a major 'technological leap' and that total reliability could not ever be guaranteed. On the financial side, SDI was a risky venture even for the richest country in the world. An initial cost of $250 billion (of which 10 per cent would be devoted to research alone) was mooted. A considerable sum, to which would have to be added an unknown, but inevitable, amount of overspending.

On the other hand, Star Wars was an instant media success and a sensational political coup, a futuristic concept with a laudable aim ('No more war') which could appeal to even the most blasé. It is hard to imagine a more seductive idea, on the face of it: a purely defensive shield to blunt the nuclear sword of Damocles. Reagan had, in fact, unleashed a particularly powerful metaphor, one that it is virtually impossible to argue against: the shield, the arm of the righteous, shall triumph over the sword, the arm of the wicked. (It is surely not accidental that the military reply to Saddam Hussein's invasion of Kuwait was at first christened 'Desert Shield', before becoming 'Desert Storm.') Opponents of the plan, in Europe and elsewhere, were quick to decry what they saw as Reagan's 'hidden agenda' – to tip the nuclear balance in America's favor by protecting strategic weapons sites – but to no avail. Star Wars had an enormous impact. It sent a message that was clearly understood: America is regaining the initiative, but its weaponry is purely defensive. Reagan could claim to be breaking new ground in the conduct of war and the pursuit of peace simultaneously.

The benefits of SDI would be reaped in other ways, too. It made possible some of the technology which assisted the US military successes in the Gulf War. Perhaps most important of all was the effect on the Soviet Union, which exceeded all expectations. Towards the end of the 1980s, a number of Soviet officials admitted, Glasnost permitting, that the formidable technological and financial challenge that Star Wars represented became a decisive factor in the ideological surrender of the Soviet system. This time, Moscow knew it would not be able to keep up; the stakes in this gigantic poker game of military spending had gone too high. Meanwhile, America would reap the pure profit of the technological leap forward that SDI would provide. Space, information technology and lasers were sure to be part of the winning combination that would make America the unchallenged world leader of the twenty-first century.

The Reagan administration was also actively working in other spheres of diplomacy and foreign policy. Support for American allies was aggressively pursued, whether by bringing cruise missiles into Europe to counter the Soviet SS-20s, or by financing anti-communist movements in Angola, Afghanistan and Nicaragua. Everywhere, Reagan's stated goal of rolling back Soviet influence was being proclaimed in the most unambiguous terms. America is back!

The international comeback was to be accompanied, on the domestic front, by a determined and unashamed revival of good old-fashioned all-conquering American capitalism. Reagan and his team praised the entrepreneur and heaped scorn on the federal government for its wastefulness and, above all, its appetite for taxes. Taxation was the scourge of initiative, the rack upon which America's vitality was being broken. Reagan's America would come back to its senses and once again be the land of opportunity, of dreams come true, but on one condition: the sacrosanct laws of free enterprise must be allowed free reign. The wealth accumulated by a few individuals would ultimately be of benefit to all, according to Adam Smith and the founding fathers of economic liberalism, whose notion of the 'invisible hand' is more familiar to us as the 'trickle-down' effect. Get rich, Reagan told Americans. And let the rich get richer. Let the poor get to work and stop depending on government handouts and welfare schemes, which are merely an alibi for laziness. The truly needy, the really hopeless cases, will be seen to by charity, not by the state: a simple message, enthusiastically received.

If this old credo could suddenly flourish anew, it was surely because the ground had already been prepared by a series of economic reversals and a crisis of faith in Keynesian doctrine which culminated in the recessionary seventies. The approach which had once been so successful (stimulation of demand, reliance on deficit spending) – Europe's 30 years of post-war prosperity were its most eloquent testimony – now looked increasingly obsolete. America, indeed, was not alone in burying Keynes.

A short digression is necessary at this point. We shall see in a later chapter that Reagan's reforming zeal was mainly directed against government intervention, and deregulation was the preferred method for curtailing it. In one area, however, he not only boosted government action but set out a high-priority, long-term plan for the nation. This was in the realm of defense. That he more than achieved his aim is apparent, as recently illustrated by the Gulf War. Crucially, it is this very notion of long-term planning which Reagan ignored in every other sphere, but which elsewhere turns out to be the key element underpinning the economic success of Germany and Japan.

Keynesian economic theory was moribund, then, even in Europe, where policies of stimulating consumption had failed to produce a French recovery in 1975, or a German one in 1978, as Jacques Chirac and Helmut Schmidt learnt to their cost. A whole body of economic orthodoxy was put in doubt: contrary to what had been unquestioningly taught in every university, it seemed that unemployment and inflation could, in fact, coexist. The Phillips curve, a model refutation of this possibility, was of no help in the face of the new economic reality: stagflation. However ungainly the name, the symptoms were unmistakable and the malady was spreading far and wide.

It seemed that the old school of economic thought had become obsolete almost overnight. In its place new, radical theories were emerging and Reagan would be their standard-bearer. Supply side economists and the monetarist school, led by Milton Friedman, had put forward a model of the economy which turned Keynesianism on its head. They advocated a package of measures based on tax reduction, strict control of the money supply, deregulation and privatization. The goal was to renew America's enterprise culture, putting the self-made man back in the driver's seat and government intervention firmly in the boot.

A number of spectacular reforms were planned, with the Economic Recovery Act (ERA) as the spearhead. A three-pronged attack was soon launched. The first objective, deregulation of the oil, banking, telecommunications and air travel industries, and the freeing of competition generally, had already been in Jimmy Carter's sights since 1978; Reagan would now pursue the policy more vigorously.

The second target was the tax structure. A sweeping reform was adopted, under which the income tax system was considerably simplified by abolishing a large number of deductions and reducing the tax rates, especially in the higher bands. The third goal was to lower inflation through tight management of the money supply.

Implementation of this policy fell to the Federal Reserve Board and its chairman, Paul Volcker (a Carter appointee), who put such energy and skill into his task that the cost of borrowing rose dramatically, almost overnight. The days of easy money were over: interest rates climbed to unprecedented heights, exceeding 20 per cent in 1980–81. Consequently the value of the US dollar went through the roof, soaring above 10 French francs by early 1985. The White House was then able to argue that the dollar's strength was a reflection of a healthy US economy.

As a complement to the ERA, the Reagan administration set about reducing spending on social programs while sharply increasing the defense budget. The choice of priorities was made unflinchingly, and though debatable it was at least clear. The logic behind it ran thus: cutting back on welfare signals a return of confidence in the individual and the laws of the free market, while a stronger military will reinforce America's position and give the Chief Executive the means to carry out his ambitious plans for the nation.

With these shock tactics, the 'conservative revolution' (to borrow from the title of Guy Sorman's 1983 study) was under way. Soon the whole world would become fascinated, if not entirely won over, by the Reagan whirlwind.

America, America

America is back, bigger and better than before! The message was at first greeted with scorn and derision by those who winced at the thought of a Hollywood cowboy occupying the White House. Incredulity gradually gave way to a more guarded attitude, followed by curiosity, and finally a mixture of surprise and admiration. Even among traditionally sceptical European intellectuals, there were some who climbed aboard the Reagan bandwagon.

Granted, much of the new president's appeal could be explained by his long experience in front of the camera. As a broadcasting professional himself, he was uniquely well equipped to exploit the incalculable impact of the mass media in getting his message across. Of course he was assisted by a team of communications specialists, but his own gifts were considerable. By carefully controlling the media dosage, he built up a consistent image of the affable boss, the down-home American in love with his ranch and his adoring wife. Constantly in the spotlight, he nevertheless remained cool and collected – unlike Jimmy Carter, who grew visibly exhausted the harder he applied himself. This was a president who had time for his afternoon nap. . . yet he could show courage under fire, quite literally: shot by a would-be assassin on 30 March 1981, he got back on his feet, cracked a joke for the cameras, and sailed through the subsequent operation without a complaint. They were soon calling him the Great Communicator: he had created a starring role and an image that could be exported to the four corners of the globe.

Ronald Reagan possessed an intuitive genius for capturing and shaping the economic trends of the 1980s. European-style social democracy was running out of steam, Adam Smith's capitalism was ripe for a comeback: he knew it, and he knew just how to stage it, even if a little makeup and a few mirrors were required to make the show convincing. Reagan was particularly adept at the illusionist's art of concealment. The grey areas, the weak links, the unflattering images were kept out of sight: a staggering budget deficit, for example, which grew year by year to become the most colossal debt in history, or the covert aid provided against Congress's express wishes to pro-Western insurgencies in the Southern hemisphere.

No matter! Despite these few blemishes, Reagan's reborn America soon reached an unassailable peak of influence. This, surely, was the New Jerusalem of messianic capitalism, and the irresistible good news could not fail to enlighten the darkest redoubts of the unbeliever. Reaganism took to the skies. Europe was its first landfall, followed shortly thereafter by the developing countries, where a dramatic shift toward market forces, open competition and private enterprise was brought about by the combined efforts of the World Bank and the International Monetary Fund (IMF). Europe and the South were soon privatizing across the board; monetary policy, based on the US Federal Reserve Board recipe, was adopted wholesale in an attempt to reign back the galloping inflation that was eating away at property values and earnings and exacerbating social injustices.

The mid-1980s saw Reagan's America shining as brightly as the stars on Old Glory. The USA was again a force to be respected (or feared), a model to be emulated, an object of envy. America was once more synonymous with world leadership.

The cornerstones of American power

In spite of the rosy picture painted above, doubts were already beginning to surface. Was this spectacular revival based on anything more solid than Mr. Reagan's skilful sleight-of-hand? Did America's recent successes stem from the ideological and philosophical virtues of Reaganism, as widely claimed, or were they *primarily* due to certain specific advantages (one might say privileges) already built into the equation? The question almost answers itself, for on close examination it becomes abundantly clear that the Reaganite boom so admired by the world's movers and shakers bore little resemblance to the genuine economic miracles of which West Germany, Japan or South Korea could boast. The comparison is invidious, because America was not playing with the same deck – and the cards were heavily stacked in her favor.

When Ronald Reagan entered the White House in 1981, the USA already possessed economic, financial and technological assets that

dwarfed those of all other contenders. It is perhaps useful to be reminded of the scale and diversity of those assets.

Capital investment

To begin with, the post-war years saw an unparalleled accumulation of
investment, both at home and abroad. Reagan inherited a colossal network of modern infrastructures ranging from airports and motorways to
factories, universities and property developments of every description.
Foreign investment was equally awe-inspiring: US multinationals had
acquired vast assets abroad. These remain substantially undervalued due
to an accounting system which looks at acquisition costs and ignores
current revaluations. US holdings overseas thus totalled $215 billion in
1980, rising to $309 billion by 1987 (see Paul Mentré, *L'Amérique et
Nous*: Dunod, 1989). They brought in considerable revenue, of course,
but the point is that they put America streets ahead of its nearest competitors. In 1988, for example, the level of direct investment abroad by
American companies was three times that of Japanese firms.

Natural resources

The USA is blessed in this category, with vast reserves of raw materials
and energy (coal and natural gas in particular) and lacking only a handful of strategically vital metals and minerals. There is no doubt that its
human resources, too, can be counted as natural wealth. With the
fourth largest population in the world – but first among developed
nations – the USA is unlikely ever to be short of a work force. Compared to Japan, for instance, whose ageing population is crowded into a
small territory utterly bereft of raw materials or sources of energy,
America is evidently sitting on a gold mine.

Technology

Again, America enjoys a huge comparative advantage if only because
the world's top scientists, engineers and students come to work in the
USA, Reagan or no Reagan. They bring with them the kind of capital
that everyone agrees is the most precious: grey matter. A single statistic
makes this plain: the number of Nobel Prizes regularly awarded to
American scientists. Year after year, the brain drain provides the coun-

try's laboratories and universities with the keenest minds and the finest intellects; they come because America allows their talents free reign. It is an advantage that has been hard, and fairly, won. And its importance is usually underestimated – everyone, it seems, knows that the famous Patriot missiles contained a few Japanese-made components, but the fact that Sony could not make its cam-corders without a supply of Motorola microchips is, oddly, not equally notorious.

Monetary privilege

This is another crucial factor. Since the Bretton Woods Conference of 1944, the dollar has been the currency of reference for virtually all international transactions. It is also the principal reserve currency held by the world's central banks. In what amounts to an imperial privilege, America can everywhere make payments, take out loans and finance its spending operations in its own currency. In practice, this privilege has repercussions which go further than one might think. John Nueller, an American economist, uses a striking analogy to illustrate some of the consequences: imagine for a moment, he says, that everyone you have to pay accepts all the cheques you write. Then suppose that the beneficiaries of your cheques, all over the world, use these same cheques to pay off their creditors, instead of cashing them. Your finances will be affected in two ways: first, because everyone takes your cheques, you will never have to use cash. Your cheque-book is all you need. As a second consequence, you will be happily surprised when you ask to see the balance of your account. There will be more money in it than you had reckoned on after deducting what you had spent. Why? For the very reason that, as stated before, your cheques are never cashed but continue to circulate from one bearer to another. In practice this means that you will have 'extra' money on hand for investments and purchases. The more use everyone else makes of your cheques, the more resources are available for your use.

This process, argues Nueller, has already put at America's disposal some $500 billion over and above the taxes it collects and the government loans underwritten by American (and foreign) savers; $500 billion is hardly insignificant: it is the equivalent of 31 years of American aid to the developing countries!

America's monetary privilege is thus considerable, and the effects are far-reaching in a broader financial sense. It has been estimated that a total of $1200 *billion* circulates each and every day within the US financial network – more than France's annual gross domestic product (GDP). America is sitting on a mountain of money, its own as well as others'. The dollar is both the badge and the instrument of her enviable privilege.

American cultural domination

This is a trump card largely unaffected by the vicissitudes of history. It simply goes from strength to strength, as if the Americanization of the entire planet possessed an unstoppable and self-sustaining momentum which easily overcomes any pockets of local resistance and shrugs off the carping of critics. For thousands of millions of people throughout the world, in communist China as much as anywhere else (if not more so), the American way of life, and of thinking, is the only authentic test of what it means to be modern.

This formidable cultural hegemony is based on at least three crucial factors, of which the first – the English language – should be glaringly obvious. English is the nearest thing we have to a universal language, an Esperanto of immense benefit not only to tourists but, more importantly, to scientists and businessmen. There is no product in greater demand worldwide than this, the language of America, of the new empire. It is particularly galling to the French-speaking people of Québec, for example, that the immigrants to their province, whether from Asia or Latin America or elsewhere, want to learn English and only English. More specifically, what has evolved is a universal medium for business and technical communication which not only takes the form of the English language but borrows its content from ideas and concepts developed in American universities. Thus a whole body of values, assumptions and thought processes intimately linked with the USA is broadcast on a permanent basis from one end of the earth to the other.

America's second cultural weapon, perhaps its most powerful one, is the pervasive influence of the US higher education system. The best and brightest minds in the world are irresistibly drawn to the constellation of prestigious American universities such as Harvard, Stanford, Berkeley, Wharton, Yale, UCLA and so on. The quality of their teaching, the wealth of resources, the sheer magnitude of their influence, all bring together in a few select places the world's intellectual élite. More than a source of pride, this represents an incalculable long-term benefit for the nation: its culture, values and methods are eventually propagated, everywhere on earth and at the very highest levels, by an army of foreign graduates who return to lead their own countries. Most of the new crop of Latin American leaders, for example, are alumni of American universities, and this is already having a positive effect on the development prospects of nations like Mexico and Chile.

For the new breed of young European technocrats, as well, the lure of a Masters in Business Administration stamped 'Made in the USA' cannot be overestimated. America still enjoys a virtual monopoly over economic and business education. Its efficiency and influence are so great as to eclipse any other system or model among international economic circles; the German concept of the social market economy is practically unknown to trained economists and the wider public alike.

What it all adds up to is an instrument of cultural power and privilege whose effects are much more significant than is generally imagined. The advantages accruing to America can be likened to those provided by England's mineral wealth in the nineteenth century.

A final element in the cultural equation is the mass media. As the most visible and spectacular vehicle of Americanization, it is also the most decried. Without going into the interminable debate over 'national culture' and the threat of American 'subculture' (every country on earth seems to have its own version of this hardy perennial), the overwhelming dominance of American film and television is a fact of modern life that cannot be denied, for better (at times) or for worse (more often), but in any case for profit. America reaps huge rewards from its productivity and professionalism in this field, and the current worldwide trend towards privatization of TV broadcasting plays right into American hands. Multimedia communications groups in Europe and elsewhere are far more attentive to questions of short-term profitability than the old state monopolies ever had to be; the fact that an American series can be imported at a fraction of the cost of making one's own has put paid to many a local or national production.

At a more subtle level of influence, the plethora of contests and game shows made locally for the home market in Italy or France or Spain are ideal (if unwitting) vehicles for the propagation of the neo-American economic system, on which they are directly modelled. Just switch on your television and see for yourself: America is back!

But had America ever really gone away? There is a fundamental ambiguity here which is at the root of a great many contradictions, misinterpretations and illusions regarding the triumph of Reaganism. True, America had suffered a relative decline by 1980. But a step or two backwards could not undo the work of decades: the advantages won by the genius of the American people, and the ensuing privileges granted by history, remained intact. Somewhat too hastily, the pundits credited Reagan and his philosophy with a string of successes which had rather more to do with America's basic, enduring strengths than with the qualities of its leaders or the pertinence of their policies. In short, an extraordinary optical illusion was created, whereby the USA, sliding dangerously out of control, appeared to reach the turning point of the Reagan years and then effortlessly negotiated the U-turn towards recovery and renewal. In fact, the country was able to draw on massive reserves of power and privilege, a long-established fund of cultural supremacy, and a store of credit (both literal and figurative) in every sphere. But what the rest of the world saw was a seemingly miraculous rescue operation, which was diversely greeted with acclaim, or astonishment, or envy.

Miraculous or not, it was a feat of legerdemain which skirted the real issue: were Americans under Reagan's leadership making the best of their considerable heritage? Was it being used wisely and productively? With the benefit of hindsight, not everyone is convinced that the Reagan years were quite what they seemed, and some would even argue that the 1980s actually saw the nation squander a significant portion of its heritage. Seen from this angle, the brilliance of the 'Reagan renaissance' more closely resembles that of a shooting star, a decadent empire going out in a blaze of glory. Outside observers will applaud the spectacle, but they have been tricked by the illusion of power, and by the power of illusion.

Ten years after its glorious return, America is discovering that some of the party lights have gone out. The land of opportunity, birthplace of

Mickey Mouse and brave new world of space shuttles, Star Wars and leveraged buyouts is not the Eldorado some still imagine it to be. Behind the Hollywood scenery and the glare of the spotlights, the true picture is quite different.

Chapter 3
America backwards*

Not far from some of the most splendid landscapes on earth, the great American cities, reputable centers of business and finance, beckon to the visitor. What do they find there today? Rubbish and rust, damage and deterioration of every description. They may happen to notice that the tin-roofed pedestrian walkways along their route are there to protect them from the hazards, not of any new buildings going up, but of the stone crumbling away from old buildings about to collapse. They may be forgiven for thinking they are in, say, Prague – but in Prague, of course, they have had 40 years to get used to it. No, this is New York, the very image of the Great Modern Metropolis itself.

Deterioration, in a word, describes both sides of this strange new America: a land deteriorating *physically* (which is apparent at first glance) and, on closer inspection, *socially* as well. America now leads the advanced nations in drug abuse and crime, while in such matters as vaccinations or voter turnout it is at the bottom of the league tables. What happened? More importantly, why did it happen?

Like everyone else, I feel a compelling need to find some answers to these alarming questions. The first step, then, is to have a close look – and compare.

How far has the rot set in? To start with, both capitals (the political and the financial) are virtually bankrupt. Washington DC was some $200 million shy of its budget by the end of 1990; its mayor, Marion Barry, had been sentenced in August to 6 months in prison for possession and use of drugs. In the summer of 1991 the new mayor of New York, the Hon. David Dinkins, facing another huge deficit in *his* budget, had little recourse but to begin sacking 30 000 city employees

---

*Many of the arguments and figures presented in this chapter are drawn from a study by Professor Christian Morrisson of the University of Paris (I), Panthéon-Sorbonne.

(including 4000 teachers) – 10 per cent of the municipal workforce. Cost-cutting measures ranged from the merely inconvenient (closing all the city's public lavatories) to the more sinister: the drug treatment centers, in a city of half a million addicts out of a total population of 7 million, were to be shut down, along with most of the shelters intended for some 80 000 homeless. The list goes on: Central Park Zoo and 30 public swimming pools would have to go, a household waste-recycling project was put on hold for a year; even street lighting would be reduced by a third – hardly encouraging news in a city whose crime rate continues to rise steadily.

Nearly every major American city finds itself in a similar plight. Even the airports are shabby! Whole districts, in the Bronx, South Dallas and elsewhere, display a kind of gangrenous urban blight the likes of which no modern Briton or German can recall. In San Francisco, the 'new homeless' roam the streets in their cars, which are the only homes they can afford, despite holding down a regular job. Property speculation has put even rented accommodation out of their reach. The vast urban tracts of 'uncities' (H. G. Wells's coinage seems particularly apt) such as Houston, Washington and Los Angeles are being ravaged by 'crack wars' and crime generally; Black ghettoes are once again coming to the boil, as they did in the sixties. 'Blacks are paying the bills for the Reagan years,' says actor–director Spike Lee. 'The civil rights movement has simply been wiped out.'

Crime – especially Black crime – has reached terrifying new heights. New Yorkers are murdered at the rate of five a day, but in at least ten other cities the rate is higher. Washington's newly elected mayor, Sharon Pratt Dixon, took office at a time when the city had just managed to break its own record for the third year running, with 483 murders in 1990. The country as a whole recorded an astonishing 21 000 murders in 1989 and was expecting some 23 000 in 1990. A million Americans are currently in prison; more than 3 million are on bail or probation. In only 10 years the US prison population has more than doubled to reach an overall proportion of 0.426 per cent (beating the previous world record-holder, South Africa's 0.333 per cent, by nearly a third). Our language as yet lacks a word for this kind of 'Gulag', and the question resurfaces: What on earth is happening to America?

Look further, and another change is apparent. Twenty years ago, the

'American challenge' was to be an inspiration to both West and East. True, the multinationals which spearheaded it continue to invest abroad; but nowadays hardly a week goes by without the announcement of another Japanese takeover, whether of some prestigious landmark (Rockefeller Center springs to mind) or a further slice of Hollywood and the entertainment industry (MCA now belongs to Matsushita, CBS is owned by Sony). Look at NASA and its space shuttle program, which only a few years ago still embodied the pioneering spirit of adventure launched by John F. Kennedy's New Frontier: now it too must grapple with repeated setbacks and spectacular failures. The celebrated Hubble telescope, launched into space at enormous cost on 24 April 1990, will be sending back hopelessly blurred views of the universe due to a faulty manufacturing process. Look, again, at the airports: crashes and near misses are not infrequent, and luggage is routinely lost or stolen.

What of the 'golden boys', those symbols of the affluent Reagan years in their $2000 suits, who were lionized for their knack of amassing fortunes in a matter of months? Today, many are in trouble, and some are in gaol. The massive failure of hundreds of Savings and Loan Associations (once the darlings of an ebullient Wall Street) is history's largest financial collapse. It leaves a gaping hole in the nation's accounts which could conceivably end up costing the taxpayer (naturally) some $500 billion – the equivalent of $2000 for every man, woman and child in the USA.

What *is* happening to America?

If we are to believe the historian Paul Kennedy, in *The Rise and Fall of the Great Powers* (Random House, 1988), the USA is entering a phase of historical decline comparable to that of the Hapsburg empire in the eighteenth century, or of Britain at the end of the ninteenth. Whether Kennedy's diagnosis is too pessimistic is at least debatable. Turning to political scientist Joseph S. Nye, Jr (in *Bound to Lead: The Changing Nature of American Power*, Basic Books, 1990), a number of counterarguments may be advanced:

- Only the USA can claim to maintain a significant presence in every field. It is still both a military and an economic power, boasting both

high technology and vast natural wealth.
- It has a crucial superiority in space, in communications, in culture and in science. Where are the Japanese Nobel winners?
- Even the brightest proponents of the decline theory, some of whom have strong anti-communist credentials, have shown a distressing eagerness to apply the argument to the USA while somehow overlooking the Soviet Union. (We French are no longer so quick to praise Sartre, for instance. . .)

Nye does, however, come up with one common factor in every historical decline: woe to any government unable to control its indebtedness, or, in other words, government that cannot persuade its taxpayers to pay up. This is a fair description of what we see happening today: Americans behaving as if the national legacy of comfort and prosperity which they have inherited amounts to a permanent tax exemption. The prospect of any increase in taxes commands no support among the American public, as Walter Mondale found out in the 1984 presidential election. The Democratic candidate was unable to erase the merest hint of an impression that maybe, one day, *some* taxes might have to be put up. He lost 49 out of 50 states on polling day.

My own opinion is that the dividing line between nations on the rise and those in decline is to be found in a society's desire to build for the future, and thus to progress, or instead to enjoy the present – and thus to decline. Later on, I will explain how a national preference for one or the other is revealed in terms of taxation, borrowing and interest rates.

Historical decline or not, there is no mistaking the current feeling of anxiety, almost of desperation. This has at least spawned a new growth industry, as the economist Bernard Cazes wryly observed, namely, an abundant outpouring of opinion and speculation on the subject of 'The Decline'. Serious commentary ranges from the stoically resigned and the darkly foreboding to the reassuringly upbeat. For those whose tastes run to the baldly apocalyptic, bookshops are bulging with best-selling fictions of that genre (the same is true, relatively speaking, in Moscow). Elsewhere, the recent boom in the turnover of accountancy firms specializing in liquidations and bankruptcies is being shadowed, so to speak, by a surge at the box-office for films like *Ghost, Pacific Heights,* and *Desperate Hours*, which play quite explicitly on the dread fear now haunting so many Americans: that of losing their homes, through sheer inability to meet the interest payments on their loans.

Another sector of recent, dramatic growth is, sadly, the gigantic drugs economy, spurred by the arrival of crack, a cheap derivative of cocaine. One thorough study in the spring of 1988 found that 23 million Americans had taken drugs on at least one occasion in the previous month. These included 6 million more or less regular users of cocaine and half a million heroin users. In schools, half the pupils had smoked marijuana and one in seven had sniffed cocaine. The same year, a report by the National Narcotics Intelligence Consumers Committee (NNICC) put at $22 billion the market value of cocaine sold to users in America (and Europe, whose share is almost negligible). And on 9 January 1991, the International Narcotics Control Board, an organ of the UN, issued a massive survey of the drug problem from its headquarters in Vienna. Among its findings, the cost of drug abuse to the American economy and society as a whole was estimated to have risen to $60 *billion* a year – a sixfold increase since 1984. The report did admit that drug use seemed to have peaked and was now falling somewhat, allowing George Bush to point with justifiable pride to the early success of a range of very tough measures now being implemented. Yet the figures are still far too high. The report also notes that the use of amphetamines is actually increasing. What cannot be avoided in each of these reports and studies is the feeling that they point to an increasingly desperate America, a nation seemingly adrift.

This desperation not only haunts individuals, each facing some private terror – whether in the form of street crime or drug dependency or unemployment, or racial hatred, or even a stack of unpaid bills – but seems to have a grip on society as a whole. The American Dream itself is slipping out of reach, the very dream which has fuelled the nation's forward march since the days of the Pilgrims. Already, the melting pot, in which immigrants from the four corners of the earth were to have mixed and finally blended in – the dream of assimilation – is but a dim memory. America in the 1990s is well on the road to 'retribalization', as each ethnic community in turn barricades itself around its linguistic and cultural differences.

The barricades are up everywhere you turn in today's America. On my first visit, in 1960, I was amazed to find that people would leave their doors unlocked, even if they were going to be away for a fortnight. It was explained to me that, as break-ins were almost unknown, even in town, it was enough simply to shut the door. On my most recent visit, I had dinner in a flat looking out over Central Park where the security arrangements were rather more substantial: the 75 tenants of this apartment building paid for 20 guards to keep watch, 24 hours a day, in teams of 5.

The visitor to America in the 1990s is sure to come away with more than a few raw, disturbing images of a society under stress. To explain them, we must look beyond the surface glare and glamor of the Reagan era and try to understand what really happened during the past decade.

A house divided

Something has come unhinged in this new America, and journalists, sociologists and criminologists have come up with a term to describe it: 'polarization'. Formerly a buzz word used only by observers of the developing countries, the concept neatly fitted certain countries such as Brazil or South Africa. It designates a kind of *de facto* segregation, or 'economic apartheid', underpinning a cruel and irrevocable social split. In such a two-tiered society, the different sections of the population are virtually living on two separate planets, and the gap between them widens year by year.

Polarisation in America is by now a widespread, generalised phenomenon, thanks largely to the ultra-liberal policies of the Reagan administration. And it is not only the polarization of rich and poor, but of whole institutions: prestigious universities on the one hand, a public educational system in tatters on the other; gleaming, modern hospitals and clinics in stark contrast to a bloated, obsolete medical infrastructure. The economy itself is polarized: one need only compare the high-tech industries (mostly tied to the federal defense budget), which put the USA at the very top in some fields, with a number of other areas where America is falling further and further behind.

The most significant outcome of Reaganite liberalism is almost certainly the widening gap between the rich and the poor. This was supposed to be the 'price worth paying' in order to 'reinvigorate' the nation; a very high price indeed, in view of the lacklustre economic

results. Even after a modest recovery, and despite the forecasts of supply-side theorists, the last 10 years did not bring down the number of
poor. In fact, their numbers increased slightly, while the number of millionaires actually tripled. Some 40 million Americans at the low end of
the scale saw their income drop by 10 per cent in as many years. Taking
a definition of poverty as living on a disposable income of less than half
the national average, we find that 17 per cent of the American population are poor, as against 5 per cent in the former West Germany or in
Scandinavia, 8 per cent of the Swiss and 12 per cent of the British.
Some experts do not accept this method of calculation, and estimate
that the poor now account for fully *20 per cent* of the US population.
The figure is the highest in the industrialized world – and it does not
include the growing ranks of clandestine immigrants, most notably in
California.

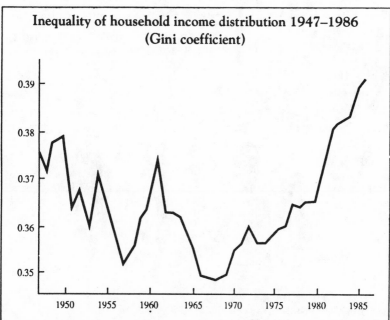

**Inequality of household income distribution 1947–1986
(Gini coefficient)**

The Gini coefficient measures the degree of inequality in the distribution of income
within a society. At a theoretical value of 0, income would be equally distributed
among members of society; as its value increases towards a maximum value of 1, it
reflects increasingly unequal income distribution.

SOURCE: *US Bureau of Census*.

A comprehensive report of official statistics compiled by the Congressional Budget Office, published in 1989, concluded that 'the gap between rich and poor grew wider in the 1980s, to the extent that by 1990 the total net income of the $2\frac{1}{2}$ million wealthiest Americans will be about equal to that of the 100 million at the lower end of the scale'.

It should come as no surprise, then, that images usually associated with the southern hemisphere are an everyday part of the modern American landscape: mini-slums springing up next to sumptuous estates; queues of the unemployed snaking down pavements past the ostentatious shop-window displays of luxury goods; the homeless, stamping their feet to keep warm in doorways cluttered with rubbish and overturned bins. Even the middle class, America's pride and the source of its stability, is shrinking year by year. The depressing new social geography sees the poor, growing poorer, facing the rich, who are growing richer. What, we ask again, has happened to America?

Predictably, this polarization has heightened social tensions, leading to a kind of sporadic, anarchic 'class struggle' undreamt of by those young professionals in post-Soviet Moscow who have only just earned their liberal Reaganite credentials. As affluent Americans wake up to increasingly unsafe cities and a 'deteriorating environment' which is the inevitable consequence of there being more and more poor on the streets, some entrepreneurs can nevertheless take heart: from night watchmen and bodyguards to virtual private armies, the security services industry is booming, while the trade in firearms is breaking all records. Times are tough, and Americans are worried. They are also armed to the teeth.

In 1990, *Time* magazine interviewed New Yorkers about their personal safety. Sixty per cent said they *always*, or often, felt threatened by crime, while only 26 per cent seldom felt so. For 68 per cent of them, their quality of life was now worse than it had been 5 years ago. Among the new merchandise in New York's shops, one should not be too surprised to find bullet-proof satchels and children's underwear. After all, the murder rate for young men in US cities ranges from 4 to 73 *times* greater than it is in Bangladesh, one of the two or three poorest countries in the world.

It all amounts to an extreme reluctance on the part of the 'well-to-do', barricaded inside their mansions, to come to terms with the fact that they no longer live in a country which bears comparison with Sweden or Switzerland. Rather, on venturing out, they encounter a sort of Third World on their doorstep: more developed than the other one, of course, but becoming every bit as inequitable. It is a 'Third World' where a great many people are nevertheless extremely well off, and where any notion of social justice is condemned as subversive, if not obscene. The 'War on Want' is only palatable as a charity fund-raiser in today's America; any suggestion that social security should be extended to one and all is viewed as a frontal assault on the ruling classes themselves.

The Bonfire of the Vanities

When it appeared in 1987, Tom Wolfe's novel *The Bonfire of the Vanities* was recognized for its stingingly accurate portrayal of the fears and fortunes of Americans confronted by this new polarization. For those who have not read it, the story is one which any American will confirm is perfectly emblematic of the 1980s. (Tom Wolfe more or less invented the New Journalism, as it was called in America, and his novel bears the reporter's stamp.)

A young Wall Street broker (McCoy) drives out to Kennedy airport to pick up his lover, Maria. On the way back to town, as night falls, he accidentally joins the wrong exit queue on a motorway interchange. Since the traffic is bumper to bumper, he is unable to leave the queue and has to exit into the Bronx. . . at the wheel of his $48 000 Mercedes. Soon he is lost, going in circles until he spots a motorway access ramp. He hesitates: it is clearly the wrong direction but, as Maria notes, 'at least it's civilization'. Once on the ramp, however, a makeshift roadblock of old tyres forces him to come to a halt. He gets out to clear the way, when two young Black men approach. Fearing the worst, McCoy hurls a tyre at one of the youths, who throws it back, and jumps into the car where Maria, terrified, has taken the wheel. As she zigzags among the tyres and rubbish bins in a desperate attempt to escape the trap, McCoy hears a distinct 'thok!. . . the sound of the rear fender hitting something'. The second youth has disappeared from view. Finally they get back onto the motorway.

Once Maria has calmed down somewhat, McCoy reminds her of the 'little sound' and wonders if they should inform the police. Once they are safely back in his 'White Manhattan' flat, he reminds her again: they might have hit one of the youths; maybe they should report it. Maria explodes: 'I'm gonna tell *you* what happened. I'm from South Carolina, and I'm gonna tell you in plain English... Two niggers tried to kill us in the jungle, and we got outta the jungle, and we're still breathing, and that's that.' McCoy weakly gives in to her insistence that they should drop the whole matter; for one thing, he must keep his wife from finding out about his affair with Maria. His fate is thus sealed. Innocent, he is nevertheless well-off and white, and will be made to bear the full force of all the stored-up hatred which he and his 'class' have earned.

Henry Lamb, the young Black man hit by McCoy's Mercedes, lies in a coma for a year, then dies. The police trace the owner of the car; Maria denies that she had been at the wheel; Lamb's accomplice, the other Black youth, makes a false statement accusing McCoy. Now McCoy begins his descent into hell, becoming a pawn in the machinations of three people who are determined to destroy him: a Black preacher from the Bronx, the local prosecutor and a British reporter. Each has his own reasons for seeking the conviction of a rich white man (or, in the case of the reporter, for milking a great 'story': Wall Street Bond Wizard Kills Black Youth and Flees).

Always looming in the background of the novel is the surreal contrast between opulence and power, on the one hand, and the deprivation and wretchedness of the Bronx, on the other. McCoy is a graduate of Yale with a six-figure income and a luxury flat worth $3 million. Each morning as he leaves his apartment building (under an awning which is itself a status symbol), he can admire the thousands of yellow tulips planted on the median strip of Park Avenue and paid for by the residents' association. The office building where he trades in bonds shows the same attention to sumptuous detail. Like all the other golden boys, he knows himself to be one of the 'Masters of the Universe'. Yet just across the river is the Bronx, where young Blacks are dealing in drugs and shooting up by the thousands in dingy stairways where sex, violence and addiction are the stuff of daily life. It is a 'neighborhood' where moving house means keeping the neighbors at bay, lest they steal your furniture out from under you. McCoy's unintended victim happened to be an exception: at 18, Henry Lamb had been a model student and could actually *read*. This achievement was notable enough to earn him a place at New York City College.

This contrast between Park Avenue and the Bronx is no less flagrant than that which divides Soweto from the garden suburbs and swimming pools of Johannesburg. The only human bridges linking the two worlds are the teachers, the police and the judges; and in the Bronx, the judges dare not stray more than a few yards from their courthouses as they scrape a meagre living on a miserly wage.

Caught up in a grotesque political and media 'event', McCoy becomes a symbol, and a convenient scapegoat. Poor, rich McCoy, with all his charm, crashes to earth just as so many other American vanities have fallen from past glory. Inequality is nothing new to America, of course. The Bronx was a sinkhole long before Reagan entered the White House. But as the polarization of rich vs poor became more entrenched in the 1980s, its very nature has changed. In his recent bestseller, *The Politics of Rich and Poor*, Kevin Phillips asserts that the good old days, when the rich could grow richer with total impunity, are over once and for all. He does not rule out the possibility that future revolts by the have-nots could plunge the country into turmoil – a scenario also mooted by *The Economist* in a long and exhaustively researched article (4 May 1990). What, indeed, is happening to America?

On the critical list: education, health and democracy

It is not only in terms of rich and poor that American society now finds itself dangerously polarized. Ominously, the same polarization has spread to a number of vital areas which until recently could be counted among the nation's great strengths.

Let two points – two facts – illustrate what is probably the most disturbing development of all: a declining democracy.

Fact number one: voter turnout in American elections is the lowest of all the Western democracies. Non-voters outnumber voters two to one, regardless of the issues or candidates involved. Moreover, this amounts to a *de facto* disenfranchisement of the least privileged sections of society, who would seem to be so inhibited or so alienated that they no longer grasp the importance of an electoral process which will, in some way, decide their fate. Voter apathy may not be new, but it has never before been so widespread. The same pattern can be observed in most of the Western democracies, in fact, and it may well be related to certain features of the neo-American model. In former times, the poor revolted; today, dulled to a stupor by the drab ordinariness of their squalor (which never appears on their TV screens), they do not even bother to vote.

Fact number two: since ancient times, one of the distinguishing marks of a civilized country was that it could count its inhabitants (e.g. the biblical account of Herod's census). Yet 10–15 per cent of the American population – not including those who actually have reason to hide from the authorities – now 'go missing' from the national census. What degree of civic responsibility, one inevitably wonders, does that reflect?

Turning to education, the present situation is almost unbelievable. True, the American system of higher and postgraduate education still leads the world: in any given year, the USA accounts for more than one-third of all published scientific work. The number of research scientists actually doubled between 1976 and 1986. The great universities, with their highly selective admissions policies, have managed to maintain standards consistent with their reputations for excellence. The financial and human resources on which they can draw remain the envy of the rest of the world.

Yet alongside this prestigious (and, for parents, very expensive) upper echelon we find a primary and secondary education system which simply does not measure up. Recent studies that assessed the scientific knowledge of pupils at ages 10, 13 and 17, found that Americans scored *lowest* of all the industrialized countries. Most receive no scientific training whatsoever after the age of 16. In other areas the results are no less disappointing: in geography, for example, American students aged 18–24 came last in a comparative study of eight countries.

Hardly surprising, then, that 45 per cent of US adults are unable to locate Central America on a map, while more than half cannot place the UK, France or Japan. And in an even more crucial matter, it *is* surprising to learn that at 18, the age when young Americans go off to college, fully 40 per cent admit that they cannot read properly.

The whole problem of illiteracy is a particularly vexed question in today's world. The new orthodoxy, which presumes that everything works if the market works, hardly explains why the UK literacy rate is lower than Portugal's, or why Americans are more likely to be illiterate than Poles.

In the end, we must ask whether or not the overall quality of a nation's education system represents a fundamental asset, an absolute value; and if so, whether the decline in American schooling over the past few years may have much to do with the economic pattern (the neo-American model) of which it is part and parcel. Current trends in European mass education (i.e. the state schools, for the most part) provide some clues: the systems there, too, are showing signs of decay. This is especially true of some of the most highly developed economies – France, Italy, the UK – the very ones which stand outside the Rhine model and are therefore more susceptible to neo-American influences.

America's polarized education system, offering first-rate graduate studies for the very few and inferior compulsory schooling for the many, differs radically from that of countries such as Germany and Japan, where most pupils reach respectable, if average, attainment levels – and outright failures are almost non-existent. Even where the American system excels, the same polarizing forces are evidently at work. Out of a total of 3600 colleges and universities, only about 200 are highly selective in their choice of students.

One revealing statistic which shows up in study after study is the amount of time students in the USA devote to homework: seldom more than 1 hour per day, as compared to an average of 3 hours spent watching television. It is hard not to conclude that the days when America was a paragon of modern civilization, leading the insatiable human quest for knowledge, are receding further and further into the past.

The education 'patient' was already so ill by 1983 that President Reagan set up a national commission to study the symptoms. In their report, unambiguously entitled *A Nation at Risk*, the experts agreed that the level of education in the USA had already fallen *below* what it had been in 1957, the year the Soviets launched the first Sputnik and a shocked America began to question its own abilities. When a dozen specialists were brought together at Columbia University in 1990, under the auspices of the American Assembly (a legacy of Eisenhower), they came up with some significant conclusions about America in the

1980s (see *The Global Economy: America's Role in the Decade*, Norton, 1990). Three in particular are worth mentioning here, because they are not unrelated: 'The American education system is on the verge of collapse'; the savings ratio in America is shockingly low; and that is only a logical outcome of the Reagan administration's 'persistent view that the trade deficit is a sign of economic health'.

Robust good health – in the physical sense, at least – is something we still associate with America, on the evidence of those rosy-cheeked, athletic teenagers who populate the world of TV advertising. Behind the glowing images, however, is yet another case of polarization, made worse by Reaganism and now severely affecting the entire health care system. On paper, the situation may not look bad: the USA still spends more on health than any other OECD country (10 per cent of GDP), and many outstanding hospitals and clinics are world leaders in their chosen specialities. Medical research still flourishes, with new drugs and treatments being developed in some of the world's most advanced laboratories.

But these peaks of performance cannot disguise a much poorer level of general health care than is generally realized. A few recent statistics are real eye-openers:

- Infant mortality: at 10 per 1000 – twice that of Japan – the US rate is only number 22 in the world, and it is not just the higher rate for ethnic minorities which accounts for this poor showing. Even the figure for White babies alone compares unfavorably with that of many developed nations.
- Vaccinations: US rates average out at 40 per cent lower than the rest of the industrialized world, and in some cases are lower than the figures for developing countries.
- Teenage pregnancies: among 15 to 19 year olds, the figure is 10 per cent, which is 10 times higher than in Japan.

All of these figures point to an increasingly fragmented and uncaring society of dysfunctional families and spreading poverty. The proportion of under-age children whose parents are divorced is higher in America than anywhere else; a fifth of its children live below the poverty line. In 1987, 12 million of them had no health insurance coverage (a 14 per cent rise since 1981). Yet, in a country where there is no national health insurance scheme, public spending on health care as a proportion of overall government spending is, at 14 per cent, the lowest in the OECD. The Reagan administration ferociously opposed any and all attempts to institute a national health plan. . . in the name of promoting family values! As a result, half the employees of the nation's small and medium-sized businesses are wholly ineligible for welfare benefits. Redundancies, when they come, are swift and merciless: on average, workers find themselves out of a job and on the streets in just two days.

As government took an axe to social programs, drastically cutting their funds or eliminating them altogether, the overall situation simply went from bad to worse. The most crippling deficit in America today is not financial (gigantic as that may be), but social. It is a gap that cannot possibly be plugged by organized charities or individual acts of kindness. In its drive to reinvigorate America by encouraging 'winners', the Reagan team consigned the losers – and the merely ordinary – to the scrap-heap of history.

Reaganism would have no truck with 'social' planning; its brief was to restore an ailing economy, from which all else would naturally flow. Alas, it was not to be.

Industry in retreat

American industry is in retreat. The only conceivable objection to this statement is to be found in the volume of overseas production realized by US multinationals (20 per cent as against Japan's 5 per cent), and even this represents a climb-down from the position of 25 years ago. One has only to recall the opening lines of Jean-Jacques Servan-Schreiber's *The American Challenge*, published in 1967 (English-language edition in 1968): 'In fifteen years' time, the third largest industrial power in the world, after the United States and the Soviet Union, may well turn out to be, not Europe, but *American industry* in Europe.' Since those words were written, the flow of investment across the Atlantic has reversed. This change grows more pronounced each year.

By September 1990, *Fortune* magazine was asking in deadly earnest if 'Made in the USA' would soon be an obsolete expression. The Reagan years did see the creation of 18 million jobs, but most of them were in services, *not* industry, and many were little better than odd jobs, with few prospects, in restaurants, shops, and most noticeably in security and protection firms. Meanwhile, industry was shedding 2 million jobs and piling up record trade deficits. American manufacturers saw Japanese competitors catch up, and eventually overtake them, in a number of fields. Take the car industry: in 1990, General Motors, the giant among giants, posted a third quarter loss of $2 billion. Ford announced its 'worst year since 1982', while Chrysler plunged deeper into an already precarious situation with a further loss of $214 million in a single quarter. Together, American car makers were running an overall deficit of some $60 *billion*.

America's resilience, its ability to turn a difficulty to its own advantage, is legendary. But there is a limit to the amount of time available for shaping a sustained recovery; how much time only becomes clear once a turnaround has been achieved – and that is not yet the case. As the Gulf War was ending, the American Council on Competition, whose membership is drawn from the top ranks of industry and higher education, concluded that by 1995 the USA would simply drop out of worldwide contention in 15 key areas of technological production (of a total of 94). It was no fluke that the famous Patriot missiles could only do their job thanks to certain Japanese-built components. The vital factor, here as elsewhere, is long-term planning. If American armed forces performed masterfully in the Gulf in 1991, it was thanks to decisions taken in the 1960s and 1970s. Since when, the short-term view has increasingly taken precedence over the more forward-looking, long-term approach.

The future is so obviously being mortgaged for present gain that even someone like Carl Icahn cannot deny it. Mr. Icahn was one of the first corporate raiders, the man who took over TWA on a gamble. Ironically, these days he deplores the 'casino mentality' of big business. The nation is living well beyond its means, he says, while 'the infrastructure is crumbling, nothing new is built and nothing old is maintained'. Icahn compares the USA to a family farm where the first generation planted, the second brought in the harvest and the third finds the bailiffs coming to repossess the lot. It is beginning to look as if the bailiffs will be speaking Japanese.

The quality of goods 'made in the USA' is falling, and so, relatively speaking, is that of its know-how. Two hundred top executives from firms which manufacture parts for Toyota were brought together in November 1990 to be told some hard facts by one of the Japanese multinationals' directors. A particularly eloquent example: American factories were turning out 100 *times* more faulty components than their Japanese counterparts. As for know-how, American companies find that they have to forge new alliances with European or Japanese firms in order to bring in the skilled personnel they cannot find at home.

The same processes are at work undermining the aeronautics industry, in spite of the massive aid which it receives, directly or not, in the form of military procurement by the Pentagon. The big American firms have lost their near-total dominance and let in the Europeans, who can now boast that the Airbus has captured a 30 per cent share of the world market. It is the same story in other vital sectors, such as electronics and information technology. America may have invented the transistor and the microchip, but American products now account for only 10 per cent of the world market, as against 60 per cent at the end of the 1960s. And when General Motors orders 100 new presses, 80 will be purchased abroad – where they are cheaper, more modern and more reliable.

It is worth pointing out, at this juncture, the extraordinary skill and courage shown by Ronald Reagan in convincing Congress, and public opinion, that the temptation to give in to protectionism must be resisted – even in the face of a traumatic industrial decline and the growing foreign penetration of domestic markets.

There are at least five reasons for this industrial eclipse, all related to the loss of the five great advantages which lay at the heart of the postwar boom. These were studied in detail by the authors of a report, *Made in America* (Michael Dertouzos, Richard Lester and Robert Solow: MIT Press, 1989), which was prepared on behalf of the celebrated Massachusetts Institute of Technology.

1. The relative size of America's home market has shrunk, leaving manufacturers in no position to capture new foreign markets in the face of competition from Japan and Europe.
2. America's technological dominance is over. More and more innovations now come from overseas, and new products and processes are introduced at a much faster rate in Europe and Japan than in the USA (4 years vs 7 years, for example, in the automotive industry).

3. In the race to train a highly skilled work force, the USA is losing its former edge over foreign competitors.
4. The USA could once afford to take up almost any challenge – such as putting someone on the moon – on the basis of its immense accumulated wealth. This, too, has gone.
5. Finally, American management techniques no longer set the standard for the rest of the world. Again, Europe and Japan have caught up and often surpassed their former mentor, to the extent that US companies now copy methods pioneered abroad, such as 'pull' production systems, 'total quality management' (TQM) etc.

There is another factor, too, which became particularly significant during the 1980s: 'Stock Market Mania'. The irresistible lure of speculative trading and windfall profits ultimately worked against US industry. America's best and brightest college graduates, dazzled by the golden boys and their multimillion-dollar gambles, felt little incentive to choose the hard road of manufacturing as they stepped into the job market. A glamorous Wall Street caricature of capitalism was to prove a knife in the back of capitalism itself. As high finance beckoned, manufacturing industries accumulated a 'skills deficit' and went into a tailspin.

In April 1991, the Trilateral Commission (composed of business and trade union leaders, politicians and economists from North America, Europe and Japan) held its annual meeting in Tokyo. The Japanese hosts announced that, on the basis of the above, they had reached certain inescapable conclusions: having already helped to revitalise British industry over the last decade, Japan's next great task, they agreed, would have to be the re-industrialization of the USA.

The deficit nightmare

Industrial decline and social polarization were not the gravest threats facing America, according to Reagan. The real worry was the soaring budget deficit. That government borrowing should have reached unprecedented heights under Reagan – who had promised less government and greater national self-reliance – is one of the (many) fascinating paradoxes of his presidency.

Today, a whole new batch of American officials and politicians are losing sleep over Reagan's legacy of debt. In the 1960s and early 1970s, the radio news bulletins would begin with one grim, simple statistic: the number of American dead in Vietnam. These days, another figure is permanently displayed on an electronic signboard on New York's 42nd Street: the federal government's total debt. By the end of 1990, it stood at an unimaginable $3.1 *trillion*, the equivalent of total government revenues over 3 years, or of 35 years of annual budget deficits – which are themselves enormous, as we shall see.

There are so many other eloquent statistics and economic indicators that it is hard to choose the two or three most damning, but the following will do: the current account, more or less evenly balanced at the end of the 1970s, was running a $180 billion deficit by 1987, i.e. 3.5 per cent of GDP. It was brought down to $85 billion (1.5 per cent of GDP) in 1989, but even that represents a gigantic gap. As it happens, all this red ink flows from industry. The fact that the agricultural trade balance remains in the black is hardly reassuring: as a net exporter of agricultural produce and a net importer of finished goods, America now has a trade profile which is beginning to resemble that of a developing country!

The federal budget gives equal cause for concern. Now that we can see the results of his policies, it seems quite incredible that Reagan managed to convince voters he could cut taxes, increase military spending and maintain other government programs all at the same time. Lester Thurow, an economist at MIT, offered the following epitaph: 'Here lies Ronald Reagan, the man who took a great power from world creditor to world debtor in world record time.'

For the last few years, the annual federal budget deficit has been hovering around the $150 billion mark (3 per cent of GDP). The question is, how can it be reduced? Neither of the two branches of government in a position to do so has yet been able to summon up the necessary courage. The President pledges no new taxes and no cuts in military spending, and the voters applaud; members of Congress reap the same electoral advantage by opposing cuts in social spending. Balancing the budget is left for another day.

Oddly enough, there is a law on the US statute books which *requires* the budget to be balanced: the notorious Gramm–Rudman–Hollings amendment, which states that across-the-board cuts shall be applied automatically if all else fails. But Capitol Hill and the White House cannot even agree on how to implement the law, giving rise to the lamentable spectacle, last seen in late October 1990, of a US president having to stare down a stubborn Congress by threatening to stop payment of civil servants' wages.

The effect of mounting deficits has been political paralysis – an inability on the part of the government to act decisively in vital areas of neglect such as education, research and the infrastructure. Just how bare America's cupboards had become was poignantly illustrated at the end of the summer of 1990, when the Gulf War was set in motion. An astonished world saw the mighty USA bring out the begging-bowl and ask her allies to help finance the military operation.

Those who sniggered at America's humiliation on that occasion showed a deplorable lack of judgement, in my opinion. For the astonishing thing is not that contributions were sought at all (mainly from the Gulf Arab coalition partners), but that this had not happened sooner; and we in western Europe in particular have no cause to feel smug – we who could just as easily have shared the fate of Hungary or Czechoslovakia, had it not been for the GIs sent to defend us, at little or no cost to ourselves.

The world's largest debtor

It is, of course, only natural for the rich to loan to the poor, and for rich countries to loan to poor ones, who can then use those funds to speed up their development. This profound logic of complementary incentives is justly cited as a validation of the liberal ethic. Thus, a century ago, France and England were the two great lending nations of the world, as was America until the 1970s. But since 1980, in a spectacular and unprecedented reversal, the world's most powerful country has become its largest debtor.

There is really only one reason for the change, one which provides ample food for thought in the light of the liberal ethic so beloved of Reaganites: in a word, Americans have stopped *saving*. Rather than store up for the future, in accord with the virtuous principles laid down by their Puritan forebears, they now plunge headlong into debt in pursuit of consumer satisfaction and instant gratification. This new economic morality of the American nation, its people and government alike, is exacerbating the plight of the poor and compromising everyone's future prospects.

America's net foreign debt (i.e. the amount it has borrowed from overseas sources less what it is owed) stood at $600 billion in 1989, i.e. about half the total debt of the entire developing world. Less than 15 years ago, the USA was the world's most important lender to other countries; now it is the biggest borrower. This has had a number of consequences, the first and foremost being a loss of independence, an increasing reliance on foreign creditors.

Without sufficient savings of her own to finance investment, America has had to seek loans elsewhere (principally from Japan and Germany, whose surpluses are the mirror-image of US liabilities). Each year another $150 billion (3 per cent of GDP) is added to the mountain of debt. It is a cruel irony of history that the defeated nations of the Second World War, now eminently prosperous, should be rushing to the rescue of a profligate America. More than ironic, it is visibly humiliating: every time the US Treasury goes to set the premiums on government bonds, it must secure the prior approval of Japanese subscribers. And in order to attract foreign investors, interest rates have to be kept high – thus discouraging investment at home and further delaying recovery.

These shackles of debt are not the exclusive preserve of the federal government: business and industry are looking increasingly exposed as well. Where once they enjoyed a reputation for financial probity, thanks to low levels of borrowing, they too are having to take out loans on a massive scale. In fact, US companies have *tripled* their borrowing since 1980, and debt as a proportion of shareholder's equity has doubled over the same period. There can be no clearer evidence of their financial vulnerability, leading the Brookings Institution to calculate that in the event of a major economic recession, one in ten of America's biggest companies would be forced to call in the receivers.

In addition to everything else, America's current economic and financial debility is a dangerously unstable factor in the world at large. The interlocking of economies is such that in 1982, for example, when Mexico announced it was unable to meet its commitments to foreign creditors, a global banking and financial crisis was only averted by the narrowest of margins. Now it is America's turn to find itself in reduced circumstances. The largest banks in the land are themselves worryingly exposed through the collapse of the property market and snowballing

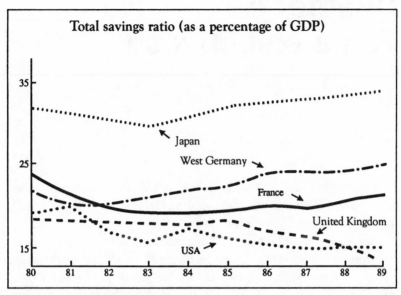

Total savings ratio (as a percentage of GDP)

SOURCE: *Direction de la Prévision,1989*.

defaults by borrowers – particularly those who were so eager to issue the notorious junk bonds, which would ultimately be their undoing.

The largest banks know, however, that they are literally 'too big to fail' and can count on a helping hand from government if the worst comes to the worst. America's political leaders would step in to prevent the crash of a major financial institution on the grounds that it could set off a lethal chain reaction culminating in widespread disaster. More than a domino theory, this is the so-called 'butterfly wing' effect: the beating of a butterfly wing in, say, Tokyo or Chicago might end up as a tornado in Paris.

Thus, in yet another intriguing but ominous irony of history, 10 years of ultra-liberalism have resulted in a US financial system whose future may only be assured with the help of federal government hand-outs. As part of a larger picture bursting with paradoxes and ironies, it is highly symptomatic of what Paul Mentré, paraphrasing Milan Kundera, has elegantly termed 'the unbearable lightness of strength'.

Chapter 4
Fame and finance

As the Boeing touched down at Kennedy Airport, the passenger next to me said, 'What a wonderful country! Here, at least, you can still make a fortune, and make it fast'.

Not a very original remark, but one that leads to an intriguing question. Just how does one go about 'getting rich quick'? Apart from the casino, there are really only two sure routes. The first is through industry, i.e. by inventing and selling; the second is through trade, i.e. by buying and selling. But no traders worth their salt simply sell a product in the same state that it was acquired in: some extra value or service is added. Finance is virtually alone among trades in allowing the dealer to make a profit by selling his or her goods (securities and commodities) unchanged. The crucial problem for the financial trader is, therefore, how to raise the money to buy the goods in the first place.

The problem can be solved in only three ways: (1) self-financing; (2) borrowing; (3) increasing capital.

Self-financing

This method calls upon the financial resources that a company has left once it has made provision for depreciation, paid its shareholders their dividends and settled its tax bill.

From company directors' viewpoints, there is no better method. Self-financing leaves them beholden to no one, free to do what they like with the money they have earned. Many industrialists who love their work but loathe getting entangled in questions of finance choose this route and stick with it. But not the true financial dealer, for whom this approach is simply too slow. It is not enough, in the financier's world, to generate internal growth; outside resources must be recruited in order to achieve the quickest possible expansion of the business.

Traditionally, the English-speaking countries were always the champions of self-financing. Recently, though, they have been overtaken by Germany, where some 90 per cent of financing is self-generated. Japan, on the other hand, has one of the lowest rates (70 per cent), while continental European countries, including France, are generally somewhere in between these two extremes. In any case, self-financing is the method of choice, whereas outside financing (mainly through borrowing) is seen as a secondary resource, a less-preferred option, except by a few daring individuals – those who are willing to face any challenge, take any risk, in order to 'get rich quick'.

Borrowing

A company can usually choose one of two paths when it decides to borrow: either it goes privately to its own bankers, or it goes public by issuing bonds on the market. (A relatively new third option of debt securitisation can be ignored for the sake of argument.) Taking the second path, the public one, depends on at least one important condition being fulfilled: the bond issuer must be known, and esteemed, by those he or she hopes to sign on as subscribers. The more recently established the firm is, the greater the requirement of a good reputation and a high profile.

Borrowing has three distinct disadvantages: first, the amount raised varies in direct proportion to the borrower's own capital stock. In other words, lenders would rather lend to the rich. Secondly, borrowing is an expensive business, and never more so than in recent times, when the real rates of interest in the industrialized nations have consistently broken all the records set during the last 200 years. The final drawback to borrowing is that loans are time-bound. The recipient is expected not only to pay interest but, eventually, to repay the principal as well.

All of which is terribly restrictive and exacting; financiers need something more dynamic. And that is why, in the English-speaking countries where deregulation has taken place, dealers have thought up a variety of new techniques that allow the borrower to raise considerable sums, as long as his lenders are convinced that their investment will rapidly yield sizable profits under his management. The borrower's strategy is thus to buy in ever-greater volume in order to increase the volume and profitability of sales, and the means most commonly used are junk bonds and leveraged buyouts (LBOs).

These new techniques are only of marginal interest to the big, well-established financial firms. But what if you are young, ambitious and talented, and your goal is to make a quick personal fortune (thereby contributing, in Reaganite parlance, to the 'democratisation' of an economy dominated by old wealth and numbed by the complacency of the establishment)? To this question, a brilliant financier named Fred Joseph, chairman of Drexel Burnham Lambert, provided an answer in 1983 which will go down in economic and financial history.

Fred Joseph devised a three-stage plan which unfolds as follows:

In stage one, using your flair and talent, you find a company whose stock market rating happens to be well below the monetary value of its assets.

In stage two, your banker (who is as ambitious and talented as you) does you a threefold favor. First, he talks up your reputation on the market: in effect, he provides the publicity which is the psychological glue needed to make your plan stick. Finance and celebrity are indissolubly wedded in this system. Your banker then issues junk bonds on your behalf: these are not (as the name wrongly implies) worthless, but merely expensive, on account of the higher risk they carry. And the risk is high precisely because you, the talented but not very wealthy borrower who has issued them, have few assets of your own to back up your ambitions. Since you are about to launch yourself almost single-handedly into this precarious operation in order to make your fortune, it is entirely reasonable for the market (i.e. those who subscribe to your bond issue) to charge much higher interest rates than they would to, say, IBM. This is clearly the most difficult phase of the proceedings: you have to convince people to let you borrow huge sums of money, despite your obvious inability to provide surety for the loan. This is where your banker's third favor comes in, one that is specifically designed for this very situation. He makes you a direct loan – again, at a high rate of interest – and, in doing so, demonstrates to the rest of the market his confidence in your abilities. Having obtained this loan, you can now buy the company identified in stage one. The relatively weak purchasing power of your own assets has been multiplied, the way a lever concentrates physical force: thus the term 'leveraged' buyout. Now it is up to you to squeeze enough profits from your new acquisition to satisfy your banker, and yourself!

The new ingredient in Fred Joseph's recipe for success is to be found in the trade-off between high risk and high interest rates. Banks have traditionally been extremely wary of brokering such arrangements: their chief concern has always been to limit risk, to obtain guarantees for their loans. As credit institutions, their behaviour is shaped by considerations of long-term security and stability. To lend on a high-risk, high-interest basis marks a radical departure from this scenario by granting priority to the short-term, i.e. the immediate rate of return provided by interest payments and the consequent profits that can be displayed. Never mind the long-term perspective, the high-risk banker seems to be saying. The future is not my department; my only concern is to be today's winner, to score instant success, to make my mark right now.

Here, in a nutshell, is the theme that will recur throughout this book: the combat between the two major forms of capitalism is fundamentally that of the short term vs the long term, the present vs the future.

And now for stage three of the game-plan. Having secured a 'war chest' through borrowing, the future golden boy will adopt the tactics of the raider by swooping down on the prey with a vengeance. First they must satisfy the shareholders of the newly acquired company by paying them more than the previously quoted share price, but still less than the monetary value of the assets. Then comes the process of asset-stripping. (To European ears, the term sounds highly pejorative, because we think of a company as something more than a piece of merchandise. Americans attach no such emotive value to it.) This allows the borrower to repay the loan, but more importantly to reap instant profits which he shares with his banker. Act I of a personal success story is complete.

The outside observer may be forgiven for thinking that he or she has accidentally strayed onto a film set. In fact, according to Felix Rohatyn, senior partner and manager of Lazard Frères (the firm which once rescued New York City from financial ruin), Wall Street is now 'worse than Hollywood'. And not just because the fate of so many companies, stripped of their assets and employees, is the stuff of melodrama. Whole sections of the American financial system have been plunged into crisis as a result of the rapacious new techniques. A particularly revealing illustration of the problem has been provided by Michel François-Poncet, chairman of Paribas, who notes that the developed world's monetary authorities imposed a series of preventive measures, following the 1987 crash, aimed at restricting the amount of credit which banks could extend, using a formula known as the Cooke ratio. This worked so well in the USA that the proportion of overall company financing by banks (the intermediation rate) fell from 80 per cent in 1970 to only 20 per cent by 1990.

One of the consequences of this policy is shown by another dramatic statistic: whereas 8 American banks could be counted among the world's 25 biggest in 1970, by 1990 the largest American bank, Citicorp, was ranked number 24 in the world. As they wound down their credit facilities, however, American banks were forced to step up their involvement in high-yield (i.e. high-risk) operations in order to maintain their profitability. By 1990 the total of their LBO investments had reached $190 billion, or three times the amount earmarked for loans to developing countries ($64 billion).

Those who have been reading the specialized press since the stock market crash of 19 October 1987 will know that there has been an alarming rise in bankruptcies among US financial institutions. To compensate for a declining volume of business, and in accordance with the very logic of the American capitalist system itself, they have had to throw themselves headlong into high-risk activities in a frantic search for quick profits. And at the end of this rocky road it is the American taxpayer who will foot the bill.

Increase of capital

To return to the saga of our ambitious young people, intent on becoming lords of the financial universe: they know that the real wizards, those who have penetrated the inner circle, eschew both of the paths described so far. Rather than exploit their own savings or borrow those of others, they go to the open market and, on the sole strength of their name and reputation, obtain an increase of capital – money which has the apparently magical qualities of being both inexpensive and eternal. Unlike borrowed money, this sort goes on forever: a company's capital stock is not refundable. What is more, its cost is well below that of borrowed money, because dividends seldom exceed 3–4 per cent of share value, whereas the interest rates on loans in the developed world currently vary between 8 per cent and 12 per cent or more.

As for the risk factor, shareholders know that the are liable for unlimited risk. The question naturally arises as to why any potential investors would stake their money on a lone individual, no matter how clever or ambitious, as opposed to the safe option of an experienced, respected firm. The answer lies in the ability of the golden boys to promote their own image, to market themselves. What they are selling, in the end, is hope.

In the value system which creates golden boys, self-financing is a bore; buying with borrowed money is rather more exciting; raising capital on the money markets on the strength of one's reputation alone is the prerogative of true heroes. More glamorous than any of these, however, are the fully fledged divinities called investment bankers, who actually invest little and take few risks themselves. Their role is to persuade others to do the buying and selling, and for this they must possess star quality, projecting absolute conviction and a complete mastery of the ins and outs of finance. Their skills are richly rewarded, because they receive a commission on every completed transaction, whether purchase or sale. Quite rightly, for the service they provide is valuable: they draw the maps that show where to dig for treasure. It is also here that we must seek the germ that leads to such phenomena as financial 'bubbles', not to mention the increasing 'financialization' of the economy, or finance-led capitalism. Beyond dollar values on the stock market, there are psychological values which the market attaches to its champions, its revered demigods. There is nothing intrinsically wrong with this; the hope of gain and profit is the oxygen which capitalism must have in order to thrive. Without hope, there can be no enterprise. But even the Stock Exchange needs to keep a sense of proportion.

'A kind of frenzy'

More than ever – and more than others – the English-speaking economies are subject to 'Stock Market Mania'. It is a trend which began to snowball in the 1980s. The Alpine countries, where banks continue to play the leading role in company financing, have remained largely unaffected.

The stock exchanges have always wielded great influence in the American economy, but the financial climate of the 1980s proved to be particularly favorable for their expansion. It was a decade that saw the Dow–Jones index triple, while the futures and options markets grew steadily. The volume of business on the Chicago exchanges is now twice or three times greater than that recorded on Wall Street. The markets, the world of high finance and all its trappings, enjoyed a prolonged boom which led to a profusion of new financial services. . . and new millionaires. The more ambitious financial houses became overnight media darlings: the press had an insatiable appetite for the stories of spectacular deals and meteoric careers which came out of new or little-known firms with names like Drexel Burnham Lambert, Shearson Lehman Hutton, and Wasserstein Parella. Henceforth IBM, Apple or Colgate made for dull copy. Wall Street combined the excitement of gambling for high stakes with the glamor of show business. America being what it is, this media celebration naturally focused on individual success stories which seemed to illustrate the triumph of finance over industry.

Market traders and raiders who had amassed colossal fortunes virtually overnight became celebrities in the grand Hollywood tradition. People like Michael Milken, dubbed 'the king of junk bonds', and Ivan Boesky, the wizard of arbitraging who drove a pink Rolls-Royce, were constantly in the news – long before they came to be tried and sentenced (to 10 years in jail in Milken's case, to 3 years and a $100 million fine in Boesky's). And then there is Donald Trump, perhaps the king of self-aggrandizement, whose Taj Mahal was built entirely through junk-bond financing. These larger-than-life characters were elevated to the rank of super-heroes of the American Way of Capitalism. Rarely, if ever, did the media stop to ask just what sort of capitalism was being glorified, or whether the omens for the American economy were really so favorable.

Not everyone was blinded by the glitter: Maurice Allais, recipient of the 1988 Nobel Prize for Economics, asserted that the American economy 'seems to have given itself over to a kind of frenzy of speculative finance which produces enormous incomes based on nothing really solid, and whose demoralising consequences have been seriously underestimated'.

One especially demoralising consequence is, to use the vocabulary of American story-telling, the proliferation of 'bad guys' and 'outlaws' in this new Wild West of finance: namely, the corporate raiders, whose speciality is the hostile takeover. Once the company has fallen victim to their 'ambush', it is dismembered and sold off piecemeal for huge profits. Not all remain 'bad guys' forever; just occasionally, someone like Carl Icahn will emerge – the raider who terrorised the market place, bought up TWA, then discovered the virtues of corporate responsibility and became a model manager and employer. Others, like Irwin Jacobs, follow no other law or logic than that of maximum profit in a minimum time. Still others, such as Jimmy Goldsmith, are fired with the crusading zeal of the true believer in economic liberalism and scourge of creeping state intervention. When Goldsmith made his bid for the tyre giant Goodyear, or succeeded in his hostile takeover of the conglomerate Crown Zellerbach, it was, he said, for a worthy cause: to defy and dismantle the bureaucracy which was smothering initiative, and to weed out slothful managers who lived like parasites on the company's back, indifferent to the interests of shareholders. But he did not turn up his nose at the fabulous profits which resulted from his schemes.

Takeovers, buyouts and mergers are not exactly newcomers to the American business world. Contrary to popular perceptions, the number of such operations during the 1980s (2000–3000 per year) was actually half that recorded between 1968 and 1972, with an all-time peak of 6000 occurring in 1970. But if one examines, not the number but the total monetary *value* of such operations, then the Reagan years do indeed signal an explosion of activity: from $20 billion annually in the 1968–72 period, to $90 billion per year between 1980 and 1985, to $247 billion in 1988 alone. Another way of looking at mergers and acquisitions is as a *percentage* of GDP: again, by 1983–85 the annual proportion had doubled since 1968–72 (see Prot and de Rosen, eds., *Le Retour du capital*: Odile Jacob, 1990).

But the most telling indicator is the way in which the very nature of these operations has been transformed since 1982, and the emergence of the adjective 'hostile' to qualify them. As explained by Edward J. Epstein in a 1988 article entitled 'Who Owns the Company?', there is a long tradition of takeovers in the USA, almost all of which were 'friendly' – i.e. they had the approval of both firms' boards of directors – essentially because the fusion or takeover procured some advantage for each party. Benefits might be expected from diversification, improved cash flow or reduced taxes. In any case, there were numerous laws to protect the public interest in these matters. They varied from state to state, but their main thrust was to allow government to intervene to prevent takeovers by acting on behalf of even a small number of shareholders. When the US Supreme Court struck down one such law, the Illinois Business Takeover Act, in June 1982 – simultaneously invalidating many others – the situation changed dramatically. The takeover game became much easier to play. The classic variant, in which a conglomerate welcomed a smaller firm into the group, had *expansion* as its principal motive. In the hostile gambit, the object is to dismember the targeted company in a bid to increase its quoted market value.

The spiral of bluff

The 'star treatment' lavished on financial companies and their top dealers was to prove irresistibly seductive to the country's intellectual élite. As they flocked into finance, industry's loss soon became apparent. Already hard-pressed to recruit the new engineering and financial staff it needed, manufacturing industry was soon losing those it had to banks and brokerage houses, where the pay was incomparably better and no one had to get their hands dirty (or even their shoes!) on a factory floor.

This domestic version of the brain drain was in no way an exclusively American phenomenon. A cursory inspection of the payroll of any Parisian bank or investment firm will reveal that the young Olympians of high finance are earning two to three times more than their colleagues and former classmates who happen to be working in less specialized – and less speculative – departments of a single company. Same qualifications, same talent, different risk factor: presto! A salary differential of three to one. It is on such specific points of divergence that the daily battle of one capitalism against the other is being fought.

The stage was soon set for another Great American Show: rags-to-riches success stories, fortunes gambled and won, cloak-and-dagger deals became the daily bread of the mass media as they turned their attention to Wall Street. In no time at all, finance was promoted from the back pages to the headlines, and not just in the *Wall Street Journal*. Not a day would pass that the press failed to report the next sensational instalment of the latest thriller: here a devastating takeover bid, there a fiendishly clever stratagem, everywhere a pot of gold to be borne off by the conquering hero – not to mention the juicy details of these same heroes' turbulent private lives. (Who could be unaware of Donald Trump's marital problems when his wife's claim for divorce – and half his fortune – was emblazoned on the cover of every glossy magazine?)

Finance, and the economy generally, were henceforth firmly in the public spotlight, for better or for worse – mostly for worse. The effects of this intense media coverage were felt far beyond Wall Street itself, in the boardrooms and managerial suites of American companies. Executives – those valiant captains of industry – could hardly ignore the fact that the press was portraying them as the new comic-strip heroes and dragon-slayers of the video age, facing down the perils of stock-market manipulation. Their perceptions of themselves and their reactions and behaviour were to change subtly as a result, as did the very jargon they used. The warlike vocabulary which gained currency in the 1980s highlights the 'Dungeons-and-Dragons' approach to finance and business: white knights, black knights, poison pills, golden handcuffs and golden parachutes sound as if they feature in a video game rather than in corporate affairs. All of which made for a much more exciting media spectacle than the dull facts regarding productivity rates in the car industry or the ups and downs of international computer technology markets.

Cast in their new public role as warriors engaged in titanic duels with the raiders of the stock market, high-profile managers and company directors took on the aura of demigods, manipulating vast sums and incalculable assets, masterminding the movements of armies of workers, able to leap over international frontiers and defy mere governments. Not surprisingly, some of them believed the hype. Delusions of grandeur fostered by the media blitz would soon influence their management style, their methods and decisions. It would be naïve to imagine that mergers, acquisitions and takeovers are the result of purely rational choices. Pulling off a stunning corporate coup might have more to do with the Chief Executive Officer's ego or his craving for publicity than with good business sense; it may stem from management's desire not to appear cowardly or conservative in the eyes of its own workforce; it may simply be justified as a prestige-building operation.

This upward spiral of celebrity, of bluff and counter-bluff, of the financial power-play, brought Reagan's America to its feet to applaud the new super-heroes of Wall Street. Finance set the tone for the whole nation. Atop the new Olympus of the financial markets, the gods of finance could demand any sacrifice. Economic policy was subject to the whims of Wall Street: with a sneeze of the Dow–Jones or a hiccough in the prime rate, all America felt feverish. The markets themselves could go into a spin on the basis of a poor showing in the monthly trade balance or a rise in unemployment. The impact on Wall Street of a given event would far exceed the importance of the event itself. Thus, a downturn in exports or a disappointing quarterly output figure is not of grave concern in and of itself; what *is* worrying is when the financial markets overreact to a single piece of news.

The laws of the market

In the context of this financial extravaganza, manufacturing industry has been cast in the role of the country cousin whose old-fashioned wardrobe and homely appearance provoke a condescending smile. The Massachusetts Institute of Technology (MIT) issued a report in 1990 which analysed the often unhealthy relationship between finance and industry. Successive waves of takeover bids have sapped the latter's confidence in itself. There is no hint of anything resembling an industrial strategy in the machinations of corporate raiders; their sole concern is immediate profit. A company's only defense against such predators, according to MIT, is to pour all its efforts into short-term profitability.

The result is that the financial markets have assumed almost dictatorial powers over the economy in general, and private enterprise in particular. Businesses are increasingly forced into adopting strategies and behaviour patterns which simply do not make good industrial and economic sense.

In the first place, the Stock Exchange makes heavy demands on a firm's capital stock, whose profitability must be demonstrated at all times and in all circumstances. Under pressure from its shareholders, who must be appeased with profits lest they decide to withdraw their support, the company must do everything in its power to pay out 'competitive' dividends. At the same time, it strives to keep its share price as high as possible in order to discourage any hostile takeover bids. Thus the company will move heaven and earth to maximise short-term profits and present a glowing report to its Wall Street overlords. This must be done every 3 months: in what has come to be called the 'tyranny of the quarterly report', the financiers will comb through the balance sheets of every firm listed on the exchange, comparing, analysing, criticising. Every 3 months! There is no respite, no allowance for momentary slippage.

Any manager will tell you that the only way to increase profits quickly is to cut 'non-essential' expenses. Advertising, research, training and development of new business are the usual targets for such cost-cutting exercises. Yet these are the very items in the budget which allow firms to prepare for the future. They are the key to new product design, improved production techniques, a more skilful workforce and the opening up of new markets to new goods. To starve these activities of resources is, ultimately, to jeopardise the company's long-term prospects. Financial logic in this instance clearly contradicts industrial logic.

Then there are the unsavoury consequences of 'takeover mania': any firm caught up in a takeover bid (whether as buyer or target) necessarily takes on new debt with which to finance the operation, or repel it. The balance sheet inevitably reflects this, and the financial fallout may persist for years. An example: the RJR Nabisco Group found itself chained to a $22 billion debt contracted in the course of its takeover by KKR; this weighed so heavily that, in the end, the new owner was forced to sell off Nabisco's many subsidiairies to BSN.

The rewards of defeat

The constant threat of takeover and other forms of corporate raiding is the source of more than just financial headaches for US companies. Senior management finds itself caught up in a kind of persistent guerilla warfare which makes exorbitant demands on its time and energy. The obvious priorities – producing and selling – have to be sacrificed to the planning of elaborate defensive manoeuvres and the marshalling of vast armies of (well-paid) legal advisers. Never mind productivity or customer satisfaction: the talk in the boardroom is all of poison pills and golden parachutes. The latter may serve to illustrate a point: how much company time was devoted by Nabisco to the protection of its chairman and Chief Executive Officer from the unfortunate consequences (for them personally) of the firm's takeover by KKR? We may never know; but what is well known is the cost of stitching together these golden parachutes: $53 million and $45 million respectively. The consolation for finding themselves out of a job was handsome indeed! Invested at a rate of 10 per cent annual interest, each man would be assured of a yearly income in the neighborhood of $5 million. By way of comparison, the best-paid company directors in France earn between $500 000 and $1 000 000 a year. Such, in the new America of takeovers and buyouts, are the rewards of defeat.

In a further twist of this paradox, shareholders may also find that the company's loss is their gain. The golden rule among investors in the new American model of capitalism is, again, that of grabbing the quickest and fattest profit. Taken to its logical extreme, the practice of never refusing a bargain or a higher bid leads to shareholder disloyalty, and this in turn constitutes a major handicap for businesses, who benefit most from a stable, secure capital base.

The shareholder is king (to borrow an expression coined by de Juniac and Mayer in *Le retour du capital*), and he shows a regal indifference to the company in which he has invested. He demands dividends and profits; the rest (the company's long-term interests, for example) is anecdotal. Paradoxically, this tendency is especially strong among institutional investors (pensions funds and insurance companies, for the most part), who wield tremendous power on the stock exchange, because they account for 40–60 per cent of Wall Street capitalization. Unlike their Japanese or, to a lesser extent, European counterparts, who help regulate and even 'police' the market, American institutions are hell-bent on increasing the value of their portfolio, whatever the cost. The single overriding concern, for them, is to earn high returns for their own investors, whose savings they have been entrusted with, and to win pride of place in the annual league tables of successful investment houses.

When a takeover bid is launched, these institutional investors become key players – and potential 'traitors' – in the process. In their obsession with short-term profit, they may decide to support a hostile bid for a company, even one whose pension fund they manage, simply because there are substantial capital gains to be had from the transaction which will look good in the institution's annual report.

With shareholders like these, who needs enemies? Things have come a long way since the word 'company' meant, as its etymology suggests, a community of interest, a mutually beneficial partnership of employers, employees and investors. Gone is the *esprit de corps* implicit in incorporation; companies are now merely cash-flow machines, subject to the whims of finance and exposed to the cruellest elements of stock market speculation.

Capitalism without owners

It is difficult for many Europeans, who feel an almost sentimental kinship with their colleagues and companies, to face this logic and its implications. For it *is* a kind of logic: for the new dominant breed of 'rational' American shareholder, the company represents nothing more than 'a bundle of shares' (to paraphrase Keynes) and, like everything else in the USA, it is up for grabs – if the price is right. As the French philosopher Michel Serres (who teaches in the USA) remarked, 'In America, money is the *goal* and things are the means to achieve it, while in Europe our goal is to achieve things, with money as the *means*'. Buying a company, for the American capitalist, is ultimately no different from buying a property or a painting. It is therefore perfectly logical for the shareholder-kings to do as they please with the company they have just purchased, breaking it up and selling off the segments which do not interest them. Its employees and managers are treated in the same way as its capital: all are forms of disposable merchandise.

Does capitalism really demand that workers be treated as goods? Can a capitalist business survive without an owner? Both are serious questions deserving serious debate; the latter, though, seems tantalisingly paradoxical, almost facetious. Yet even in the sober columns of *The Economist* the question of 'ownerless capitalism' in the context of the Anglo-American economies has recently been raised.

If the *Wall Street Journal* had a lonely hearts section for businesses, the messages would read: 'Company seeks mature owner' and 'Attractive firm seeks faithful shareholders'. The crowning achievement of contemporary American capitalism is, bizarrely, to have done away with genuine ownership by destroying the logic of shareholder stability.

Profitability now. . . or later?

Among the many paradoxes posed by late twentieth-century capitalism, there is one which suggests that Karl Marx might be sharing a private joke with the ghosts of history past, present and future.

The soul of capitalism is profit, and its legitimacy is now hailed everywhere on the planet, though only yesterday it was, for many, the ultimate taboo. In France, where the socialist government had already fallen in line by 1982–83, the utopian vision of a durable socialist–communist partnership now seems as remote, and as believable, as Shangri-La; meanwhile, the overnight collapse of communism in Eastern Europe has given rise to an undiluted faith in the market. The principle of profit-seeking as the best incentive for creative enterprise is, in short, universally acknowledged. Profit is not only legitimate, it is the very engine that drives the economic machine. How curious, then, to discover that America – capitalism's adopted homeland – should now provide a new object lesson, an important corollary to the guiding principle: namely, that profit can also *weaken* free enterprise; it can be damaging to the economy; it can hinder development. Just as few would argue with the proposition that too much taxation will eventually lead to diminishing tax revenues, so it may be argued that too much emphasis on today's profits can jeopardise tomorrow's.

Except for the occasional fluke of fashion or good fortune, the long-term success of a product is the culmination of sustained, day-by-day effort. It depends on a variety of factors: production techniques and distribution networks must be fine-tuned; customers and consumers must be won over on a number of counts, not the least of which is after-sales service. It took 6 or 7 years for the personal computer, for example, to conquer the wider public, while videos and cam-corders took even longer – more than 10 years. Such tenacity implies financial sacrifices: the manufacturer accepts that profits, if indeed there are to be any, must be preceded by losses. The launch of a product can be relatively expensive – particularly when the product itself is initially inexpensive, as is often the case when the maker hopes to capture a large market. It is an elementary strategy, as perfected by the Japanese. Step 1: flood the lower range of the market with goods whose low price tag reflects low profit margins. Step 2: as your competitors are squeezed out and fixed costs depreciate, you move gradually up the product range. It is worth recalling what Japanese cars were like, only 15 or 20 years ago: small, plain, flimsy and charmless – but cheap. Today, of course, Japanese cars compete with the most robust German models and the elegant Italian makes. Japan is, in fact, the world's leading producer of cars. Not by accident: success on this scale had to be engineered with equal amounts of skill, determination and costly sacrifice.

Profit vs development

American manufacturers seem to have forgotten this well-tried formula for success. More often, they have concentrated too narrowly on the high-tech, high-profit end of the market; at other times they have retreated from markets they once dominated, when faced with strong competition. Only rarely have they planned and executed long-term industrial and commercial strategies for winning whole markets – or winning them back. In the field of medical imaging, for example, it was American firms who originally launched scanner and ultrasound technology. Their mistake was to focus exclusively on the top of the range, which meant confining their sales to the small market niche consisting of the most advanced research centers and the most modern hospitals. Middle-range production was handed, by default, to the Japanese, who wasted no time in snapping up the larger market of average, unremarkable hospitals and clinics. This, in turn, provided a solid base upon which to improve their products, expand their range and, in the end, compete directly with American manufacturers at the prestigious high-tech end of the market.

A similar difference in strategies has been evident in the field of electronics, where American companies virtually gave up on mass production for a mass market and concentrated instead on advanced military technology, or, in some cases, turned to altogether different ventures with a potential for quick profitability (financial services, for instance, or even car hire).

The plain-spoken President of Sony Corporation, Akio Morita, does not hesitate to voice harsh criticism of American business leaders and their absence of forward planning. Americans are good at making money through mergers and acquisitions, he says in substance, but they no longer know how to produce new goods. The Japanese plan things 10 years in advance, while Americans seem to be interested only in the profit to be made in the next 10 minutes. If it goes on like this, according to Morita, America will be left with the economy of a ghost town. There are Americans who agree with him, in less vehement terms perhaps, such as Richard Darman, Director of the US Office of Management and Budget. His condemnation of 'now-nowism' included this definition of the problem: 'the impatience of the consumer, not of the creator, and of the egotist rather than the pioneer.' Keynes can be credited with a kind of prescience when he expressed the fear that the spirit of finance might overtake and supplant the spirit of enterprise. Today, even the largest and most successful American corporations can attest to the 'tyranny of finance'. At IBM, for example, nearly 50 per cent of the profits are distributed as dividends, while at Rank Xerox the figure is over 60 per cent.

The banks that finance Japanese firms are, by comparison, considerably less greedy. Because they often belong, directly or indirectly, to the same business group, and usually own a significant slice of the capital stock, they are in an excellent position to understand that it would be counterproductive to charge the company the highest interest rates on loans, or to demand the fattest possible dividend. In short, they have the good sense to wait for the swings to deliver what has been lost on the roundabouts. In such a climate of give-and-take, everyone wins. Japanese businesses are able to design, and finance, long-term projects without the suffocating weight of high-cost capital crippling their efforts.

This is not the case for so many American companies, constantly looking over their shoulders at a ravenous pack of shareholders and investors, and consequently wedded to the drive for quick profits. It is hardly surprising, given such a hostile climate, that American entrepreneurs are increasingly hesitant to get involved in any risky industrial venture, as the MIT report (*Made in America* – Michael Dertouzos, Richard Lester and Robert Solow: MIT Press, 1989) makes clear. Yet what could be more inimical to capitalism than this refusal to take a gamble, to bet on the future? By definition, capitalism and free enterprise are synonymous with risk-taking. The American Dream itself presupposes it; the industrial venture is a continuation of the pioneer adventure.

Excess of caution, reliance on short-term profit, retreat into safe, secure positions: these are not the qualities Ronald Reagan had in mind when he declared, on a 1984 trip to China, 'We are a nation of optimists. Like you, we have inherited vast stretches of land and sky, of great mountains, fertile fields and boundless plains. Everywhere we turn, we discover new possibilities, and that gives us hope'.

It is hard to imagine an irony more cruel than this unexpected side effect of Reaganism: the tyranny of finance is threatening the spirit of free enterprise. For America, this is not merely inconvenient, it is extremely dangerous. Past experience tells us that the really big industrial successes are the product of equally colossal risks taken and won. In their study of Japanese business strategy (*Kaisha: the Japanese Corporation*, Basic Books: New York, 1985), J. Abegglen and G. Stalk highlight the amazing Japanese capacity for taking financial and industrial risks. It is not unknown for firms to initiate mass production of goods even before their saleability has been established, a tactic which allows fixed costs to be quickly recouped while introductory prices for the consumer are kept low. What better example than the Walkman, the brainchild of Akio Morita, which was already being mass produced before a single unit had been sold?

Profit is, in the final analysis, the petrol that fuels the capitalist engine. If the blend is too rich, or it is added too quickly, the engine may seize up – or explode. In the view of Akio Morita and other Japanese industrialists, their American counterparts have too long ignored this key concept, sacrificing the needs of the workforce and the demands of production on the financial altars of Wall Street.

This last point requires further explanation, because it implies that a sound industrial strategy must be based on enlightened management of human resources as well as product strategy. The Japanese are not the only observers to deplore the failings of so many American bosses in the field of employer–employee relations. The French Institute for International Relations, in its 1990 report (*Ramsès*: Les Editions Dunod), based its conclusions on a number of American studies:

'American employers are heading in the opposite direction from that which all past experience would suggest is the right way. All the evidence – case histories of top performers, academic studies of the social factors hindering productivity, the conclusions of independent consultants or of in-house brain trusts at companies like IBM, 3M or Hewlett-Packard – points to one fact: the diligent and devoted management of a stable workforce is one of the decisive ingredients for achieving a competitive edge.'

The frantic dash for profits thus induces behaviour patterns which fly in the face of good human resources management; in the wider context, the whole social fabric of America is being threatened by the consequences of unbridled greed and arrogant affluence.

The new perils of the almighty dollar

Money and wealth have always been seen as cornerstones of American society, where Europeans have trusted in rank, culture and honor as the prime values; not surprising, perhaps, for a young, industrious republic founded on the Protestant ethic which, as Max Weber so lucidly demonstrated, could easily accommodate itself to the theory and practice of capitalism. It is simply a commonplace to note that money is king in the land of the almighty dollar. But it is all too easy to forget that this spirit of competitive individualism and brash materialism is accompanied, and held in check, by a number of other keenly felt values and hallowed institutions. If America has, from the very start, venerated the dollar sign, it has nevertheless always kept one hand on the Bible and the other on the Constitution. The USA is not only a deeply religious society, as everyone knows, but also one in which a true civic sense is enshrined in the Constitution, and where the rule of law enjoys a more exalted status than in any European culture.

In the USA moral tradition implies a number of implicit restraints and unwritten obligations. Rockefeller once said that it was shameful for a rich man to die rich. The vitality of charities, public-interest groups and other elements of the 'voluntary sector', and their importance as social shock-absorbers, has already been mentioned. On the whole, it seemed that America had devised a successful balance between competing and conflicting principles, at the most fundamental level.

It is now clear that this delicate equilibrium has been upset. Like any sovereign, 'King Dollar' had never exercised absolute, unlimited authority, but nowadays its power extends into virtually all social activity. Professor Alain Cotta, in his recent study *Le Capitalisme dans tous ses états* (Fayard, 1991), identifies three characteristics of the 'new' capitalism: it is finance-led, media-obsessed and corrupt. Fame, it seems, has taken fortune by the hand and led it straight into corruption. There is even a school of neo-conservative economic thought which holds that corruption is at times the 'rational' response to management problems: in other words, a thief is merely someone who is not yet powerful enough to be bought off, to be worth corrupting. This new strain of cynical capitalism has simply swept aside the inhibitions of traditional Western morality and made even more intolerable the glaring contradictions and inequalities at the heart of American society.

Can it possibly be right and proper, to take but one example, for Michael Eisner (head of the Disney Corporation) to earn more than the combined salaries of all 4000 gardeners employed to keep Orlando's Disneyworld green and tidy, and 100 times more than, say, the Chief Executive Officer of Peugeot? What are we to think of the $550 million income declared in 1988 alone by the junk bond king, Michael Milken? Such questions are beginning to trouble some American consciences, as evidenced by the proposal to put a legal ceiling on top executives' pay (a bill to that effect was put before Congress, and even *Business Week* magazine has wondered if 'bosses are too highly paid'). The US Senate heard testimony from one expert, M. Graef Crystal, to the effect that the head of a large American company earned, on average, 110 times the average salary of his employees. In Japan, the ratio is 17:1, in Germany, 23:1. Why, then, should American bosses earn five or six times more than their Japanese of German counterparts? According to market forces, such differences ought to reflect the competitive superiority of American firms; alas, this is not the case – quite the reverse. So much for the laws of the free market, once the monarchy of money has been firmly established.

Dig deeper, and the story becomes more sordid. Wall Street in the 'roaring eighties' witnessed every conceivable form of duplicity and misconduct, with the profoundly worrying consequence that the code of professional practice has been severely undermined. The hallowed motto of bankers and financiers, 'My word is my bond,' can no longer be taken for granted. The new super-heroes of finance would rather trust in another slogan: 'any means to an end.' The means may include paid informers or even professional detectives hired to 'get the goods' on the heads of companies targeted for takeover. Wall Street is increasingly distrusted, even as it absorbs more and more of the world's savings and investment on which America now depends.

Here, then, is the ultimate paradox: morality – or at least ethical behaviour – is not just a luxury, a decorative afterthought. It is a structural necessity for the proper functioning of a capitalist system. The business community – even on Wall Street – is fully aware of this, and the backlash has begun. In some cases, the reaction against the excesses of the recent past has been more vigorous and exacting than anything we can imagine in Europe, notably when the Securities and Exchange Commission (SEC) decides to prosecute stock market misdeeds. Judges in a number of trials have not shirked from imposing stiff sentences, sending wrongdoers to gaol. And suddenly – whether as a fashion, an alibi or a long overdue reordering of priorities – courses in business ethics figure prominently in university curricula (notably at Harvard Business School). There has been a recent flowering of 'ethical investment funds' which guarantee not to invest their clients' savings in companies of dubious virtue; at the same time, some 40 American states have passed legislation to curb the worst effects of takeover mania. The Pennsylvania state congress, in April 1990, went so far as to punish shareholders who sell out within a year and a half following a takeover by providing for the confiscation of their profits.

Across the country, a popular wave of revulsion against the speculative wheelings and dealings of the giant investment firms can be felt; it is part of a more general tide, a powerful moral offensive which, in its puritanical zeal, also commits a few outrages. Revelations (or just hints) of financial impropriety have destroyed a number of political careers in recent times, including Geraldine Ferraro, the 1984 vice-presidential candidate; Michael Deaver, former White House chief secretary; John Tower, nominated (unsuccessfully) to become George Bush's Defense Secretary; Jim Wright, Speaker of the House of Representatives; and so on up to the present day and tomorrow's headlines. America has become hypersensitive to 'questions of money' and their moral implications.

Morality, then, is beginning to reassert its fundamental importance, and as such can be seen as a good investment. America is responding to a real threat. For all its celebrated splendour, finance has tyrannised and debased both the economy and society as a whole, and America has begun to react. The new moral crusade is, in reality, only one episode in the first act of the great conflict now being staged between two systems, two forms of capitalism, and whose outcome is not a foregone conclusion. As the saying goes, 'Never sell America short'.

Chapter 5
Insurance: a study in contrasts

The American model of capitalism described in the previous chapters is a relatively new phenomenon, so many changes having taken place in recent times. Less than 25 years ago the 'organizational man' described by Burnham in his 1941 classic, *The Managerial Revolution*, still reigned supreme; technocrats, not investors, had the upper hand. Thus John Kenneth Galbraith could write, in 1967, of the apparent power shift within companies and corporations away from shareholders and manipulators of capital, towards the nucleus of versatile, production-oriented teams and individuals steeped in the modern culture of technological innovation (*The New Industrial State*: Houghton Mifflin Co.). What seemed at the time to be the wave of the future, the hallmark of progress and modernity, was diametrically opposed to the trend of the Reagan years, which have seen the ascendancy of financiers over engineers and the media taking over the role of the trades unions.

Is this 'resurgence of capital' therefore an inevitable, irresistible tendency of modern industrial economies? Is there any evidence that another model of capitalism really exists, as I claimed in my introduction to this study? My answer is that it does, because I have encountered it in my own professional field, that of insurance. It is an area which in many respects epitomises the rivalry between the two systems. Virtually all the important issues faced by decision-makers within the insurance industry boil down to a conflict between two fundamentally differing approaches: the Alpine model vs the Anglo-Saxon model.

The two cradles of insurance: the mountains and the sea

It was during a visit to the Swiss subsidiary of my firm, Assurances
Générales de France (AGF), that I was first alerted to the unique features of Alpine capitalism.

I had always thought of Switzerland as the very incarnation of liberal economic philosophy and laissez-faire capitalism. Thus I was baffled
when, to my question about the firm's approach to setting vehicle
insurance rates, the managing director replied that there was no company policy in the matter – there could never be – because all Swiss
insurers had to comply with the law and offer the same rates. I could
hardly believe my ears: having for many years advised the French government on economic policy, and having always championed the abolition of price controls, I was forced to conclude that France was a far
more liberal country than Switzerland, on this question at least.

Later, in the course of a business lunch, a Swiss banker told me that
he was confident no American bank would ever gain a significant
foothold in personal banking in his country. I was intrigued: why not?
Because, he answered, American banks are so obsessed with making
constant personnel changes. 'One simply can't imagine the Swiss
entrusting their savings to people they don't know!'

And so I was initiated into this strange new landscape of bank
accounts which were more than mere financial operations, but social
exchanges as well; where the insurance markets were determined, not
so much by rivalry over differing rates (even in those areas where price
controls had not been imposed), but by competing services and standards of customer care. I was discovering a form of capitalism in which
the price tag, the material aspect of a product, was secondary to the service being offered – in other words, the whole web of non-material,
subjective, even emotional factors woven into the product.

What originally struck me as a paradox, a contradiction in terms, is
in fact one of the best illustrations of the conflict between the two
models of capitalism. An analysis and understanding of its significance
requires some delving into the past, and the emergence of the insurance industry from two very different birthplaces.

The earliest form of insurance springs from the upper valleys of the
Alps, where villagers first organized mutual aid societies around the
turn of the sixteenth century. This Alpine tradition gave rise to a host

of community organizations charged with the protection of common interests, such as guilds, corporations, professional syndicates and mutual benefit insurance groups. The distinguishing characteristic of such organizations is the sharing of risk: the cost borne by each member remains more or less independent of the probability of his or her own personal risk factor actually occurring. There is a kind of solidarity, leading to a redistributive exchange within the community. This tradition continues to be strongly upheld in its geographical cradle (Switzerland and Germany), but can be observed in other parts of the world as well: notably in Japan, where the 'community spirit' is equally powerful.

The other birthplace of modern insurance was the sea: originally, this took the form of loans which backed the maritime ventures of Venetian and Genoese traders. London eventually became the true home of this kind of insurance, finding its most celebrated expression in the tavern of a certain Mr. Lloyd, where a system was devised to insure the cargoes of tea aboard English ships. A very different system from the Alpine conception: rather than security, solidarity and redistribution, its operating principle was the profitable management, through speculation, of individual risk.

Both models point to the fundamental choices which different nations and cultures make in shaping their societies. In the Alpine system, insurance is a means of organizing community solidarity; in the 'maritime' system which grew out of marine insurance, it tends to work against that very solidarity, on the evidence (as we shall see) of the precarious and fragmented nature of the contractual arrangements. One strengthens the social glue which binds individual interests together, while the other helps to dissolve it.

The origins of these two 'schools' of insurance shed a revealing light on the development of the two economic models prevalent today: on the one hand, Anglo-American capitalism with its investor-king, its emphasis on short-term profit and personal financial success generally; and Rhine capitalism, on the other hand, with both its overriding concern for the longer term, and the primacy it accords to the company as an expression of the partnership of capital and labor.

True to their respective birthplaces, these two variants of the insurance business continue to fight it out today on the stage of the European Community. Since the earliest days of the EC, and more than ever since 1985 and the Single European Act, the issues and arguments over the future of European insurance reflect the age-old differences, and imply the existence of separate socioeconomic models.

A particularly striking characteristic of each system is the way it deals with road accident indemnity insurance: in Germany, Austria, Switzerland and Italy, it remains compulsory for a universal, undifferentiated rate to be offered to drivers. In Britain and other English-speaking countries, rates are unregulated, although third-party insurance itself is obligatory. What this 'maritime' approach does is to divide the captive market into fine segments and apportion risks individually (rather than pool them, as in the Alpine system).

If symbols are needed, then each model again provides its own striking example. It is no coincidence that the Alpine cities of Zurich and Munich are the world centers of the reinsurance industry – a business which depends on security and continuity. Companies such as Münchener Rück, not to mention the largest European insurer Allianz, attest to the Bavarian capital's importance in this field, while Zurich boasts Compagnie Suisse de Réassurance, the Zürich group and Winterthur. Trieste, at the foothills of the Alps, also belongs to this insurance 'family' and is home to companies such as Generali and RAS (Riunione Adriatica Sicurità). These, then, are the three capitals of a clearly recognizable Alpine model of insurance, and they remain strong in their home base. But the 'maritime' model is beginning to push its way in, benefiting from the ascendancy of the neo-American economic model which it mimics.

The living symbol of the 'maritime' model is, naturally, Lloyd's of London. Its origins in marine insurance are still evident in the way its investors, or 'names', are required to stake their entire personal wealth against the risks they may incur. Despite its worldwide reputation, Lloyd's is currently (and notoriously) in the throes of a crisis stemming largely from the names' loss of confidence in their agents, too many of whom are apparently underwriting huge, ill-judged risks. Again we see the effects of the 'fame and finance' syndrome: brokers were only too happy, in the short term, to sign any deal, no matter how speculative, in order to take whopping commissions and enhance their visibility in the market. Unfortunately for their investors, the long term is about to catch up with the high rollers. Lloyd's, like America, faces a bleak day of reckoning in the not-too-distant future.

The Alpine model: a vulnerable giant

The basic principle of Rhine capitalism in general, and of its insurance industry in particular, is that of the community of interests, both within the company as well as between company and consumer.

A recent study by the Institut de l'Entreprise concluded that 'German businesses owe the efficiency of their operations to a broad consensus which, by and large, keeps the social peace, as well as to the solidarity between owners and management in determining policy and protecting company interests'.

These interests are further protected by the German Board of Insurance Control (BAV), who take the view that what is good for insurers is good for policy-holders. The insurance sector is in fact not subject to the ordinary rules of competition, as enforced by the Bundeskartelamt (Federal Monopolies Board) – whose chairman complained in 1988 that 'the BAV seems to believe that consumer protection boils down to guaranteeing the solvency of the insurer. All its energies go toward making certain German insurance firms do not lose money: in other words, requiring them to be profitable. The BAV can thus hardly claim to be acting in the best interests of the customer. There being no one else, it is my duty to take on this role'. An uproar followed, but nothing has really changed. On the eve of the Single European Market, price controls are still in place in Germany (and Switzerland) in the sensitive area of compulsory third-party vehicle insurance. The Swiss manage this through a joint commission which includes representatives of policy-holders; in Germany, companies submit their pricing proposals to be approved by the BAV. A maximum profit margin of 3 per cent is left to the discretion of the insurer. Profit-making is optional under this system – not, as elsewhere in the business world, a necessity or even an end in itself.

What this means is that German drivers, good, bad and indifferent, will all pay the same premium to insure a given make of car, no matter which insurer they choose. The latter may compete with other firms over the quality of service – prompt payment of claims, more generous compensation etc. – but not over premium rates. Risk is evenly spread, and the principle of solidarity firmly upheld. But in practical terms this means that the good drivers end up paying for the careless ones.

In 1985, one large German insurer decided to challenge this situation by proposing that premiums should vary according to nationality, on the statistically unimpeachable grounds that German citizens had a much lower accident rate than immigrants. Under the proposal, everyone would pay the base rate, but a supplementary charge would be levied on foreigners: 25 per cent more in the case of Greeks, 50 per cent extra for Turks, and a 100 per cent surcharge for Italian drivers! Predictably, the plan contravened EC anti-discrimination rules and had to be dropped. The compulsory universal rate remains in force in the Alpine countries – as it does in Japan, where even the number of insurance companies is limited by law (to 24 in insurance and 31 in assurance). As ever in the case of Japanese enterprise, the solidarity of the 'keiretsu', the extended family of workers and bosses, customers and suppliers, is paramount. The big insurance firms are founded on it, and they thrive.

Another factor helping to keep Alpine insurance businesses comfortably well-off is the durable customer base. Until 1988, the 10-year contract for comprehensive household insurance was standard practice in Germany. The European Commission had this reduced to 5 years; yet in most countries the contract is renegotiated annually. In life assurance, the average German policy runs for 30 years, while in Britain 6 years is the norm.

Clearly, there are aspects of the Alpine model of insurance which suggest inflexibility, and would seem to work to the detriment of the consumer. But it would be unwise to condemn the system out of hand: it is part and parcel of a whole nexus of social values in which a steadfast clientèle proceeds from a basis of mutual trust and stable contractual arrangements.

While such a system supposes that the company's interests take precedence over those of the customer, the corollary is management's authority over that of shareholders and investors (a principle that extends well beyond the insurance industry). Management derives its strength in part from its structure as a collective body headed by a board of directors. A supervisory board has the power to appoint or to dismiss members of the board of directors, and oversees the interests of both shareholders and employees; the latter have their own representatives on the supervisory board, who may in fact be trade union officials unconnected with the firm. The end result is a surprisingly stable mixture with a pronounced preference for the long term.

The modern nemesis of long-term management, the takeover bid, is virtually unknown in Japan, Switzerland and Germany. Approximately a third of German companies issue registered shares which may not be sold or transferred without the express authorisation of the company. What is more, the board of directors (in its capacity as legal representative of the firm) may in some cases withhold its reasons for turning down a share-transfer request. This prerogative is a highly effective delaying tactic: you can perfectly well buy shares on the Stock Exchange but find that you have no vote and no right to join in an increase of capital for as long as the share transfer has not been approved by the company in question. In a well-known example, the Swiss insurer La Genevoise refused to authorise the purchase of 14 per cent of its shares by its rival Allianz, who thus found itself with no votes and no voice in company policy; meanwhile, the Zürich stepped in and took over nominal control of La Genevoise.

It is easy to see why the Alpine model of insurance has come increasingly under attack, especially from Brussels. There are a number of awkward questions to be answered: what guarantees that insurers' interests will always coincide with those of policy-holders? To what extent do fixed-price, single-rate premiums stifle competition? What prevents German insurers, for whom there is no clear incentive to reduce administrative costs and increase productivity, from acting against the best interests of their customers? The EC commissioners have concluded that the cosy Alpine insurance market is ripe for a shake-up. The so-called 'third stage' directives already in the EC pipeline are designed to open the markets up to genuine competition; the unspoken assumption is that the Anglo-American 'maritime' model of insurance is to be imposed.

In the Alpine model, insurance is first and foremost an institution, and the markets must be strictly regulated to suit its needs. The Anglo-American variant reverses the equation: insurance is primarily a market and, as such, must be subject to the basic laws of open competition, unregulated and unrestricted apart from the obligation to stay within certain solvency margins. Alpine insurers thus find themselves in an enviable, and unique, position of financial strength which allows them to undertake ambitious programs of outside expansion wholly financed through their own equity capital. Conversely, the basic premise of 'maritime' insurance, while ideologically sound (and growing in influence), can lead to serious financial difficulties for even the most prestigious and powerful firms.

These contrasts are brought out most vividly in the realm of third-party car insurance, if only because in the developed countries, where driving is an almost universal activity, it has been made compulsory and thus affects virtually everybody. On close inspection, it is a field in which the extraordinary diversity of the insurance sector stands revealed as a paradigm of the great sociopolitical issues now facing the industrial democracies.

The British experience: the costs of the invisible hand

In the English-speaking countries, insurance rates are wholly unregulated. Let us first examine the British variant, based on the rationalisation of premium levels.

Given that the customer is king (but then, so is the shareholder), the British broker offers his client the best possible quote in the most rational form: a host of individual criteria (make of car, type of employment, even the home address) are weighed up in assessing the policy-holder's rating (i.e. the premium level corresponding to his or her individual profile). The full range of quotes on offer can then be instantly called up on the broker's computer screen. These are displayed in order of increasing cost to the client. The commission is included, but not specified, in the offer price; again, each broker is free to charge whatever he wishes in commission fees.

This represents a significant departure from the Alpine system, in which each company reigns supreme over its network of exclusive distributors. In the 'maritime' model, it is the broker who 'navigates' from one insurer to another. Brokerage houses can thus become extremely influential, not only through capturing a large share of the market, but in their capacity as advisers, case managers, or even product designers. The insurance company is little more than an incubator of identical products which it must try to sell, segment by market segment, at competitive prices, and within the limits defined by solvency margins. And although this system of brokerage distribution is based on competitive pricing, the question today is whether the consumers' long-term interests might not best be served through a certain harmonisation of the different distribution networks.

The crucial point is that, in a system where information circulates in real time, and where the products are by definition the same (since the broker's computer display lists them in ascending order of price), there is no particular advantage to be had from innovation. In fact, were the system to reach its logical outcome, any given product would be strictly indistinguishable from any other within air-tight market slots: in which case, producers would actually *avoid* innovating. Here, practice confirms the theory that the comparative advantages of innovation tend to fade in any system where information circulates in real time. The principles of 'perfect competition' state that in any market where a given commodity is negotiated, buyers and sellers are so numerous that no single individual can influence the price. In other words, the price is an absolutely reliable sign-post which provides all the information needed by producers and distributors to achieve an optimum allocation of the commodity on the market.

Where the Alpine system assumes, as we have seen, that 'what is good for the company is good for its customers', the Anglo-American model is based on the premise that 'the customer can be trusted to know what is good for him, and to choose between different companies'. Or, to put it another way, one society conceives of insurance as a quasi-public service provided by tightly regulated institutions in a moderately competitive environment; the other sees insurance as a self-regulating market similar to any other, in which companies fulfil two roles: offering competitively priced products, and providing a minimum of security.

This minimum is not always enough. In 1970, one of the leading British car insurance firms – Equality & Security – went bankrupt in spite of a million-plus customer base. At the time, there were exactly five officials in the whole of the UK who were responsible for regulating the British insurance industry. In the end, the UK had to accept the 1974 EC directive requiring tougher regulatory measures.

British insurers, then, have to fulfil two conditions if they are to prosper: their product must be competitively priced, yet it must also be comparable to rival products, i.e. as standardised as possible. The only way round this apparent conundrum (production and management costs being equal) is, therefore, to concentrate on market segmentation. Companies pour all their creative resources into the development of sophisticated pricing schemes. It is not unusual for a British insurance firm to have 50 000 different policies on offer. Schedules are drawn up in which every conceivable factor is taken into account. The successful insurer trades on a single skill: the ability to create increasingly refined market segments, to find the market niche whose added value is the result of new permutations and combinations of variables that no one had dreamt of before.

The inner logic of this system turns on the precise calculation, through refined statistical analysis, of the price of each and every individual risk. The denial of mutuality, of the 'community of policy-holders', is total. This process of extreme segmentation and differentiation harks back to the maritime origins of the system, in which the insurer takes on a specific bet. The policy-holder pays a premium (a form of savings) which corresponds exactly to the probable risk involved. He neither benefits from, nor helps bear the cost of, any sharing of risk.

In practical terms, what happens in the case of an automobile accident? When two cars collide in France, the drivers will exchange statements, and each then sends his own claim to his agent or broker, who provides immediate compensation under the provisions of a multilateral scheme in which all companies participate (the 'Insured Loss Compensation' system). In the UK and America, the procedure is utterly different: the policy-holder informs his or her broker, who in turn deals with the insurer who issued the policy, who in turn negotiates with the other driver's insurance company on a case-by-case basis. The results are, to put it mildly, erratic.

Yet this procedure fits in with a larger pattern of relations between the insurer and the insured. Poor customer service partly reflects a low level of customer loyalty. Given that extreme market segmentation rules out solidarity among policy-holders, who are bound by their individual risk factors alone, there is nothing to foster the 'privileged relationship' between company and customer. Purchasing insurance coverage becomes an exercise in comparative shopping, not unlike 'zapping' from one television channel to another. The customer turnover rate for car insurance is in the 10–15 per cent range for most French companies; it exceeds 30 per cent in the UK. Again, the operative model is Lloyd's marine insurance: coverage for ships in high-risk zones may be renegotiated hourly in some cases.

This 'zapping' by clients in search of the best deal results in an ever-increasing rate of price variation: insurers end up devising special offers and bargain premiums; this encourages even greater customer turnover, which in turn increases administrative costs. As the company pours more and more money into canvassing for new clients, the extra costs are passed on to the consumer in the form of higher premiums. Prices are thus in constant upheaval; the dizzying pace of such cyclical variations can become unmanageable, and the more vulnerable companies simply go under.

The inescapable conclusion is that, in the absence of all notions of customer loyalty, the British insurance business is showing visible scars from the high cost of the 'invisible hand' that theoretically regulates a free market.

The Californian experience: the extremes come together

California was Ronald Reagan's launch-pad: his successful bid for the Presidency was fought on his record as a governor who pioneered deregulation and privatization in his home state. Yet, in this arch-conservative land of private-sector utilities and transport services, the insurance business is now subject to a degree of state regulation that makes a mockery of free enterprise and the market economy. What on earth could have caused this great leap backwards?

My own experience in the field may shed some light on this puzzle. Several years ago, my firm, AGF, purchased a stake in Progressive Corporation, an American insurer who specialised in increased-risk automobile insurance, i.e. coverage for drivers whom no other insurer wanted to touch. Remember that in the Alpine system, these drivers would pay the same basic premium as everyone else; but in the Anglo-American context of price freedom, the high-risk drivers insured by Progressive Corp. had to pay an average yearly premium roughly equivalent to the value of the car itself. Were this situation to prevail in France, where the average premium is FF 2000 ($325) per year, drivers in this category would end up paying something like FF 50 000 ($8300) – the average value of a car – in other words, a sum equivalent to the annual minimum wage! No wonder, then, that drivers in California (and in other states) took up the battle against exorbitant car insurance rates as part of the general movement towards consumer rights and protection. Virtually no one could be found to defend a system whereby a driver with two accidents on his record (who was likely to be young, Black and earning the minimum wage) was required to spend his entire income on car insurance. Moreover, the almost inevitable consequence of this Catch-22 situation was a huge increase in the number of uninsured drivers – reaching 15 per cent in some areas of the USA – whose eventual victims would be deprived of compensation for any damage or injury.

The groundswell of public outrage at this untenable state of affairs reached its apotheosis in 1983 with the adoption of the notorious Proposition 103 in a statewide referendum. California entered the realm of the absurd in the application of state control over insurance: under the new law, all companies had to reduce their rates by 20 per cent – except for those who seemed too financially vulnerable to withstand the shock. The current regime sets strict upper limits on insurers' overall profitability. Meanwhile, under a barrage of consumer litigation, the courts have opted for the old motto *summum jus, summa injuria*, according to which fairness to the victim should take precedence over the letter of the law. In a contest between two parties, one of whom is a wealthy insurer and the other an impoverished victim, the judge may well dig into the 'deep pockets' of the former regardless of the latter's proven culpability or negligence.

The consumer protection movement, presumably unaware of the Alpine model of vehicle insurance, has made this issue one of its top priorities, and not only in California. Cures worse than the complaint are springing up in other states: the New York State Insurance Commission can block any rate increases above 15 per cent and has actually imposed fines on companies that cut their rates too drastically. Things are now moving backwards, towards old-style government interventionism, at an astonishing rate. American insurance companies are already so alarmed at the profusion of laws going through the state legislatures that they are pressing for the federal government to get involved!

The fascinating aspect of all this, for Europeans, is that the only ideas currently in fashion in Brussels (and in Paris, to some degree) are those of Thatcherism, circa 1980. It is a particularly salient example of the general tendency, when the two capitalisms collide, for the less efficient neo-American model to triumph *ideologically* over its objectively more efficient Rhine rival (see Chapter 10).

Another example of this tendency can be seen in the new techniques of assets management as practised by a number of insurance firms in the English-speaking world, and most notably in the USA. When British insurers invest fully half their assets in the Stock Exchange, alarm bells should begin to ring; the noise should have been deafening when American insurance companies plunged gleefully into the junk-bond market or underwrote mortgage loans of the most dubious nature, all to the tune of hundreds of billions of dollars.

In the Alpine model, the reduced volatility of the financial markets, with their emphasis on debenture stock, means insurance companies can pursue financial policies based on continuity and security. They can keep the tyranny of the quarterly report at arm's length: nobody expects them to produce the brilliant short-term profits that are symptomatic of over-extended risk.

The French experience: a synthesis in the balance

It is ironic to note that the French insurance industry, so prone over the years to a debilitating inferiority complex, still fails to appreciate the qualities of its own peculiar mix of approaches. Yet this synthesis, the fruit of empirical observation and practice, manages to combine the best features of Alpine stability and Anglo-American flexibility.

By the mid-1980s, once the Single European Act had been adopted, French insurers were convinced that the arrival on their home ground of foreign competitors, especially the British and the Americans, would be their ruin. But in spite of bearing the developed world's highest tax burden (except in life assurance), French companies have prospered on every front.

In the domestic market, foreign companies have failed to establish a secure foothold in spite of the lifting of all financial and trade barriers. This applies even to the high-risk industrial sector, where their market share has actually declined over the last decade. Nor have they successfully challenged French firms (notably the friendly societies) in the liability insurance market. And in the one area of weakness for French companies, the life assurance market, it is not competition from overseas which has seen their market share dip but rather new challengers at home: banking groups, for the most part. By way of compensation, French insurers have stepped up their investments abroad, in what is surely the most surprising success story of recent years. While British and American companies have tended to fall back on their home markets as a result of the pressure exerted by their shareholders, the two countries that have been especially active in expanding their overseas insurance operations are France and Switzerland.

As for automobile insurance, British firms no longer deserve their reputation for the cheapest coverage in Europe. Considering that French taxes are higher and that French firms offer a superior service, it is reasonable to assert that British car insurance is significantly more expensive than the equivalent French product. The explanation lies in the production and distribution system which has evolved in France: it is a uniquely balanced approach which does not discourage innovation. Pricing methods, for example, are a blend of the best features of the Alpine and 'maritime' models: although insurers are free to set their own prices, the surcharge for new drivers is limited to 140 per cent and loading (i.e. charging extra premiums) may not exceed 25 per cent per at-fault accident. As for distribution, the situation at AGF may serve as a representative example: each of its three sales vectors (general agents, direct dealing, brokers) accounts for about a third of domestic turnover.

There is, nevertheless, one major weakness in the French insurance system. The taxpayer has not yet woken up to the fact that the level of compulsory social security contributions is higher in France than in other industrialized economies of comparable size, and for one reason: employers' contributions are fixed at an exceptionally high rate. Yet nothing could be more crucial in building up a country's competitive edge, as well as in the fight against unemployment and the promotion of national solidarity, than the sustained development of supplementary pensions through capitalization – but on the sole condition that these pension funds are managed with the 'creative caution' typical of the Alpine model (whose institutional investors provide stability, unlike those in America and elsewhere who have succumbed to the lure of short-term speculation).

True, the cautiousness typical of the Alpine insurance system, and the comfortable position it enjoys in the economy, put it in danger of becoming far too set in its ways. But it is equally clear that insurance in the Anglo-American vein can find itself locked into a vicious circle in which public hostility may play an unpredictable part, and which ultimately works against the grain of the free market economy: efficiency may be compromised by instability, and an obsession with the bottom line can lead to poor standards of customer service.

Given these parameters, it seems wilfully perverse of the French insurance industry to show itself so eager now to climb aboard the Anglo-American bandwagon. This trend seems all the more illogical when one looks at the wider picture, which shows the Rhine model of the economy to be more just and more efficient on a number of levels than its English-speaking rival – as the next chapter will demonstrate.

Chapter 6
The other capitalism

In economics, as in entertainment, the spectator is more likely to remember an outrageous, over-the-top performance than a quietly understated one. In other words, the glitter of Wall Street and the gladiatorial drama of the casino economy enjoy a worldwide notoriety denied to the subtle balancing act of the German *Sozialmarktwirtschaft* (social market economy). In their dreams of a capitalist nirvana, the downtrodden inhabitants of Tirana or Bratislava or Ulan Bator naturally conjure up visions of a prosperity made in America, and packaged by Hollywood; dreams made all the more legitimate and credible now that the fulminations, falsehoods and false hopes of half a century of communist propaganda have been firmly swept aside. When, in the summer of 1990, a few dozen Albanians managed to escape the last European bastion of Stalinism and find refuge in France, it soon emerged that their true destination was America: the America of Dallas, Chicago and Wall Street. And when the Budapest Stock Exchange was inaugurated earlier that same year, it was cause for national celebration. Hungarians at last had tangible proof that the capitalist Eldorado was just around the corner.

It would certainly come as a shock to most people in the former communist countries, then, to learn that capitalism is not one and indivisible, that market economies – like cars – come in different makes, and that the most efficient one is not necessarily the glamorous American model. One who would not be surprised, though, is Lech Walesa. Poland's new President has openly talked of his quest for an ideal model which would reconcile the supposed prosperity and efficacy of American capitalism with the relative security, in social welfare terms, of the old regime (see Guy Sorman, *Sortir du socialisme*: Fayard; 1991); a model which would allow people, in the words of a much-quoted Warsaw witticism, 'to live like the Japanese without having to work harder than the Poles'.

Were President Walesa to look over his shoulder to Germany, he would find something not unlike his ideal system. To take but one example, the former West German states could boast an average of 1633 hours per year of real working time per employee in manufacturing industry. Joking aside, this does fit the description of 'working less than the French while producing as much as the Japanese' (see *Futuribles*, January 1989). German metalworkers already enjoy a $36\frac{1}{2}$ -hour working week, and it is quite possible that the 35-hour week scheduled to be introduced in 1995 will (in spite of the enormous controversy it has aroused) eventually become the norm. The point is that, of all the great industrialized nations, Germany can lay claim to both the shortest working week and the highest wages, while at the same time building up an enormous trade surplus with the rest of the world.

Yet Germany is but one example, one particular incarnation, of the 'other capitalism', the Rhine model – largely unrecognised or, at best, misunderstood – which extends from northern Europe to Switzerland, and partially includes Japan. Like its rival, the neo-American model, it is indisputably capitalist: the market economy, private property and free enterprise are the cornerstones of both systems. In the last 10 or 15 years, however, the neo-American model has begun to veer off in another direction, a trend described by sociologist Jean Padioleau as 'the speculator gaining the upper hand over the industrial entrepreneur, and the race for easy, short-term profits undermining the collective wealth built up through long-term investment'.

The Rhine model represents a very different vision of economic organization; it presupposes different financial structures and social controls. It is far from perfect, but its characteristic features combine to produce a stable, yet dynamic (and remarkably powerful) system. The same aphorism may be applied to it as to democracy: it is the worst system in the world, except for all the others. And although it has never received anything like the public recognition and international prestige of the neo-American model, there is evidence of a greater awareness among economic decision-makers. A survey of 300 European company directors, carried out by the French polling organization SOFRES in August 1988, makes for interesting reading in this respect.

Asked to name their preferences if they had to subcontract more work abroad or purchase more foreign goods, they opted for West Germany (as it was then) by a huge margin, in spite of its higher salary costs – of which they were, naturally, well aware. (France, incidentally, was their second choice, with the Benelux countries coming in third.)

Let us now turn to some of the fundamental aspects of the Rhine economic model, those which distinguish it most clearly, and in many cases radically, from the neo-American model.

The role of the market

Just as there can be no socialist society in which all goods and services are free, so can there be no capitalist society in which all goods and services may be bought and sold. Some assets, by definition, cannot be transferred from one owner to the other. They may be personal (love and friendship, generosity and honor, for example) or collective (democracy, public freedoms, human rights, justice etc.). They are what may be termed non-negotiable (or non-exchangeable) goods, and they are basically the same for both models of capitalism, with one major exception: religion.

Where the models diverge significantly is in the realm of negotiable goods (i.e. commodities and services that can always be exchanged), and in that of mixed goods. The two diagrams on page 102 will give a rough idea of the market status of certain types of goods in each model.

The differences are clearly visible: the neo-American model gives pride of place to negotiable goods, while the Rhine model has a preponderance of mixed goods (those which are partly negotiable on the open market and partly dependent on public-sector initiative). It is worth examining each item in turn.

Religions

In the Rhine model, religions do not generally function as economic institutions; in Germany, for example, pastors and priests are paid out of public funds, just as if they were civil servants. In the USA, it would seem, religious movements are increasingly run as mixed-economy institutions, often using the most sophisticated methods of marketing, publicity and media-management.

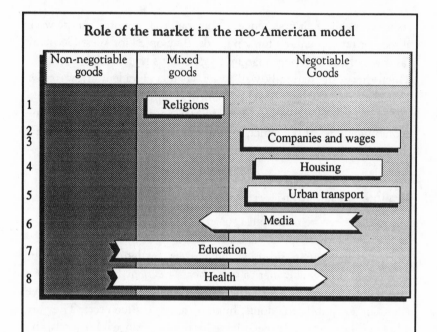

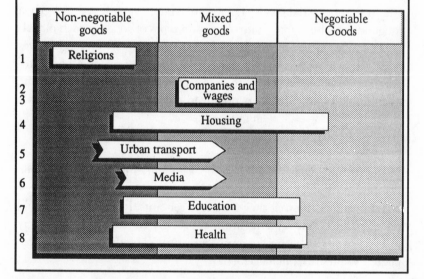

Companies

In the neo-American model, a company is a negotiable good like any other, whereas for the Rhine economies it is not just a commodity, but a community – in other words, a mixed good.

Wages

The same holds for wages, which, in the neo-American model, are increasingly subject to the prevailing winds of the market at any given moment; the Rhine system, however, tends to base wages on factors not directly connected with worker productivity, such as qualifications, seniority and nationally agreed pay scales. They are thus negotiable goods in one case, mixed goods in the other.

Housing

Housing is also almost exclusively a market commodity in the USA. In Rhine economies, by contrast, public sector initiatives account for a significant proportion of housing and rents are often subsidised.

Urban transport

The situation in urban transport is analogous to that of housing, although even in the USA it is subject to some public regulation; one of the few places where untrammelled competition prevails in this sector is Santiago, the capital of Chile, where, thanks to General Pinochet's 'Chicago boys', anyone can set up a bus service and set fares at will. As a result, bus traffic there is the heaviest in the world, and pollution levels are worse than ever.

Nevertheless, the many deficiencies of municipal transport services in Rhine countries have put them under increasing scrutiny, and moves toward privatization are on the increase. This is indicated in the diagram by an arrow pointing in the direction of the 'negotiable goods' category.

The media

Similarly, the media – especially television – which have traditionally belonged to the public sector in Rhine economies, face increasing privatisation. Oddly, this is the one case where the American trend goes against the grain; its all-commercial broadcasting sector is experiencing a new growth of 'community-run' television stations financed through public subscription. Thus the arrows in the diagram point in opposite directions for this commodity.

Education

This spans all three categories of goods in both models. Nevertheless, it is readily apparent, in the case of the neo-American model, that the proportion of educational establishments subject to market forces is enormous, and still growing steadily (as indicated by the arrow in the direction of 'negotiable goods').

Health

Like education, health embraces the three different categories of goods in both models, but in the Rhine model, where a greater role is accorded to public hospitals and mutual benefit schemes operating in tandem with Social Security, there is as yet no sign that the authorities are keen to transfer many of their prerogatives to the private sector – as is increasingly the tendency in both English-speaking and Latin countries. It is a point which needs underlining, as it admirably illustrates capitalism's potential for both short-term wealth creation and long-term erosion of social values. The latter may occur if public authorities fail to exercise their supervisory role, and when there are no other strong social values to compete with that of money and wealth. As the late French economist François Perroux once wrote:

> For any capitalist society to function smoothly, there must be certain social factors which are free of the profit motive, or at least of the quest for maximum profits. When monetary gain becomes uppermost in the minds of civil servants, soldiers, judges, priests, artists or scientists, the result is social dislocation and a real threat to any form of economic organization. The highest values, the noblest human assets – honor, joy, affection, mutual respect – must not be given a price tag; to do so is to undermine the foundations of the social grouping. There is always a more or less durable framework of pre-existing moral values within which a capitalist economy operates, values which may be quite alien to capitalism itself. But as the economy expands, its very success threatens this framework; capitalist values replace all others in

the public esteem, and the preference for comfort and material well-being begins to erode the traditional institutions and mental patterns which are the basis of the social order. In a word, capitalism corrupts and corrodes. It uses up society's vital life-blood, yet is unable to replenish it.

Le Capitalisme, in the 'Que sais-je?' series: 1962

These are prophetic words indeed, and any number of concrete examples may be found to illustrate them. To take but one which concerns us all (directly or not), let us examine the American legal process, which has begun to take on all the characteristics of a marketable, negotiable commodity.

In Japan, it is considered somewhat shameful to bring a lawsuit; every avenue of negotiation and compromise must be explored before resorting to such an extreme measure. In the European tradition, the legal profession – like all the other professions – frees its members from the need to chase profits and calculate prices, in order to be able to concentrate in a disinterested fashion on serving the public good. It is this notion of service to a higher ideal – whether this be defined as 'justice' or 'health' or 'education' – which in turn defines the code of professional conduct: in a word, honor. Honor is the key concept, as the term 'honorarium' (payment for professional services) clearly indicates.

This ancient tradition (stretching back to Hippocrates, in the case of medicine), fundamental to the liberal professions, is the cornerstone which anchors them firmly *outside* the market place. But in the USA, a radical change is under way. The legal profession is now more aptly described as 'the lawsuit industry'.

This latest victory of a certain brand of capitalism has been fully documented in Walter Kolson's study, *The Litigation Explosion* (Truman Talley Books: New York, 1991). In his review of Kolson's book in *The New York Times* of 12 May 1991, former Supreme Court Chief Justice Warren Burger notes that this unprecedented change began to gather real momentum in 1977, when the Supreme Court ruled that lawyers should be allowed to advertise their services on television. The immediate upshot of this decision has been the exponential growth of contingency fee agreements, whereby a prospective plaintiff in a lawsuit hires the services of a lawyer on the following terms: no fee will be payable if the suit is lost, but if it is won and damages are awarded, the lawyer will take a percentage cut of the damages. Such arrangements are now routine in road accident cases, so much so that an injured victim is not surprised to find a lawyer by his side in the ambulance, urging him to sign a contingency fee agreement before they reach hospital.

According to the statistics, there has been a 300-fold increase in the number of malpractice suits against US doctors and hospitals since 1970. Given that the resultant cost of malpractice insurance may reach the equivalent of £30 000 per year for some doctors, it is no wonder that aggressive profit-making is the order of the day in the medical profession as well – as innumerable American women (to take just one example) could testify on being advised by their gynaecologists to undergo a hysterectomy on the sole grounds that the onset of menopause has made the uterus 'redundant'.

Another statistic speaks volumes: the number of federal judges found guilty of corruption and tax evasion in the 1980s exceeded the total of the previous 190 years of US history. The judiciary, too, is swaying to the siren song of the profit motive. Do not imagine, however, that dark irrational forces are at work: your lawyer, who sees you as a rich vein of potential lawsuits waiting to be mined, is working to a logical plan which begins and ends with maximum gain; your doctor is merely following the same capitalist reasoning, in which you are a biological generator of profit. But here's the rub: in such a system, who can you trust? And what is a society really 'worth' if it systematically breaks down trust?

Bank capitalism

In the Rhine model, the 'golden boys' and their breathless exploits on the floor of the Stock Exchange are conspicuously absent. Banks, not stock markets, are the principal guardians of the capitalist flame in Germany and Switzerland: one has only to compare the Frankfurt or Zurich Bourse with their heavyweight British or French counterparts. Frankfurt's total capitalization is a third that of London, and nine times smaller than Wall Street or Tokyo. It is only recently that options and futures markets were introduced on the German exchanges, which remain narrowly focused and decidedly unglamorous. German companies in search of financing are far more likely to talk to their bank than to raise funds on the financial markets or through public subscription.

Some – including giants like Bertelsmann, the biggest European press and publishing group – are not even listed on the stock exchange. Just the opposite, in other words, of what we see in the UK and the USA, and all the more striking a contrast in the light of Germany's economic power and influence.

It is the strength and vigor of German banks that explain this situation. While everyone has heard of the Deutsche Bank, with its commanding position in the German economy, and of others such as the Dresdner Bank or the Commerz Bank, few suspect how very powerful they are. Crucially, they may (unlike American banks) conduct all types of business; no regulations restrict them to a single activity or sector. German banks are 'universal' institutions: they make ordinary loans and have ordinary depositors; they deal in stocks and bonds, and manage company treasuries; they also operate as commercial banks, providing investment advice and carrying out acquisitions and mergers. And finally, they maintain whole networks of economic, financial, business and industrial information for the benefit of client companies. The result is a special relationship between bankers and their customers in which mutual cooperation is constantly reinforced.

Above all, German banks have assumed the role of company financiers, which elsewhere has been taken over by the stock markets. Most firms have their 'house bank' to whom matters of finance are entrusted; one can almost imagine the German banker telling his client, the company president: 'You just take care of improving production and increasing sales, and leave the financial problems to us!' In Japan, as mentioned earlier, the symbiosis of industry and banking is even more pronounced, with many industrial groups owning their own banks. It is almost possible to reverse the equation and say that the Japanese banks (and insurance companies) own their own industrial groups.

Mutual-interest networks

In Germany, too, the common ground shared by banks and industry goes some way beyond purely financial considerations. As important company shareholders, banks enjoy a privileged status and their views are listened to, on at least two accounts: first, through direct ownership of a portion of the capital; and, secondly, through voting rights exercised on behalf of shareholders who bank with them. Combining these two levers of influence gives German banks a considerable say in board-room decisions. Thus, Deutsche Bank owns a quarter of the shares – and with it a minority veto – in the automotive giant Daimler Benz (which also makes engines and aircraft parts), as well as in Philipp Holzmann (Germany's premier construction firm) and in Karstadt (the leader in volume retailing). Dresdner Bank and Commerz Bank simi-larly have a 25 per cent or more stake in a dozen major companies.

Conversely, the banks' largest single shareholders tend to be these same industrial groups (although this seldom represents more than a 5 per cent holding in each case). And there are other links, such as the supervisory boards which oversee banking activities: big business usual-ly has its seat on these, too. Again, both conditions apply to Daimler Benz vis-à-vis Deutsche Bank.

This interpenetration of banking and business interests forms the warp and weft of an industrial–financial fabric which is both stable and highly resistant to outside factors. There are at least three conse-quences of this marriage of interests for the economy as a whole, and all are beneficial.

To begin with, the banks tend to have the long-term interests of business at heart; unlike the brokers of Wall Street, for whom regular quarterly profits are the sole criterion, German banks see their stake in a company as an enduring commitment. They accept that risks must be taken, involving large sums over long periods of time, as the price for backing a difficult but potentially rewarding venture. Why else would the Swiss banks have invested heavily in the watch-making industry at a time when it appeared to be in terminal decline, and what else explains Metallgesellschaft's ability to increase its holdings in the min-ing industry when raw materials were synonymous with doom and gloom?

A second positive consequence for managers of businesses, and for the economy generally, is that banks make for stable shareholders. Their basic loyalty gives management room to breathe, secure in the knowledge that no sword of Damocles (in the form of a hostile takeover bid) is hanging over their heads. Corporate executives are free to devote themselves to managing the firm; their time and energy are not being lavished on interminable, and unproductive, legal wrangles and the devising of anti-takeover strategies. It is one of the reasons German companies continue to be highly competitive on world markets. The same can be said of Japanese, Swiss or Dutch firms: their managers do not live under the constant threat of a sudden restructuring imposed by outsiders, although not always for the same reasons. Japanese capitalism has a number of quasi-feudal characteristics of its own, which will be explored in a later chapter. In Switzerland, the role of the three great banking groups is rather different from that of the German banks. It is through the restrictive rules governing shareholders' voting rights that the capital stock of Swiss firms is protected from would-be predators. As for the Netherlands, a whole battery of anti-takeover measures ensures that CEOs and executives sleep peacefully.

This relatively secure set-up does not mean that managers in the Rhine economies can afford to relax on the job or that their mistakes go unnoticed. There is always a nucleus of principal shareholders (banks and others) who take their supervisory powers and responsibilities seriously, acting as a counterweight to executive prerogatives. They do not shrink from punishing cases of management negligence or dereliction – and thus, indirectly, also help protect smaller investors.

The third consequence of banking's pre-eminent role in the economy is that the sheer density of the web of mutual interests cannot be easily penetrated by outside forces. It is fair to say that the German economy is driven by consensus (rather than commanded – nothing horrifies German decision-makers more than the idea of a command economy) involving a relatively small group of people, who all know one another well and travel in the same social circles. Personal relations are a decisive factor in protecting the German economy from the unwanted attentions of foreign investors. When a firm is under threat, its bankers will quite naturally seek a home-grown solution to the problem rather than look for help from abroad. Deutsche Bank, for example, stepped in to rescue the ailing Klöckner-Werke group; and when the computer firm Nixdorf ran aground, the banks were instrumental in arranging for its takeover by the electronics giant Siemens. If mergers and acquisitions are handled this way, one can imagine the difficulty, for any foreign investor who might be contemplating a hostile raid on German property, of getting past the vigilant front lines of the banks.

There are exceptions to every rule, of course. German companies are perhaps no longer as invulnerable to foreign takeover as they once were; of the 3000 West German firms which changed hands in 1989, 459 were acquired by foreign investors spending an estimated total of $3 billion – which is twice as much as the figure for 1988. (French investors accounted for 63 acquisitions, a threefold increase since 1986.) Yet these figures should be treated with caution, for on closer inspection they show that the vast majority of foreign takeovers involved small or medium-sized businesses. In 1989 a single acquisition (that of Colonia by the French insurer La Victoire) accounted for more than half of the total French investment in West Germany. Meanwhile, German investors made twice as many acquisitions in France as vice versa, and there is every reason to think that the imbalance in Germany's favor will continue to grow.

Rhine companies thus enjoy financial stability and benefit from a host of safeguards which promote long-term development and enhance competitiveness. But it is not only in the management of capital that they excel; the very structure of company management also plays an important part.

A well-managed consensus

In a 1986 report to the EC President entitled 'Federal Germany: Its Ideals, Interests and Inhibitions', W. Hager and M. Noelke wrote that German society showed 'a tendency to avoid contentious issues and questions that might jeopardise the social consensus'. The same statement applies to Japan, and this is no coincidence: both defeated in World War II, they remain, in their new capacity as economic superpowers, keenly aware of their own vulnerability. In both countries, political democracy and economic prosperity are too recent not to be somewhat fragile, making it easier perhaps to enforce a particular social discipline typical of the Rhine model.

Turning to the power structure and patterns of organization within companies, it is clear once again that the emphasis in the Rhine model is on mutuality and shared responsibilities. In Germany, all parties are invited to participate in company decision-making: shareholders, employers, executives and trade unions alike cooperate in a variety of ways to achieve a unique form of joint management (the German term, 'Mitbestimmung', is perhaps best translated as 'co-responsibility'). A

SOURCE: *Plantu, Un vague souvenir, Le Monde Éditions, 1990 p. 40. (Reproduced with permission.)*

1976 law makes it compulsory for all firms of 2000 or more employees to implement this system of shared decision-making at virtually every level.

At the top, to begin with, there are two key bodies: the board of directors, responsible for company management as such, and the supervisory board, elected by shareholders in the AGM, whose role is to oversee the activities of the board of directors. Both bodies are at all times required to assist one another in ensuring that company affairs run smoothly. Real checks and balances are thus brought to bear, allowing equal time for each side (owners and investors on the one hand, management on the other) to put its views and be listened to, yet without either one dominating.

To this top-level division of powers is then added the distinctive German brand of industrial democracy referred to above as co-responsibility. Workers' participation in management dates back to 1848 and is thus a well-established tradition. It takes the form of committees which may be likened to British works councils (or French *comités d'entreprise*), but with real and wide-ranging powers. All issues of concern to the workforce are referred to these councils: training, redundancies, schedules, methods of payment, work patterns etc. It is in fact *mandatory* for senior management and works councils to come to an agreement on these matters. But co-responsibility does not end there.

Employees have another means of influencing decisions in the form of the company supervisory boards, to which they elect delegates. Since 1976, German firms employing more than 2000 workers must allocate an equal number of seats on these boards to employees as to shareholders. Although the supervisory board will always have as its chairman (who casts the deciding vote in split decisions) a representative of the shareholders, it is nevertheless remarkable that employees should have such a strong voice on one of the most important executive organs. In the German view, dialogue between partners is the indispensable oil that keeps the wheels of business turning and reduces the likelihood of destructive social friction.

From the French standpoint, this mode of decision-making and supervision would appear so heavy-handed, and so time-consuming, as to paralyse all initiative. Yet this is manifestly not the case. Not only are German firms as dynamic as their competitors, if not more so, but they benefit from the enhanced sense of belonging which co-responsibility fosters. The company is seen by *all* its members as a community of interests, a true partnership. American sociologists have christened this the 'stakeholder' model of organization, as opposed to the 'stockholder' model. The latter concentrates exclusively on those who own shares (stock) in the business, while the former treats everyone as a partner with a personal interest (stake) in the company's fortunes.

In Japan, a different set of concepts, not always clear to Western eyes, produces the same result: a feeling of belonging to a community, almost a family. For example, under the term *amae* – virtually untranslatable – are grouped notions of the need for solidarity and protection, and the search for emotional fulfilment which the company must satisfy. Another word, *iemoto*, describes the leadership which an employer must display and carries familial overtones. According to sociologist Marcel Bolle de Bal, '*Amae* and *iemoto* are mutually complementary notions: one is distinctly charged with feminine principles of love, feelings, emotions, and the group; the other carries a masculine charge embracing concepts of authority, hierarchy, production, and the individual. Both are inseparably united in the ongoing effort to build a durable organization' (see *Revue française de gestion*, February 1988).

We in the West are constantly being reminded of the peculiar characteristics of Japanese corporate life – guaranteed lifetime employment, pay based on seniority, in-house trade unionism, group incentive schemes etc. – which are the concrete manifestations of unique cultural values. Unique they may be, but the result is the same: a collective feeling of belonging. The 'company spirit' is as strong in the Japanese variant of the Rhine model as it is currently weak in the neo-American economies.

As the world becomes a more and more uncertain place, immaterial factors like trust and belonging are increasingly important. It becomes essential for all corporate enterprises to ensure that their members play the same game by the same rules, share the same views and fit into the same patterns, so that in the end decisions can be taken by consensus and energies can be mobilised naturally, spontaneously.

Stability at home is all the more valuable when uncertainty and instability are abroad; far from stifling change and adaptability, domestic harmony can be turned to competitive advantage. It is worth noting, at this juncture, that just as America is not New York (and New York is not just Wall Street), so the largest American corporations have successfully avoided the trap of short-termism in their management of human resources, if not always in their financial management. Companies such as IBM, ATT, General Electric and McDonald's have, as far as possible, steered clear of the 'casino economy' mentality which currently disfigures the neo-American model and which sees employees as so many poker chips in a high-stakes game. They have understood that in order to build and consolidate a multinational endeavor, it is better to gamble on stability, incentive and even co-responsibility.

Training: the loyalty factor

The German brand of power-sharing is thus highly rewarding to companies; but, equally, it is of immense benefit to their employees. Purely
in terms of wages, to begin with: German workers are among the best
paid in the world, at an average DM 33 per hour as against DM 25 in
the USA and Japan, DM 22 in France (at 1988 rates). Moreover, the
gap between the best-paid and the lowest-paid workers is not as wide as
in other countries (see B. Sausay, *Le Vertige allemand*: Orban, 1985),
making Germany a far more egalitarian society than America or even
France.

Surprisingly, wages and salaries account for a smaller percentage of
German GDP – 67 per cent in 1988 – than is the case in other leading
EC member states (71 per cent in France, 72 per cent in Italy and 73
per cent in the UK). Although partly explained by Germany's huge
trade surplus (pre-unification), this little-known statistic is highly
revealing: it means that German companies manage to pay out the
highest wages in Europe (keeping industrial unrest to a minimum) and
still have more funds left over for self-financing than their competitors.

German workers are not only better paid than their American or
French counterparts but, as previously noted, they work fewer hours.
What, then, of their overall career prospects? The litmus test for promotion is, in the Rhine model, based on qualifications and seniority.
Thus the twin priorities for an employee who wishes to 'get ahead' are
clear: company loyalty and further training. Not coincidentally, the
pursuit of both is beneficial to all.

It is not unusual to find that senior managers of German (and
Japanese) firms have spent their entire working lives in the same company, having moved up the ladder of promotion from shop floor to
executive suite. Nothing could be further removed from the attitude
now prevalent in America, whereby job mobility and frequent career
changes are seen as proof of excellence and individual initiative.
(France has not been immune to this 'nomadic' bug: as with so many
fashionable trends imported from the USA, the concept was widely,
and enthusiastically, adopted. Recently, the pendulum seems to be
swinging back towards greater career stability – except in the lecture
halls of the top business schools, where 'self-affirmation through mobility' is still being taught.)

If proof were needed that the German system of power-sharing and co-responsibility could be decisive in moulding a more competitive national economy, the recession years of 1981–82 provided a striking example. Employers and trade unions agreed to keep wage settlements down, so as not to further penalise companies in distress; in some cases, they even negotiated salary cuts amounting to 3 per cent or 4 per cent of purchasing power. (Even greater sacrifices were conceded by Japanese workers following the oil crisis of 1974–75.) The resulting recovery was extraordinarily vigorous: by 1984 the German economy had begun to grow again, creating new jobs and winning back its share of world markets. And when, in 1984, a major strike was finally brought to an end, the workforce as a whole mobilised itself in order to make up the losses.

Co-responsibility, if skilfully applied, can be a potent weapon in the economic armory; it may even prove to be the decisive edge of one competitor over another. Training and education provide a further illustration of the benefits of the Rhine vision of devolved management.

Vocational training and skills upgrading are now widely recognised as supremely important for business and industry, whose real wealth lies, not in capital or plant, but in the knowledge and expertise of the workforce. In the European context, it is again Germany which has taken the lead in this endeavor, and again the approach is based on close cooperation between management and employees. Long a matter of top national priority, training in the German workplace (and outside it as well) is based on three fundamental principles:

1. It must be widely available. Only 20 per cent of the working population in Germany have no paper qualification, as opposed to 41.7 per cent of the French. The German apprenticeship system is particularly remarkable in that it absorbs half of all school-leavers; the disappointing figure for both France and the UK is 14 per cent. As a result, the proportion of German school-leavers who find themselves unemployed or in a job involving no further training is a mere 7 per cent, while in France it is 19 per cent, and in Britain. . . 44 per cent! Furthermore, there is strong emphasis on vocational studies (leading to the equivalent of a City and Guilds qualification, for

example), involving some 53 per cent of the German workforce, as compared with only 25 per cent in France.

2. Training must not be restricted to the élite. While it may be that the USA boasts an educational system which, at its best, is unrivalled anywhere (see Chapter 2), and even France has a better-educated élite than Germany, the reverse is true of intermediate levels of training. According to the DGB (the largest German trade union), in a representative sample of 100 people and their qualifications, the top 15 in France are educated to a higher standard than the top 15 Germans; but the other 85 are far better trained in Germany. This emphasis on a more egalitarian pattern of education means that Germany has been able to build a dynamic, competitive economy on the bedrock foundation of a generally well-qualified workforce, as a report commissioned by the French Department of Industry admitted in 1990. In France, as in the English-speaking world, professional training is like polo: a sport for the élite. In Germany, it is more like angling or jogging, a popular activity that anyone can do.

3. Further education is for the most part financed by employers, with help from government subsidies. As for its content, the emphasis is on behaviour and attitude: training is designed to impart values such as accuracy, reliability, even punctuality. As such, it meshes perfectly with the qualities needed for advancement. The pathway to promotion in Germany almost always involves an itinerary of further education and qualification: nine out of ten apprentices finish their training and are awarded a certificate; 15 per cent of those will then go on to do more training. It would seem that, in the final analysis, professionalism is more highly esteemed in Germany than elsewhere. As one report put it, 'In West German companies, one does not usually reach executive level until the age of 40 and only then on the basis of proven performance, not just diplomas. But there are solid links between business and higher education: virtually all the top business leaders take on some teaching duties' (Michel Godet, *Futuribles*: April 1989).

If only because it is a factor in determining company loyalty, training is of the utmost importance for both models of capitalism. It is an issue that can no longer be ignored: it concerns literally every worker and every workplace. To sum up, the 'battle' pits two rival systems against one another:

- The Anglo-American model of employment, in which a company seeks to maximise its competitiveness by sharpening the competition between individual employees. This entails a relentless drive to recruit the best and brightest, whatever the cost, and then to keep them by paying the 'going rate' as dictated at any given time by market forces. Salaries, like jobs, are fundamentally individualised, and highly negotiable.
- The Rhine–Japanese model has an entirely different set of priorities. It rejects the notion that employers have the right to treat staff as so many productive units or raw materials to be bought and sold on the market. The company-as-community has an obligation to ensure a certain level of job security, to earn its members' loyalty, and to provide educational and training opportunities – which do not come cheaply. As a result, it may not be able to pay each worker at his or her current market value; what it can do is lay the ground for a lasting career, and smooth out some of the rough spots along the way. In this model of employment, there is no virtue in promoting cutthroat (and ultimately destructive) in-house competition.

Ordo-liberalism*

Attitudes in the former West Germany on such questions as economic liberalism (strongly in favor) and the power of the state (deeply suspicious) mirror, or even surpass, those of the USA. Government interventionism is officially portrayed as the authoritarian regime's mark of Cain, notably for its association with Nazism. Beginning with the monetary reform championed by Ludwig Erhard in 1948, the Federal Republic formally rejected the notion of central planning in favor of a particular variety of liberal capitalism known as the social market econ-

---

* I wish to thank Jérôme Vignon for providing me with many of the arguments put forward in this section.

omy (*Sozialmarktwirtschaft*), as espoused by the Freiburg school of economics. The social market economy posits two fundamental principles:

1. A dynamic economy depends on the market being as free as possible, notably with respect to prices and wages.
2. Market forces alone cannot govern all aspects of society: there are certain non-negotiable social requirements of which the state must be the guarantor. The German unitary state is, therefore, defined by its social dimension.

There are a number of different components which interlock to form the German social market as we know it:

- The Welfare State component, along the lines set down by Beveridge, postulates that the state is responsible for social security in the broadest sense, and that management–labor relations must be decided by free bargaining.
- Within the social democratic component, inherited from the Weimar Republic, is enshrined the principle of employee participation in the management of companies and other institutions. Building on this earlier foundation, post-war Germany continued to refine the legal framework governing co-responsibility (*Mitbestimmung*); it is still the subject of vigorous debate today.
- The Constitution of 1949 posits, as its most innovatory feature, the principle of monetary control as an autonomous mechanism for ensuring stability (in other words, to fight inflation and recession). The present role of the Bundesbank, while not directly enshrined in the Constitution, is the obvious example.
- In conjunction with central bank autonomy, the structure of commercial banking in general is designed with company financing in mind. It is understood that the policy of monetary stability depends on the commercial banks taking a leading role in long-term financing of industry.
- State intervention and central economic planning are seen as abhorrent largely because they distort free and open competition. This is a fundamental principle: competitors must be guaranteed a level playing-field.

In the 30 years that I have been studying the German economy and working with German colleagues, it has never ceased to amaze me how sceptical the rest of the world is on the question of Germany's liberal economic credentials. Yet there is simply no denying that the German economy is wholly based on free trade. The one criticism that can be levelled is with regard to industry standards: it is true that German businesses have, over the last century or more, developed industry-wide standards which they defend jealously, particularly as they tend to be very high. These quality standards are recognised by a worldwide clientèle of importers of German goods – a further argument for maintaining them.

But apart from this single reservation, the basic principle of the *Sozialmarktwirtschaft* holds firm, i.e. that there are only two cases in which the state has the *right* to intervene in the economy, but that in those cases the state has an absolute *duty* to intervene.

The first case is the abovementioned 'level playing-field' which guarantees free and fair competition. This is where the Bundeskartellamt (Federal Monopolies Board) comes into its own, ensuring that leading firms do not abuse their position or that would-be competitors cannot set up cosy, mutually beneficial arrangements. Furthermore, it is accepted that small and medium-sized companies need some assistance in competing against the giant groups, and may therefore be granted special tax concessions and credit facilities (a similar situation exists in the USA under the terms of the Small Business Administration). Then there is the question of regional disparities: in order to guarantee that the laws of open competition apply equally in all parts of the country, the central government has a duty to assist the least-developed regions, notably in terms of infrastructure. German policy in this regard has been exemplary. Another area in which government intervention can be authorised on grounds of fair competition is research. If other countries subsidise an array of research programs out of the public purse – usually under the guise of defense spending – why should Germany not do the same?

The second case in which state intervention is both justified and necessary concerns social welfare generally. A telling example is provided by the mining and shipbuilding industries: when the world eco-

nomic climate made it imperative for these sectors to undertake massive structural changes and reconversions, government subsidies were
made available in order to cushion the inevitable impact on jobs and
living standards. This was the thinking behind the European Coal and
Steel Community (forerunner of the EC) which successfully transformed Europe's ailing coal and steel industries. But the central government's social brief also extends, as previously stated, to ensuring workers' active involvement in all aspects of company management – not
just on 'social' questions but in matters of finance as well.

Germany's emergence as a pillar of the Common Agricultural Policy
(CAP) within the EC can be seen as a synthesis of the different strands
of state intervention which its liberal doctrine authorises. Enforcement
of rules on fair competition, concern for social welfare, and action on
regional development: all inform German policy in this regard. It
should also be noted that German agriculture has recently made great
strides, thanks to subsidies provided by Brussels, in the direction of
environmental safeguards and protection of the countryside.

A final point: as explained earlier in this chapter, it is clear that, on
the question of company ownership and shareholding, German policy
shows a strong tendency towards protectionism.

The foregoing portrayal of a liberal economic regime in which the state
plays a vigorous but strictly limited role is what some specialists call
'ordo-liberalism'. The paradoxical result is that public expenditure as a
proportion of GDP is nearly as high in Germany (47–48 per cent) as it
is in France (51 per cent), and considerably higher than in Japan (33
per cent). In Germany as in France, transfers of public monies to the
private sector add up to about 2 per cent of GDP. For many observers,
these figures suggest that the liberalism of the federal government
serves as a smokescreen, behind which the interventionist hands of the
Länder are at work. This is not exactly the case. It is true that Germany
is a federal, and highly decentralised, state in which the central authorities must constantly seek to promote dialogue and consensus among
the constituent parts. More to the point, the federal government's powers are conferred upon it by the Länder, just as the cantons are the ultimate granting authority for the Swiss confederation. Moreover, German cities have a long history of autonomy, and they continue to exer-

cise an impressive array of powers and prerogatives. Each tier of government has a well-defined set of responsibilities, as reflected in the allocation of public spending. The federal budget of DM 280 billion goes on
general administrative services, welfare subsidies and defense; the Länder, with an only slightly smaller budget of DM 270 billion, are responsible for education and law enforcement; and local government
receives DM 180 billion to spend on social assistance programs, sport-
ing and cultural facilities, and so forth.

Devolution on this scale requires permanent consultation and a
coherent redistribution of financial resources. In the case of the individual Länder, each is guaranteed a revenue per inhabitant within 5 per
cent of the national average. Generous terms indeed, when compared
with France, for example, where there is a 30–40 per cent difference
between the richest and poorest regions. Again, there is a lesson to be
learned here, which (in my experience) the French have not yet
grasped. They assume, because France is by tradition so highly centralised, and its local authorities so powerless in relation to the state –
in spite of François Mitterand's devolutionary reforms of the early
1980s – that the fairest possible social and geographical redistribution
of national resources occurs more or less spontaneously at the center.
All the evidence indicates that this is pure fiction: those in search of
real national solidarity and concrete political action are better advised
to examine German policy on regional development. No less impressive than the redistribution of funds is the planning process, which
brings together all levels of government. Action is coordinated by
means of contracts which set out the agreed terms for undertaking specific joint projects.

All the preceding examples are intended to show just how well-
versed German politicians and institutions have become in the art of
consensus-building. It is a technique applied to virtually every sector of
public interest. Pay bargaining, for example, is not subject to direct
government intervention; rather, the authorities exert informal pressure on employers and unions alike, urging them to observe certain limits and avoid upsetting the collective economic apple-cart. When it
became clear that spending on health had to be reduced, for example, it
was the federal chancellor (then Helmut Schmidt) who saw to it that
employers, unions and managers of health insurance funds got together

and finally agreed on the necessary measures. It is a form of intervention, certainly, but still a far cry from the French experience, in which the public sector has long played a leading role in determining wage settlement levels.

Trade unions: power and responsibility

None of this dialogue and consensus would be possible if it were not for the active participation of powerful trade unions which are both representative and responsible. Such is the case in Germany, so much so that union membership is actually rising (after a slight decline in the early 1980s), whereas everywhere else in Europe a deep disenchantment with organized labor is increasingly apparent. Around 42 per cent of the working population is unionised in Germany – one of the highest rates in the world (in France the figure is nearer 10 per cent). This means that unions can boast a membership base of some 9 million workers, of which 7.7 million belong to the Deutscher Gewerkschaftsbund (DGB). With representativeness comes financial clout, given that dues are relatively high (2 per cent of members' wages, deducted at source). The German trade unions have prospered: they can afford to maintain more than 3000 permanent national staff and control considerable assets, in spite of the financial reversals suffered by their bank (BFG), their insurance company (Volkfursorge) and especially their property group. Their principal trump card, though, remains the 'war chests' which, in case of strikes or lock-outs, allows them to pay up to 60 per cent of members' wages. Obviously this is one economic weapon which wonderfully concentrates the minds of employers.

The trade unions do not leave the selection and training of their officials to chance. By maintaining their own research centres, whose analyses of social and economic issues keep key personnel informed and up-to-date, they ensure that their demands are taken seriously. Union negotiators are as well versed as anyone else in the art of presenting coherent, convincing arguments for their proposals, backed up by facts and taking account of the medium-to-long term. And there is yet another powerful means of exerting pressure, this time from within the corridors of power: a number of important members of parliament come from union ranks – up to 40 per cent of the Christian Democratic MPs elected under the CDU/CSU banner are trade union members. This interplay of the political sphere with that of organized labor is no doubt one more element in favor of consensus and the settling of differences without confrontation.

The above-mentioned report to the French Department of Industry stresses that German trade unions tend to wield their great power in a constructive way: to put it bluntly, they show a greater sense of economic responsibility towards the nation as a whole than many of their counterparts abroad. They cooperate wholeheartedly with employers in managing the system of apprenticeship; they openly discuss and debate the nature and content of continuing education; they are in charge of job-training centres which are instrumental in returning some 150 000 unemployed to work each year.

What no one disputes is that, on the whole, German trade unions eschew unreasonable, immoderate demands. They understand, and take full account of, the requirements of the whole economy, and they know that consensus and compromise pay off – literally, as evidenced by their members' wages. There is a genuine concern on the part of union leaders, as well as among the rank-and-file, not to disturb the well-tested recipe of a successful economy, particularly with regard to the great German bugbear which is inflation. Two features of the negotiation process as practised in Germany help to explain this fundamentally stable climate of labor relations:

1. Bargaining rounds are held with clockwork regularity, and the agreements reached normally cover a period of 3 or 4 years
2. For the duration of the agreement, unions pledge not to dispute its terms in a confrontational manner. The happy result is the lowest level of strike activity in the Western World. One has only to compare West Germany's 28 000 working days lost through industrial action in 1988 with France's 568 000, Britain's 1 920 000, Italy's 5 644 000 or the USA's 12 215 000.

The picture of a relatively harmonious labor landscape, in which the power of the unions is wedded to co-responsibility and the search for consensus, would not be complete without a mention of the extraordinarily vigorous voluntary sector. Some 80 000 German researchers, for instance, belong to scientific associations which disseminate information to their members throughout the country, besides defending professional interests and scrutinising working conditions. They constitute a kind of informal, flexible administrative arm of the scientific establishment. To take another example, environmental defense groups are strong not just in numbers, but in the preparation and argumentation of their cases.

In all, the voluntary sector plays a key role in mobilising and bringing together the vital energies of people from all walks of life. It is a typical reflection of the inner workings of a Rhine society, in which institutions provide a means of expression for ordinary citizens and their concerns.

Yet it is doubtful that any of these institutions, whether political or civic, could fulfil their potential if there were not a shared ethical basis upon which to found their activities.

Shared values

The countries that I have included within the Rhine model all share a particular set of values, which fall mainly under two headings:

1. They are, first and foremost, egalitarian societies. Disparities between the highest and lowest wages (the income spread) are much less flagrant, and fiscal policy aims for a far more comprehensive redistribution of wealth, than in the English-speaking countries. Direct taxation is favored over indirect taxes, and the top income bands are taxed at a higher rate than in the UK (40 per cent) or the USA (33 per cent). Moreover, Rhine economies levy tax on capital, and public opinion accepts this as right and proper.
2. The interests of the group are generally felt to take precedence over narrow individual interests. In other words, the communities to which a person belongs – whether company, town, trade union or charitable organization – are regarded as crucial; they are the structures that protect the individual and provide stability for the whole society. Examples abound: the powerful IG Metall trade union, for instance, had patiently waited for 3 years and the new bargaining round in order to press its demand for a 35-hour work week, when German unification suddenly came onto the agenda. The demand was dropped in a *voluntary* gesture of solidarity. According to IG Metall's president, it was simply more important to meet the new challenge posed by reunification.

But if the interests of the community are paramount, that in no way amounts to an endorsement of collectivism or central planning; quite the contrary. The principle of the free market is written into the German constitution. Fair and open competition, as we have seen, is strictly patrolled by the Federal Monopolies Board, which has been known to block a German firm from taking over a foreign competitor, on the grounds that it would infringe the rules of competition. One can hardly imagine the same scenario occurring in France, where each French buyout of a foreign company is hailed with a chorus of patriotic self-congratulation. Moreover, the Germans (along with the Swiss, the Dutch and the Japanese) would never dream of prescribing the sort of grandiose national economic plans favored by the French. In the Rhine view of economic life, the state may encourage the market, at most influence it in various ways, but never become an active player in it. The Rhine market is, nevertheless, a social market (as its German name indicates). This means, quite simply, that social institutions have traditionally been, and remain, hugely important. Social security as a state-run system was, after all, invented by Bismarck in 1881. Yet in today's Germany, the cost to the individual of national health insurance is modest, amounting to a 10 per cent contribution (as against 20 per cent in France and 35 per cent in the USA). Pensions, too, are more generous in the Rhine economies, mainly because they are strongly supplemented by company-managed individual savings plans.

There is a political aspect to the Rhine social balance as well: a civic sense of active participation in the political process still prevails. Voter turnout remains high – particularly when compared to America, where public disaffection with politics is reaching crisis proportions. In Germany, political parties are powerful and well-structured; party officials and candidates are kept well briefed by such prestigious think-tanks as the SPD's Hébert Foundation or the CDU's Adenauer Foundation. Politicians are required by law to be active, or at least present: fines are imposed on MPs who fail to turn up when Parliament meets. The free vote is the norm (i.e. MPs are not whipped on each and every division). And no public official may hold more than two posts simultaneously, in stark contrast to French practice. The Rhine model is a unique, and highly successful, synthesis of capitalism and social democracy. Its sense of balance and proportion is no less impressive than the efficacy of its economic performance. Yet it remains astonishingly unheralded, almost ignored, by the rest of the world. Quiet contentment, apparently, is not the stuff of fame and publicity. As Tolstoy remarked, all happy families resemble one another: likewise, the story of a happy society lacks the drama and tears that can grip the public imagination.

Chapter 7
The economic superiority
of the Rhine model

When we make a deliberate effort to remember the events of the past –
even the recent past – we again become aware of the extraordinary sur-
prises history is always waiting to spring on us. Let us examine for a
moment the situation at the end of World War II: the USA had triumphed, the atom bomb having sealed its dominion over the planet.
Spared the ravages of war on its own territory, America was both a military and an economic superpower; as such, it could afford to devote its
budget surpluses to the rebuilding of a war-torn Europe under the Marshall Plan, rather than cutting taxes at home. The Soviet Union was
not yet in a position to defy American power with any degree of consistency, as the Berlin crisis demonstrated. Everywhere, the American
Way of Life, which the GIs seemed to wear as proudly as their uniforms
and to distribute with every stick of chewing-gum, was a source of fasci-
nation. Even America's defeated foes found her culture irresistible.

But the two major Axis powers, Japan and Germany, had paid a hor-
rific price: their cities in ruins, their industries shattered, their people
in shock as they surveyed the scale of the disaster which their leaders
had plunged them into. In the rubble of Dresden and Nagasaki, in the
wreckage of Berlin and Hiroshima, the evidence of a cataclysm without
precedent was there for all to see and to mourn.

The vanquished emerge victorious

Less than half a century later, on 19 October 1987, a financial crisis
looms: Wall Street is heading towards a crash. The US Government
has to move, and move quickly, to avoid a major catastrophe. The decision is taken to administer a massive injection of cash into the financial

system: the Federal Reserve Bank opens the taps and the dollars flow. But before doing so, it was necessary to consult with, and obtain the agreement of, two institutions – the Bank of Japan and the German Bundesbank. Few observers paused, in the midst of global panic, to savour the irony of this extraordinary reversal of fortunes.

Two years later, the Federal Republic of Germany was able to achieve its longstanding goal of reunification by virtually 'buying up' the GDR, whose bankruptcy was by then manifest. Other nations may have had doubts, but West Germany had the money and the means to sweep aside all objections. By the end of 1989, with reunification a certainty, not only was Bonn seeking no aid, no outside support, but it was actually concluding an agreement with Moscow which amounted to the financing – by Germany – of the repatriation of the Red Army divisions stationed in East Germany. This meant that the Germans would eventually be paying for new barracks to be built on Soviet soil. There could be no better illustration of the fact that Germany was now so rich that it could buy its independence – and not on the instalment plan: in cash, and in full.

The two defeated nations of World War II had thus achieved the status of economic giants, challenging America's position of worldwide leadership in business and finance, all in less than two generations. Their success is not, of course, the product of exactly the same factors or motives: there are traits which are specific to the Japanese economy, others which apply only to Germany. But, though not identical, both economies have so much in common that the hypothesis of an alternative, and largely superior, model of capitalism can at least be posed.

The superiority of the Rhine model is manifold, as we shall see; but let us begin with an analysis of the economy, source and symbol of real power. In a world entirely won over by capitalism – not least because its ideological foe has simply collapsed – power will flow to those who, in the first instance, know best how to exploit the system for economic gain. From such a perspective, the Rhine economies look strong – and their strength is increasing daily.

To begin with, there is the hugely important question of a nation's monetary system, as indicated by the health of its currency. There is no denying that the US dollar continues to enjoy the prestigious status – somewhat diminished since the end of convertibility in 1971 – of a world standard currency, as conferred on it by the 1944 Bretton Woods accord (see Chapter 2). But neither is there any doubt that this long reign is increasingly under attack from the newcomers, the mark and the yen, as they nibble away at the dollar's supremacy.

The German and Japanese currencies together now account for about 20 per cent of central bank reserves worldwide – twice what they were 20 years ago. This is in spite of persistent efforts by the Bundesbank and the Bank of Japan to restrain a too-rapid expansion on the world money markets and maintain control over their currencies. It is anyone's guess what the mark or the yen would be worth today if the central bank authorities in Bonn and Tokyo had taken a more relaxed attitude.

The change is not just quantitative; it represents a psychological turning-point. The mark and the yen are now universally perceived as strong currencies, and assets quoted in them are seen as safe investments (especially in the case of the German mark). Both stand at the center of new, geographically defined monetary zones which exert a powerful attraction on the currencies of neighboring states.

HRH the Deutschmark

Perhaps the most graphic illustration of this is to be found in the European Community, whose monetary system (the EMS) goes back to 1978. On the initiative of Helmut Schmidt and Valéry Giscard d'Estaing, the EC created the notorious exchange rate mechanism (ERM) which, as everyone knows by now, meant linking the different European currencies (with a few exceptions, such as the UK before 1990) in such a way that they could no longer 'float' independently of one another, except within very narrow pre-established bands. The ECU was created at the same time to serve as the monetary unit of reference; its value is based on a 'basket' of European currencies.

The EMS had two main aims: to limit the extent of currency fluctuations, which undermined the stability of intra-Community trade relations; and to impose a uniform discipline on member states, such that their economic policies would have to be in keeping with the defense of currency exchange rates.

Both aims have been achieved, and the EMS can be pronounced a success. True, it has occasionally been necessary to readjust ERM parities, but on the whole European currencies have remained stable in relation to one another; as for the economic discipline required of member states, France itself provided an excellent example of this when the socialist government made its celebrated 1983 U-turn in the direction of 'fiscal responsibility' – almost entirely dictated by need to defend the franc by staying within the ERM and abiding by its terms of membership.

By and large, though, it is Germany which has benefited most from the EMS, on two counts at least:

1. From the very beginning, the mark has been the semi-official standard against which all the other EMS currencies were valued. Thus each member state's monetary policy is, like it or not, strictly tied to that of Germany. The Bank of France (like the Bank of England, and the central banks of the rest of Europe) monitors the mark on an hourly basis: whenever the gap between the franc and the mark begins to widen significantly, it takes preventive action. This means ultimately that when German interest rates rise, their EC partners nearly always have to fall in line and do the same. It also means that, if the European EMU (Economic and Monetary Union) is ever to get off the ground, it will only be on the condition that Germany gives it the green light. It is hardly surprising that the proposed European central bank, Eurofed, is to be modelled on the Bundesbank: Germany would not otherwise have approved the EMU scheme.

2. The strength of its currency allows Germany the luxury of keeping interest rates relatively low. As long as the mark remains in high demand because of its worldwide prestige, there is less pressure on the Bundesbank to make borrowing expensive in order to attract foreign capital. Added to the fact that low inflation keeps the mark's purchasing power fairly stable, this results in German interest rates actually being lower than those of its trading partners. By the end of 1990, for example, French rates were 1.5 points above German rates, while British rates were 6 or 7 points higher. The beneficiaries, of course, are German businesses and households who wish to borrow and expand.

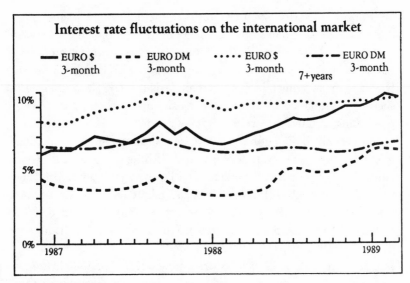

SOURCE: OCDE

A monetary 'home base'

Japan shares many of these same characteristics, if not quite so conspicuously (given that it is not a member of any exchange-rate system): the
yen is somewhat undervalued, interest rates are low and Japanese influence on the world economic scene is growing. Switzerland, too, can
count its blessings in the form of the widely admired Swiss franc, still
the world's fourth most important reserve currency. Created nearly 200
years ago, more or less simultaneously with the French franc, it has not
undergone anything like the 300-fold loss of value which its Parisian
cousin has since experienced! It should also be noted that Swiss interest rates are among the lowest in the world.

Monetary power is, for Germany, Switzerland and Japan, the equivalent of a superior dissuasive weapon which can readily be turned to
offensive purposes. The industrialists and entrepreneurs of Frankfurt,
Zürich and Tokyo, knowing that their 'home base' is secure and well
defended, can go forth on foreign economic expeditions with the
means to overcome almost any resistance. Certainly money is no
object: as Japan snaps up one American landmark or major corporation

after another, a strong yen ensures that the dollar price-tag seems a great bargain. German firms, too, can afford to 'shop' abroad, and in fact to out-shop everyone else: when the Czech car manufacturer Skoda went up for sale, no one was surprised that Volkswagen was easily able to make a much higher bid than Renault. And Swiss companies such as Nestlé and Ciba-Geigy are equally dynamic in their overseas purchasing policies, investing billions of dollars in the USA alone.

Whether by design or not, all of these overseas investments produce one very positive result, that of giving the Rhine countries a degree of control over their export markets. The Japanese strategy in the automotive sector is a well-known example. Threatened by a protectionist tide in the US Congress, Japanese exporters decided to start building car factories in the USA (and Britain). This policy of 'delocalising' production has already paid off: it is estimated that in 1992, some 2 million Japanese cars will be built in American factories. That already represents 16 per cent of the total production of US car makers. The 'American challenge' which Europeans detected 25 years ago has been turned on its head.

Companies of the Rhine type do not, as a rule, follow a policy of spectacular and speculative takeovers. They prefer to move in gradually and methodically, taking care to shape their subsidiary firms in their own image and under their direct guidance. The anecdotal evidence occasionally seems slightly fantastical, as when French workers at the Akai plant in Normandy go through their Japanese exercise routine at the beginning of each day – willingly, it would appear. The concrete evidence of Japan's successful overseas strategy is, however, convincing enough. In their US subsidiaries, they have managed to create an in-house 'micro-climate' which is responsible for productivity increases of up to 50 per cent over their nearest American rivals. What that morning exercise session also tells us is that Japanese overseas investment is part of a long-term commitment: Akai clearly has no intention of selling its French branch to the highest bidder as soon as possible, for the sake of a quick profit.

The 'slow and steady' approach to acquisitions is extremely efficient. From a solid financial base, Rhine firms gradually work towards a position of strength which shows two further advantages:

1. The new markets will not disappear overnight. The company, its goods and its brand names become established over a period of years; customers get to know them and the firm, equally, has a workforce, production site and distribution network which it knows well.
2. Delocalisation makes it much harder to draft protectionist legislation against foreign companies. It is not clear whether it is even possible, as witnessed by the debate between Europeans and Japanese over the 'turnkey factories' which the latter intend to set up throughout the EC, in an attempt to get unrestricted access to the Single Market.

Expansion on a worldwide scale, and growing political and economic influence: such are the benefits accruing from the monetary stability and financial power of the Rhine countries. And there is more.

The virtuous circle of a strong currency

Economists speak of a 'virtuous circle' of mutually reinforcing *positive* consequences which a country can expect when its currency is strong. At first glance, this may appear contrary to elementary logic: it would seem more likely that a highly valued currency must count as a handicap, because it makes goods more expensive abroad, and therefore more difficult to export. Devaluation, after all, is a favorite tactic in the drive to increase exports – examples of countries which have employed this method, or are currently tempted to do so, are too numerous to mention. The question of whether a weak currency might produce its own virtuous circle is not merely academic; it lies at the heart of the economic debate which will continue to rage throughout the 1990s, and so it is well worth taking a closer look at the arguments on both sides.

Economic theory teaches that currency depreciation will have two predictable effects on a country's balance of trade: imports, paid for in national currency, become dearer, while exports, paid for in foreign currencies, become cheaper. Logically, this takes the shape of a two-stage progression:

1. In the very short term, the balance of trade worsens. This is because imported goods, now at a higher price, have to be paid for as they arrive – demand for them does not drop overnight – whereas foreign

buyers will take some time before increasing their orders of newly cheaper export goods. There is a time lag on one side of the equation, but not on the other. This shows up as a downward curve in the balance of payments.

2. In the medium term, the curve moves upward. Consumers buy fewer imported goods because of the additional expense; exports pick up; the time lag is usually corrected quickly enough so that the losses incurred in the initial stage can be recouped. In the end, the country's overall economic position in relation to its trading partners will have improved.

This two-phased movement in the trade balance following devaluation is called the 'J-curve effect' (because plotting it on a graph produces a superb capital J). It has provided the justification for a great many economic strategies since the 1950s, notably in France (as recently as 1983) and Britain, not to mention American monetary policy since 1985. The dollar has been subject to systematic depreciation in a last-ditch effort to remedy the appalling balance-of-trade deficit; the J-curve effect was thought to be the miracle cure that could not go wrong. Unfortunately, all the signs indicate that the J-curve of devaluation is a nostrum of dubious efficacy, however elegant its theoretical construction. The facts simply do not bear out the claims made for it, and the theory needs to be overhauled as well.

The facts, to begin with: Germany (pre-unification) and Japan both maintain strong currencies and, of course, colossal trade surpluses. France and Italy, on the other hand, have not managed to generate surpluses with any consistency, in spite of repeated devaluations. And in the most glaring example, a dollar in free-fall since 1985 has not yet produced the desired effect on the US trade deficit. What could possibly explain how a mechanism that looks so straightforward on paper can go so spectacularly wrong in practice? It turns out that the J-curve theory rests on a number of hypotheses whose validity is open to question, on at least three counts.

First, there can be no iron-clad guarantee that imports will always become dearer, and exports cheaper, in the same proportions as the depreciation in the currency. Both importers and exporters can 'play' with the margins of profitability, whether to take advantage of the new situation (i.e. exporters can put their prices up, and thus increase their profit margins, without the foreign customer 'noticing') or to mitigate its effects (i.e. importers decide to sacrifice their margins and reduce prices, so as not to lose customers). This is more or less what happened in France between 1981 and 1983: French exporters saw successive devaluations as a chance to put up prices (to help pay the cost of new social measures introduced by Mitterand's first government), while foreign importers squeezed their own profit margins in order to keep prices down and preserve their market share.

A second criticism of the devaluation nostrum concerns the risk of what economists call 'imported inflation', where the increased cost of imported goods is passed down the line, eventually affecting all products and services. This is most obvious in the case of imported oil and other raw materials, as well as capital goods. At best, this means ending up back where one started; at worst, it results in rising inflation, which in turn may panic the government into another round of devaluation. The downward stroke of the J-curve clicks in, and new deficits mount up quickly. It is all highly reminiscent of the proverbial avalanche that began with a snowball.

Finally, devaluation may work as a stimulant to exports on the condition that exporting companies are willing and able to exploit the opportunity and win new markets. If for some reason they are not, the chance will be lost and the trade balance will not improve. This is not just a hypothesis: to take but one example, American industry suffers from a number of internal weaknesses that have prevented it from taking full advantage of the cheaper post-1985 dollar. There has been no significant 'clawing back' of the markets America had previously lost to Japanese and European manufacturers.

If the theoretical basis for devaluation can thus be debunked, it is still difficult for governments to kick the habit – for that is exactly what it amounts to, an addictive process whose initial 'high' is illusory and short-lived. The danger is compounded by the fact that the devaluation 'junkie' becomes increasingly blind to its own shortcomings. The French are depressingly familiar with this vicious cycle, having been locked into repeated injections of the 'miracle drug' from 1970 to 1983.

What, then, of the other path, that of maintaining a strong currency? It would seem, at first glance, to be a very hard road to travel. There is something almost heroic in taking up the challenge, for industry, of exporting products which are expensive abroad while competing with cheap foreign imports at home. The country may find its balance of payments adversely affected as a result. Yet, like all challenges, there is a positive side: energies are galvanised, complacency is banished and opportunities must be actively sought. It cannot be a coincidence that the most successful trading nations – Germany, Japan, Switzerland and the Netherlands – are those that have applied the 'strong currency strategy'.

Besides the fact that such a strategy avoids the worst side effects of devaluation, as enumerated above, it also has a number of salutary consequences. In the first place, businesses are forced to enhance productivity – virtually the only recourse available to them to compensate for the higher cost of their goods abroad. As a means of keeping management lean, keen and alert, it is rather more effective in the long run than the threat of an unwanted takeover. Take, for example, the response of the Japanese automotive giant Nissan to the *endaka* (appreciation of the yen in relation to the US dollar) of 1986–87: productivity was increased by 10 per cent a year, which meant that the price (in yen) of their vehicles dropped by the same proportion. Meanwhile, American productivity continued to decline along with the dollar, to such an extent that Paul Gray, President of MIT, admitted in an interview that 'the problem facing American industry is not so much to increase productivity as to halt any further decline' (*L'Expansion*, October 1990).

Another favorable consequence of a strong currency is that it gives manufacturers a clear incentive to concentrate on top-of-the-range goods, where the selling point is not so much price as quality and innovation, not to mention after-sales service. This in turn requires a long-term commitment to research and development – which can only be a boon for the company as a whole. The German machine-tool industry is a shining example of this approach: its products are relatively expensive, yet always in demand because of their unsurpassed quality. The same formula has worked well for German car makers such as Mercedes-Benz and BMW, who have taken on the luxury end of the market with great success (so much so that Germany now sells more cars to Japan than vice versa – an astonishing achievement).

„ MEIN GOTT, SCHON WIEDER EIN RÜCKFALL ! '

SOURCE: *Wirtschaftswoche, no. 31, 27 July 1990, p. 90 ('Good lord, he's on the skids again!'). (Reproduced with permission.)*

It should not be forgotten that Germany and Japan – today synonymous with quality merchandise – both had a pre-war reputation for producing third-rate, shoddy goods. That they have managed to turn their energies from the pursuit of war to the conquest of markets, using the arm of monetary discipline, is further testimony to the reality of a dynamic German–Japanese economic model.

In summary, the maintenance of a strong currency, however steep the challenge, brings out the best in an economy as toil, perseverance and imagination are harnessed in the drive to excel. This virtuous circle is not for the faint-hearted, but it ultimately reaps rich, and durable, rewards. To say so is no longer heresy – an encouraging turn in the economic debate – but, lest we forget, a whole generation of the best and brightest in France accepted without question the pseudo-Keynesian orthodoxy of spurring growth through repeated devaluation. While subjecting the franc to its biennial meltdown, some French economists could even be heard sniggering at the obvious stupidity of the Germans in their obstinate refusal to dope their economy with the elixir of 'controlled' inflation.

I was personally involved in the 5-year struggle by Raymond Barre (an economist who served as French Prime Minister from 1976 to 1981) to gain acceptance of the strong-currency approach; at the time, this amounted to preaching in the desert. Since 1983, however, the cause has been largely won, thanks to the support of three successive Finance Ministers – Jacques Delors, Edouard Balladur and especially Pierre Bérégovoy (later to be Prime Minister himself). That the example set by the Rhine model should have inspired this turnaround in thinking at the top is surely the nearest thing yet to a genuine economic miracle!

The dynamo of industry

Every newspaper reader knows that the brilliant results chalked up by Rhine economies have lately received a great deal of attention, and that the contrast is all too vivid when set against the trials and tribulations of the Anglo-American economies, beset by inflation and debt. Not unreasonably, there have been many attempts to explain 'how on earth they manage it' in Bonn and Tokyo; this book is one such effort. But let us be clear on one point: the strength of the Rhine economies lies first and foremost in their immense industrial strength, promoted by aggressive salesmanship.

That Rhine manufacturing industry is the best in the world is simply not in doubt. Moreover, it occupies pride of place within the national context: in Germany, Japan and Sweden, industry accounts for about 30 per cent of both GDP and total wage-earners; in the rest of the OECD, the figure is below 25 per cent (and in the USA it is under the 20 per cent mark). This superiority, as previously argued, is not just numerical but qualitative as well. Rhine-type countries have established leading positions in virtually every sector of manufacturing from the oldest, most traditional industries to the highest of the high-tech. Take any index of the top ten countries in steel making, shipbuilding, car manufacture, chemicals, textiles, electrical goods, or agro-industry: the roll of honor will inevitably include a majority of Swiss, German, Japanese and Dutch firms. Toyota, Nissan, Daimler Benz, Mitsubishi,

Bayer, Hoechst, BASF, Nestlé, Hoffmann-La Roche, Siemens, Matsushita. . . – the list goes on and on.

True, in certain high-tech industries, the Rhine economies still lag somewhat behind America, the leader; but for how long? It is already clear that Japanese and German companies are taking enormous strides to catch up with their US competitors in such branches as aeronautics, information technology, electronics and optics. Japanese advances in computer technology, for instance, mean that this field is no longer the exclusive preserve of the big American firms (who hold seven of the ten top places in the world league tables). The alarm bells are ringing in Washington as the Japanese consolidate their mastery of peripherals (monitors, printers and disks) and a near-monopoly on memories and components. It is now fair to say that the average computer bears an American brand-name, but almost everything inside it is Japanese.

So, how do they manage it? Rhine industries build on three principal strengths:

1. They pay close attention to *production techniques*, striving endlessly to improve quality, reduce costs and increase productivity – none of which would be possible without sustained investment in plant and machinery. Again, it is no coincidence that the OECD countries which invest the most in such capital goods are Germany, Japan, Switzerland and Sweden. (By 1989 Japan's investment in plant and machinery had already exceeded, in absolute terms, that of the USA, whose economy is eight times bigger than Japan's.) The Rhine countries invariably use the most sophisticated methods of production management, such as the 'zero stock' technique or the concept of 'total quality management' (TQM) – both of which were pioneered in Japan and have now been adopted by Citroën and Renault. What sets these new techniques apart is that they stimulate the creative, participative faculties of each worker and depend on a certain level of consensus through debate, thus ensuring that everyone involved in production is regularly consulted, and listened to.
2. *Training* is a priority, not a luxury (see Chapter 6). The new methods of production management represent a definitive break with the dehumanising techniques of 'efficiency engineering' associated with F. W. Taylor (and hilariously caricatured by Charlie Chaplin in *Mod-*

ern Times). But if workers are to be more than automatons, training must be more than an afterthought. True, Rhine countries spend twice as much as anyone else on their unique combination of apprenticeship and further training, but it is well worth the investment: there is no chronic shortage of engineers in Germany or Japan. The importance of all forms of vocational education as a key factor in Rhine industrial achievement simply cannot be overemphasized.

3. Company spending on *research and development* (R&D) is one of the areas where the contrast between the two economic models is most striking. For countries like Germany, Japan or Sweden, investment in R&D amounts to about 3 per cent of GDP; it is primarily aimed at developing basic technology which can ultimately benefit all branches of industry. In the USA, the figure is 2.7 per cent of GDP, but more than one-third of this investment (1 per cent) is devoted to weapons research. Rhine governments take a particularly active role in promoting civil R&D projects, often with generous subsidies. The Japanese super-ministry MITI, for example, draws up a list of ten priority areas for research which the private sector is encouraged to gear up for; this approach has already paid off handsomely, and famously, in the industry-wide robotics program launched 20 years ago, with the result that Japan is today the world leader in this sphere, producing more robots than the rest of its OECD partners put together.

Taken as a whole, the industries of Rhine countries are a formidable dynamo, outstripping all competitors. What is more, they are backed up by some extremely effective (and aggressive) sales and marketing techniques. The Rhine countries have thus become the undisputed export champions of the world. Germany has long been a great exporting nation, and Japan is now in the same premier division. The statistics are quite astonishing: the proportion of company turnover in the major German industries (automobiles, chemicals, mechanical and electrical engineering) accounted for by exports is nearly 45 per cent. In the USA, exports amount to no more than 13 per cent of GDP; in its report on American industry, MIT noted that US manufacturers suffer from a narrow, parochial outlook which causes them to miss export opportunities.

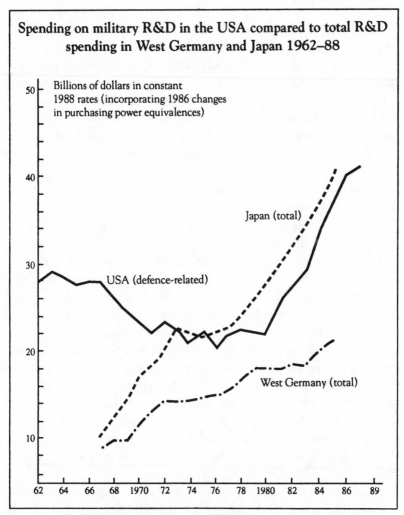

Spending on military R&D in the USA compared to total R&D spending in West Germany and Japan 1962–88

Billions of dollars in constant 1988 rates (incorporating 1986 changes in purchasing power equivalences)

Japan (total)

USA (defence-related)

West Germany (total)

SOURCE: National Science Foundation and OCDE.

There is hardly a market anywhere in the world today which has not been penetrated by German, Japanese and Swiss exporters. Even in those places where American (or British or French) firms have traditionally held sway, the newcomers are pushing ahead, elbowing their way to the top.

The economy as culture

The assertion that there can be a 'culture of the economy' may seem suspiciously vague to some, while to others it is a tautology. But if there is one word that designates a body of individual behaviour patterns shared by a whole population, enshrined within institutions, subject to agreed rules and forming a common heritage, then it is indeed *culture*. And in the Rhine model there is every indication that a specific 'economy culture' operates at every level, with its own distinctive traits.

Of particular significance is the inclination towards personal and household savings: among OECD nations, it is again Japan, Germany and Switzerland which distinguish themselves in this category. (Italy, too, rates a mention – but its savings go mainly towards financing an enormous budget deficit.) Personal savings are an indispensable source of financing in all capitalist economies; at too low a level, a foreign deficit tends to accumulate, as borrowing abroad increases to compensate for insufficient funds at home. Such is the case in America today. US households are the 'big spenders' of the Western World, buying everything on credit and building up personal indebtedness to such an extent that interest payments may add up to a quarter of their income. And just as the failure to save goes some way toward explaining America's massive foreign trade deficit, so the opposite is true of German and Japanese surpluses: very high levels of domestic savings provide the wherewithal both to finance investment at home and to make loans abroad at favorable rates of return.

The propensity to save has always featured prominently in the pantheon of factors which, according to liberal theorists, make economic progress possible. Interest rates, after all, are organically linked to levels of savings. But this propensity is itself linked to other social and cultural factors which may change over time.

Irving Fisher, the noted Yale economist, once asserted that the main cause of a drop in interest rates – i.e. a rise in savings – was 'the love of one's children and the desire to provide for their welfare'. When such feelings are dulled (as in the terminal phase of the Roman Empire, according to Fisher), impatience and interest rates both tend to increase. The result is a reckless spending spree and an attitude infamously capsulised in the supposed motto of Louis XV and Madame Pompadour: 'après nous le déluge'.

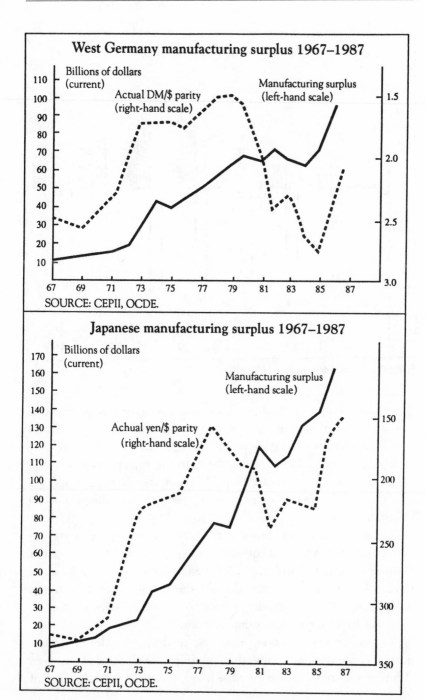

West Germany manufacturing surplus 1967–1987

Billions of dollars
(current)

Actual DM/$ parity
(right-hand scale)

Manufacturing surplus
(left-hand scale)

SOURCE: CEPII, OCDE.

Japanese manufacturing surplus 1967–1987

Billions of dollars
(current)

Manufacturing surplus
(left-hand scale)

Achual yen/$ parity
(right-hand scale)

SOURCE: CEPII, OCDE.

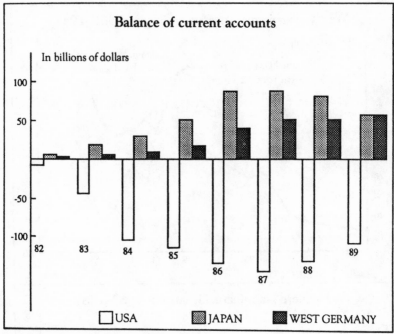

Balance of current accounts

In billions of dollars

SOURCE: *Comptes de la Nation*, 1989, p.41.

Without wishing to draw any hasty conclusions as regards 'the love of one's children', we can hardly ignore the fact that between 1980 and 1990, the level of savings decreased markedly in the USA, dropping from 19 per cent to 13 per cent of GDP. In the same period, Germany saw its savings levels increase from 22 per cent to 26 per cent of GDP, while Japan's rose from 31 per cent to 35 per cent (according to OECD calculations).

The inescapable conclusion is that the two models of capitalism diverge on the fundamental question of whether to live for the present moment – and to hell with the consequences for future generations – or to plan for a better tomorrow, though it may require sacrifices today. This dilemma lies at the heart of the ethical choices facing every society as the twentieth century draws to a close.

To return to the 'economy culture': in Rhine societies, there is a general consensus concerning the importance of all things economic. Whole populations can be mobilised, in a variety of seemingly trivial ways, for the nation's economic good; the cumulative effect of such behaviour may be enormous. When Japanese tourists abroad are found to be discreetly collecting information which might be of use to their employers, it is missing the point to cry 'industrial espionage' or to deride their single-mindedness. What such behaviour reveals is a different set of priorities, among which is a sense of duty to one's company and the national economy. Germans show a similar 'civic' regard for the economy, and a host of institutions and bodies help foster public enthusiasm and disseminate information (in Germany, the banks provide their customers with a variety of detailed economic analyses and forecasts; in Japan this task is carried out by MITI and the business firms). There is a general consensus that it is vitally important to keep abreast of new developments abroad, and firms put a great deal of time and money into finding out what their competitors are 'up to' – especially in their research laboratories. This restless curiosity and desire to learn, this openness to the outside world, can only mean one thing: a shared set of values – in other words, a culture.

The economy culture of Rhine countries undoubtedly explains the fact that they have largely succeeded in freeing their economies from the worst of the political disruptions and electoral vagaries that crop up elsewhere: not for them the classic seesaw between pre-election spending sprees and post-election belt-tightening. The near-total independence from political control of the central banks of Germany and Switzerland, for example, means that they can pursue their strong-currency policies, no matter what the political climate. The Bundesbank's founding charter even makes it compulsory for the central bankers to maintain a sound mark. Such an approach is worlds away from the traditional powers of intervention exercised by the French Finance Ministry over the Bank of France, or by the Exchequer over the Bank of England. Similarly, the five German economic forecasting institutes are utterly immune from official tinkering, and their findings can thus be confidently accepted as accurate and objective by government, employers and trade unions alike.

Ultimately, the existence of an economy culture produces a government that *serves* the economy, and tailors its policies to that end. When the cultural consensus is so wide, the result is something like 'Japan Inc.' – a whole country patterned on the company model, a nation united at every level in the constant effort to capture new markets overseas.

That the company should enjoy its exalted status in Rhine countries is a logical outgrowth of the economy culture. Unlike the neo-American view of the company as, at best, a collection of the contractual arrangements between temporarily convergent interests or, at worst, as a 'cash flow machine', the Rhine model sees the company as a social institution and an enduring community deserving of the loyalty and affection of its members, who can expect a measure of company care and protection in return.

Chapter 8
The social superiority of the Rhine model

The title of this chapter may seem surprising. Obviously one cannot define 'social superiority' as neatly as economic superiority: many of the criteria that would have to be examined are simply not quantifiable. The social achievements (not to mention the shortcomings) of a given economic model do not necessarily show up in charts and percentages; they may resist conventional statistical analysis. Any pronouncement on the social advantages of one culture or another will contain more than a hint of subjectivity. No one knows better than economists the extent to which factors such as societal types, particular value sets shared by the population, social organization and even kinship systems can introduce a whole range of distortions which significantly compli-cate the analyst's task. I therefore intend to proceed with the greatest caution.

In the search to define a set of criteria which could form the basis for a relatively impartial comparison, there are three that seem to me to have the twin advantages of simplicity and clarity.

1. The degree of *security* provided: how are citizens protected from the major risks (illness, unemployment, family breakdown etc.)?
2. The reduction of social *inequalities*: what remedies are brought to bear against the most obvious cases of neglect? How much help is available, and in what form, to the neediest members of society?
3. The extent to which it is an *'open' society*: how easy (or how diffi-cult) is it for different individuals to climb the socioeconomic lad-der, to improve their lot?

One thing should already be clear: in the first two cases, the Rhine model performs demonstrably better than the neo-American model. (It is necessary to insist here on the term *neo-American*, rather than Anglo-American, because it would be wrong to lump the UK with America insofar as the social economy is concerned. With its long-standing welfare system of a type undreamt of in the USA, Britain stands at opposite ends of the scale from today's America in this sphere.)

Granted, then, that the attempt to compare different social systems can be somewhat hazardous, the contrast between the two models of capitalism remains striking – all the more so because, contrary to certain received opinions, the social superiority of the Rhine model does not entail hidden or extra costs which adversely affect economic competitiveness. Social benefits do have to be paid for out of the public purse, of course. But those who insist that such expense is inevitably detrimental to the economy are mistaken. On the contrary: it can be plainly demonstrated that social solidarity and competitiveness in the market place make excellent bedfellows.

The high cost of health

Let us begin with a couple of anecdotes culled from the press: in the first (witnessed by French journalist Jean-Paul Dubois) a man arrives in a terrible state at the Dade Medical Center in Miami, Florida. He says he has been ill for three days, and is obviously feverish. It is Sunday, and as doctors' surgeries are closed, he has come to the emergency unit of the nearest hospital, where the receptionist is taking down his particulars: name, address. . . 'and $200 deposit, please'. She explains: 'If the doctor decides not to hospitalize you, you will be charged for the consultation and the difference will be refunded.' The would-be patient explains that he does not have $200 on him just now. And she replies that she is terribly sorry, but he will have to seek medical attention elsewhere.

In another part of the country, in a small East Coast town, an employee of a local firm is faced with a dilemma over the toothache that has been tormenting him. Should he go to the dentist? If he does, he knows that he will lose the tooth – but not because his dentist is unable to provide a more sophisticated treatment than old-fashioned extraction. No, his dilemma lies in the fact that he has no private insurance, and the cost of a crown or some other palliative treatment is far beyond his modest means. So he faces the stark choice of more pain, or fewer teeth.

Neither story is in any way exceptional. They are further examples of the polarization of American society (as described in Chapter 3); and they serve to illustrate the lack of any generalised system of social security in the USA. In proportional terms, *public* spending on health care in America is about half the level in other major Western countries. There is no compulsory health coverage: the only option is private insurance, income permitting. Approximately 35 million Americans do not, as a result, carry any form of health coverage.

Unemployment benefit is virtually non-existent, on the national level at least; but redundancy notices, once served, take effect almost immediately (within 2 days, on average, in small businesses). Family allowances are unheard of. The few social welfare programs of any note are legacies of the Kennedy and Johnson administrations of the 1960s: Medicare, which provides some health care benefits for the elderly, and Medicaid, which targets those who live below the 'poverty line'. Yet even this welfare net is designed in such a way that it inevitably misses a sizeable proportion of the neediest individuals.

The gaps in the neo-American model are, in this sphere, blatantly obvious. And there are two other grave shortcomings as well:

1. The 'litigation frenzy' which has taken hold of America has had drastic consequences for medicine in particular (see Chapter 3). Pick up any US newspaper, and you are sure to read of yet more record damages awarded against a surgeon, anaesthetist or dentist whose patient has joined the lawsuit parade, egged on no doubt by the new bounty-hunters we call lawyers. It is now common practice to consult one's lawyer before going to hospital or to the doctor's surgery; inevitably, the first person you are likely to encounter there is not your doctor or surgeon but his or her lawyer. The most innocuous treatment can become the pretext for a long, drawn-out legal battle, and the result is catastrophic for doctor and patient alike. Malpractice insurance and lawyers' fees add up to a phenomenally expensive, but indispensable, chapter in the budgets of clinics and practitioners, who pass the cost along to the public in the form of

higher bills for medical treatment. In the end, the cost of such treatment becomes prohibitively expensive for the average person.

2. Even a cursory financial inspection of the American system of private health care reveals that it is far less economical than the European-style public welfare system. Total spending on health in the
USA is, at 11 per cent of GDP, the highest in the world; paradoxically, in the UK – home of universal free health care – health spending is the lowest of the OECD countries, at less than 7 per cent of
GDP.

Social security and social responsibility

Social insurance originated in Germany under Bismarck; Beveridge
was to be his most celebrated disciple (in this one regard) in setting up
the National Health Service in Britain. France, too, had by 1946 begun
to implement its own social security system, which evolved gradually
into its present, nearly universal form of coverage (99.9 per cent of the
working population). Similarly, in Germany, Switzerland, Sweden and
Japan, the provision of health care is automatically extended to all but
a tiny fraction of the population.

Germans are broadly insured against all the major hazards (illness,
work-related accidents, unemployment) and benefit from a generous
basic pension. In Sweden, the 'flagship' of social democracy, the situation is much the same. Particularly noteworthy is the very efficient
Swedish approach to unemployment: help is available in a variety of
forms, including training and reinsertion programs. As for Japan, its
national insurance system is one of the most munificent in the world:
health care is universally available and totally free of charge.

When it comes to social security funding, the Rhine countries once
again show the way. True, before 1985 the level of health spending in
Germany was increasing much faster than GDP, and it was feared that
the system would become dangerously unbalanced. The causes were
not unique to Germany: an ageing population, technological advances
requiring the purchase of costly new equipment (scanners, ultrasound
devices, lithotripsy equipment etc.), and a general increase in the
demand for treatment, as well as for drugs – both a natural consequence
of free health care. In spite of these factors, all the Rhine countries
have managed to keep spending on health at or below 9 per cent of

GDP. But Germany in particular has distinguished itself in the exemplary way it has, since 1985, tackled – and solved – the funding problem.

This is no mean feat. Bearing in mind the previously-cited ratios between health spending and GDP (Britain's 7 per cent, Germany's 9 per cent and the USA's 11 per cent), the awkward truth seems to be that spending more does not guarantee a better system, since of these three the USA has the worst record of accessible and affordable health care provision. This seems to run directly counter to the proposition that the free market, with its built-in incentives to maximise quality and minimise cost, should be able to do the job more efficiently than the state. Heaven knows American medical facilities (privately owned and operated, in the main) use the most sophisticated management techniques – health management organization is a recognized professional category. On the other hand, there are waiting lists for some NHS operations or consultations, as every Briton knows; and it is true that the German system, in which doctors are 'tied' to mutual health funding agencies, removes some of the patient's choice. Nevertheless, the facts speak for themselves. When health care provision is market-led, i.e. driven by the personal financial interests of the providers, the resultant system is inefficient. This leads me to believe that health is one sector that definitely cannot be left wholly to market forces.

To understand how the Rhine economies achieve their unique social welfare mix of fair entitlement, public funding and efficient management, it is necessary to examine the values and priorities which are shared by society at large. There is a sense of collective responsibility in Rhine countries that does not obtain in the USA, for example. Deeply rooted in the national psyche and explicitly recognized by the political system, the trade unions etc., this feeling of community solidarity has as its corollary a well-honed self-discipline which is rather more remarkable than most people think. Naturally, there are 'welfare cheats' in Rhine societies, as everywhere; abuses do occur, and it is not entirely unknown for the unemployed to work while drawing benefit, say, or for some people to 'over-consume' medical services. On the whole, however, the general populace seems to understand that there is a danger in demanding too much of the welfare system. On the basis of this understanding, measures can be taken to remedy specific problems: in Japan, where the ageing of the population is a serious concern, a program has been launched in order to push back the retirement age; in Switzerland, for the same reasons, citizens rejected (by a 64 per cent majority in a referendum) the proposal to bring the retirement age forward, from 65 to 62.

Given this sense of collective responsibility, it is not very difficult for the government to expect and obtain the disciplined cooperation of all parties. In Germany, the authorities now require everyone involved in national health insurance (unions, employers, doctors, funding bodies, the mass of citizens or 'contributors' themselves) to get together and agree on ways to keep health spending within reasonable limits. The Swedes accept without question that those on the dole may not refuse reasonable job offers. The most radical example of self-discipline must be the consensus in Switzerland regarding income support: it is seen as a debt, not a right, and must therefore be refunded once the beneficiary's financial situation improves.

Sadly, when one examines the preceding criteria in order to determine whether France might fall within the Rhine social welfare category, the answer is broadly negative. Not because the safety net is too small, but rather that it is starting to come apart at the seams. In France, no one can resist making as many withdrawals as possible on their social security 'account', but everyone is convinced that they will never really have to pay into it. As a Frenchman, I have the right to visit my doctor's surgery every day, if I wish, and to receive an unlimited number of treatments; my doctor, too, can write as many prescriptions as he pleases; and all of this is 'free'. It is a uniquely French attempt to realize a blend of socialism and capitalism, and it looks quite attractive on the surface. Unfortunately, the long-term consequences are proving to be most unwelcome.

When reform goes wrong: an American story

In the USA, too, the government has tried to stem the continual rise in health spending, but without much success. One ambitious reform, enacted by Congress in 1984, was designed to improve hospital management while keeping a lid on the volume of medical expenses paid for by Medicare, the federal program of health insurance for the elderly.

It will serve as an object lesson in how a well-intentioned reform can go awry.

The plan was to overhaul the basic method of calculating the refundable costs of treatment. Prior to reform, hospitals would bill the government for medical care dispensed to patients by breaking down each case into separate 'treatment units' – surgery, anaesthesia, use of operating theater, tests etc. The cost of each procedure was specified on a master price list agreed to by both government and private insurers, and hospitals were reimbursed accordingly. This method had the merit of being extremely precise, but it was also very complicated and open to manipulation: an unscrupulous consultant could order repeated tests on the same patient (X-rays, for example) that were not strictly necessary, but would boost the amount of reimbursements. Insurers could hardly be expected to examine every case or even make a judgement on which 'treatment units' were essential and which were not. Moreover, new techniques and procedures were inevitably several steps ahead of the pricing schedule, with the result that doctors and surgeons could be overpaid. A meniscectomy (surgical removal of a cartilage) would still be charged on the basis of a 2-hour operation when, in fact, advances in endoscopy had reduced operating time to 10 minutes.

The new legislation brought in to correct such abuses changed all this: henceforth, there would be a flat fee for treating each illness or condition rather than for each unit of treatment. Appendicitis, for example, would attract a reimbursement of $1000 – regardless of how many different procedures were involved. It would then be up to the hospital or clinic to manage its resources and personnel so efficiently that Medicare payments would more than cover costs; anything left over would be pure profit. This new system was based on the statistically confirmed fact that 95 per cent of illnesses fall into one of 465 specific treatment categories, which can be priced on the basis of average standard costs. All of which seems, in theory, admirably simple and easy to check, with a built-in incentive to improve efficiency through better management.

It was to prove otherwise in practice, however. The badly managed hospitals instantly found themselves in enormous financial trouble; many were soon specialising in those illnesses which were more 'generously' reimbursed or in which they could be especially competitive. A few others simply turned away patients they identified as 'risky' financial propositions. This was only to be expected, after all, in the absence of any sense of *collective* responsibility for health care – hospitals were strictly on their own, bidding for the most 'lucrative' patients in order to make a quick profit. In the land of the almighty dollar, not to do so would have been illogical and impractical. A reform which seemed wholly reasonable was thus gradually undermined and distorted, with the result that, despite an initial improvement, spending on hospital treatment in the USA has continued to rise.

Those who instituted this reform might have increased the chances of its success had they first studied the way such matters are handled in Rhine countries. The same, incidentally, could be said of the French social security system as a whole – the inability to see beyond one's own borders is not only an American defect. But it seems that more than a few Americans are utterly blind to the possible shortcomings of the free market, and reject out-of-hand any 'foreign' solutions which imply an adulteration of market forces.

The logic of equality

The Rhine societies are, on a number of accounts, egalitarian: not only is the income spectrum narrower than in English-speaking countries, but the middle class is proportionally larger. Defined as those persons whose income is at or near the national average, the middle class (so characteristic of America, almost its 'trademark') now accounts for about half the US population; in Germany it forms about 75 per cent, and in Sweden and Switzerland nearer 80 per cent. Thirty years of surveys in Japan have shown that 89 per cent of the population consistently define themselves as middle class: the finding is subjective, but significant.

It follows from their egalitarian principles that Rhine countries are strongly committed to fighting poverty and social deprivation, and have organized their efforts more efficiently than either the USA or Britain. In Sweden, for example, memories of the immense hardships and endemic poverty at the turn of the century have not faded. For the Swedes there is no greater national cause than that of *trygghet* (security). Social welfare and the fight against unemployment (the gravest form of deprivation) are seen as absolute priorities. The goal of full employment is actively pursued through a variety of initiatives – not least on the part of government, which set up the Arbetsmark-nadsstyrelsen (National Employment Authority) to this end, and provides it with a generous budget.

There is no national or federal institution in the USA with responsibility for fighting the 'war on poverty': it is left to state and local governments to do what they can on the limited funds available to them. The large charities and volunteer organizations are, no doubt, as dedicated and generous as they are active and influential, but the task is still too great for them to shoulder alone. It was one of the pillars of Reaganism that individual charity and private associations should take over from the state in the sphere of social welfare. According to this reasoning, inequality is both normal and desirable; it stimulates competition and thus ultimately proves of benefit to everybody; poverty is not a political issue of concern to the state; rather it is a moral issue, and each individual must decide how and when to be charitable.

The question was widely debated in America during the first years of the Reagan administration. In Britain, Margaret Thatcher espoused the same ideology in the same terms. This was no fluke, no improvised coda to a new economic strategy: the Reagan–Thatcher dialogue crystallised the emergence of a new morality, created by and for the 'winners' – the rich who could (obviously) afford to be charitable.

To take one example of the change brought about by the new morality, it is sufficient to recall that until 1975 or so, one of the most widely discussed ideas in the USA was the so-called 'negative income tax' (i.e. a form of guaranteed minimum income). Today, just when France is implementing an almost identical system, no American politician would dare utter a syllable in support of such an outlandish concept.

Of course, there is nothing really new under the sun: the philosophical justification of inequality as expounded by 'supply-side' economists such as George Gilder has a well-established liberal pedigree. In the mid-nineteenth century, for example, Dunover wrote of 'the pauper's hell' as a necessary component of the general well-being, because it forced people to 'behave' and to work hard. Gilder, writing in 1981, was of the same mind: 'Over-taxing the rich discourages investment; by the same token, over-compensating the poor weakens the incentive to work. Both inevitably lead to lower productivity' (*Wealth and Poverty*).

Reagan invoked this argument to justify drastic cuts in federal spending on social programs, with the result that whole new 'pockets' of generalised poverty have appeared from one end of the country to the other (see Chapter 3). The same reasoning also led to the dismantling of regulations which protected employees and were thought to place too many restrictions on employers. All, it was promised, for the greater good of the economy: 'The assault on employees' rights and benefits will, in the end, be good for employment in general, thanks to the sharpening of competition which it ought to induce.' (The words are those of an EC official, Riccardo Petrella, who nevertheless goes on to criticise this view.)

In Germany – West Germany, in any case – the public attitude towards poverty is entirely different. In a manner of speaking, indigence is practically forbidden by federal welfare laws, which place the onus on society as a whole to assist those who are unable to provide for their own housing, food, health care and basic consumer goods. Social spending amounts to some DM 28 billion per year, and there is a virtually guaranteed minimum monthly income of DM 1200. According to Luc Rozenzweig, the Bonn correspondent for the French newspaper *Le Monde*, 'Welfare recipients currently number 3.3 million, or 5 per cent of the population; yet poverty is nearly invisible, despite the statistical proof of its existence. The first thing that strikes you about this country is that the vast majority of people are comfortably well-off. Street beggars are a rare sight in the big cities, with the possible exception of a few "punks" in Berlin and Hamburg, for whom cadging is clearly a sport rather than a dire necessity' (*Le Monde*, 7 August 1990).

The picture is not entirely idyllic, of course. The same newspaper notes that the increase in the divorce rate and the number of births out of wedlock has meant that poverty in today's Germany is disproportionately feminine. About two-thirds of single mothers – whose numbers are steadily rising – live at, or below, the poverty line.

In Sweden, wages and incomes are regulated by what are officially dubbed 'solidarity policies'. Their dual aim is to promote social equality and to limit the permissible income spread within different economic sectors.

It has already been mentioned that the tax structure of the Rhine model is designed to reduce inequalities and ensure a certain redistribution of wealth. One telling indication of this approach may be seen by comparing the top rate of income tax from one country to another: it is significantly higher in Germany, Japan (55+ per cent), France (57 per cent) and Sweden (up to 72 per cent) than in the UK (40 per cent) or the USA (33 per cent). Additionally, Rhine countries (including Switzerland) impose substantial taxes on capital gains.

Perhaps I should stop here, and make a full and frank admission that the implications of the preceding paragraph – i.e. a top rate of 55 per cent income tax might just be preferable to a top rate of 33 per cent – are intentional. I will let my preference for this aspect of Rhine policy serve as an unashamedly public *mea culpa*.

In seeking deliberately to reduce social inequalities, the Rhine societies can count on broad public support. The criteria which they apply in the area of incomes policy, namely seniority and qualification, are well understood by the workforce. The young bank clerk in Japan knows, and accepts, that he will have to wait 15 years before he can hope to become head of his department, though he may already be invaluable to it because he is, say, the only member of staff who speaks English. And once he is head of department, he knows that a further 15 years will be required before he can gain promotion to senior executive level, no matter how brilliant his performance! In Swiss and German firms, the command and pay structures are strictly tied to qualification levels. Wage differentials are thus seen by everybody to be justifiably based on objective, measurable criteria.

The land of opportunity versus the closed society

There can be little doubt that the Rhine success story is collective, not individual; as a model of society, it appears inflexible by comparison with the scope for upward mobility offered by the neo-American model. Does this necessarily constitute a handicap?

The USA has always been, and still is, the land of golden opportunity. The immigrants who first set foot on American soil at Ellis Island – next stop: the Promised Land! – brought with them not only pain and suffering, but dreams of a better life, dreams of freedom and prosperity, and the indomitable will to succeed. No other definition of the 'American Dream' is necessary.

There can hardly be a single American today who cannot trace his or her ancestry back to that hardy soul who decided to escape the hardships and unrelenting misery of Ireland or Poland or Italy, and try his luck across the Atlantic. And, sure enough, America opened her arms and welcomed each one. In the land of the self-made man, no dream was impossible, no ambition too great: the penniless immigrant could become a millionaire, the son or daughter of immigrants could one day be President. In other words, upward social mobility is not simply a banal fact of life in America, although it is that as well; it is an integral part of the original myth, the national raison d'être.

It is fair to describe American society as fundamentally democratic, built as it is on successive waves of immigration. Aristocratic values, still current in Europe and Japan, count for little. Social stratification, of the sort that is laid down over centuries and persists largely unchanged from one generation to the next, has not yet occurred. It may be true that WASPs (White Anglo-Saxon Protestants) form a kind of ethnic aristocracy enjoying certain advantages, but it is equally true that the same advantages have been claimed, and won, by other immigrant groups in turn. The 'hyphenated Americans' (Irish-Americans, Italian-Americans etc.) have, little by little, caught up with the WASPs or are now poised to do so.

No doubt the melting pot is not what it used to be, as has already been pointed out. Nevertheless, America continues to demonstrate a capacity for social absorption and integration far superior to that of Rhine countries, Japan included.

The fact that it is possible to 'get rich quick' in America can be seen as the grease that keeps the machinery of social mobility turning. In this sense, the primacy of money in the American value system is a positive advantage: as a social criterion, it may not be subtle but it is simple and ruthlessly efficient. The hamburger vendor can become a Rockefeller. The myth is also a present reality: the colossal fortunes amassed during the speculative frenzy of the 1980s came, in many cases, from exceedingly humble beginnings.

Germany and Japan are in another category altogether. Their immigration policies have failed to make any significant impact on the demographic time-bomb of an ageing population which both now face. Pre-unification Germany was home to more than four and a half million foreigners (7.6 per cent of the population), but they remain unassimilated and separate from mainstream German society, notably in the case of the 1.5 million Turkish migrant workers (not immigrants, as such: the German term, *Gastarbeiter*, meaning 'guest worker', is highly revelatory). Mixed marriages are usually a good indication of the degree of integration of minority groups, and in Germany such unions are very rare. There is a peculiarly German resistance to the idea of integration. The French historian and demographer Emmanuel Todd describes it thus: 'The entire legal and social apparatus has created what amounts to a separate regime for foreigners living on German soil [...]. If there is no change in the citizenship laws, or in people's habits and behaviour, the country is likely to revert to its old traditional social order. The intermingling of classes, the increasing social integration which the hardships of World War II had made possible, will thus have lasted only a few decades' (*L'Invention de l'Europe*: Seuil, 1990).

In today's Germany, the far right is more than ever the lightning-rod that attracts a strong current of xenophobia, aggravated by the influx of Eastern Europeans (Poles in particular) fleeing their own shattered economies.

The situation of Asian immigrants to Japan (mainly from South Korea, the Philippines and China) is even worse. In Switzerland, immigration has always been strictly controlled, in spite of the large numbers involved (1.5 million foreigners in a total population of 6.5 million). Swiss policy is to make it extremely difficult for foreigners to settle permanently; deportation and refusal of entry are used unhesitatingly, and borders are strongly manned. Even in Sweden, a relatively small number of immigrants are the focal point of a variety of unresolved problems.

As for the UK, the situation is not so clear-cut. The individualism characteristic of British society makes possible a significant number of mixed marriages and a large, established immigrant population – most of whom hold British passports but whose origins are in Africa, the West Indies and the Indian subcontinent. Unlike Germany, there is a distinct willingness to grant British nationality to settled immigrants. Yet, as Emmanuel Todd notes: 'Even more than in France, the tendency in Britain is one of growing segregation; communities of West Indian, Muslim or Indian origin seem to be retreating into their ghettoes [...]. British practice looks increasingly like German-style exclusion.'

Unable to absorb outsiders at the same pace as America or even Britain, countries of the Rhine model do not present the same opportunity for spectacularly rapid money-making either. Their stock exchanges offer far less scope for windfall profits, and property speculation has not run riot (except in Japan). Rhine societies are set in their ways, socially speaking. Individuals may improve their lot, of course, as in any capitalist country; but they tend to do so more gradually, and the achievement is more likely to be durable. Society is less open – but this may also mean it is better protected from sudden change, less subject to outside influences. Does this amount to a strength or a weakness? Is an open society preferable to a partly closed one? These, too, are questions which must be asked, and whose answers cannot fail to influence the outcome of the conflict of capitalism against capitalism.

The war on direct taxation

The statistic cited earlier regarding health spending in the USA and in Britain (11 per cent of GDP and 7 per cent, respectively) does not compare like with like: health spending in the USA is mainly private, whereas in the UK it is essentially a public expense – Mrs. Thatcher's privatization policies did not extend to the National Health Service.

As far as the overall American economy is concerned, the cost of the health system is immaterial. As long as individual consumers are paying for it, there is no reason why they should not spend more on health than on, say, holidays or furniture. In Britain or France, on the other hand, the public health system is financed through compulsory contributions by employers and employees, and these form part of the nation's overheads. They may thus have a direct bearing on the competitiveness of the country's products and services in the international marketplace.

Such is the line of reasoning which, beginning in the early 1980s, gave birth to the 'war on direct taxes'. The battle still rages.

At the forefront of the attack, President Reagan and Prime Minister Thatcher blamed the system of compulsory contributions for every ill under the sun: it penalised companies, discouraged individual initiative and dulled the fighting spirit of whole societies. The EC, in turn, took up these accusations in one of its periodic bouts of Europessimism. The fact that contribution levels in Europe were so much higher than in

America was thought to constitute an intolerable burden on EC economies, making it impossible for them to compete on equal terms in the dog-eat-dog arena of international trade. The levels, however, have not come down significantly in the meantime.

Before a categorical yes-or-no answer can be given to the question of whether these criticisms are valid, it is well worth looking at the experience of Rhine countries. Their record of economic performance coupled with social achievements would suggest that the question is particularly complex, and cannot be reduced to the blanket assertion that less taxation inevitably produces a more prosperous economy. A thorough analysis will have to take into account not only the level of compulsory contributions, but the way they are structured as well. First, then, the theoretical and historical background. What we call 'contributions' are actually a form of direct taxation which the state collects for the purpose of financing social programs. Since the end of World War II and the setting up of the European welfare state in all its different variants, this form of taxation has increased considerably, reflecting the growth of state interventionism and the generalisation of social welfare entitlement. The size and speed of this increase led some economists to predict that the growth rate of government spending (and hence of state revenues) would soon outstrip that of the economy. If left unchecked, they warned, an infinitely expanding public sector would eventually swallow up the entire national wealth: in other words, collectivisation by the back door.

The liberal reaction to this dangerous slide down the 'road to serfdom' (in Friedrich von Hayek's words) was to unleash a ferocious attack on direct taxation, whose negative economic effects outweighed the intended social benefits. The best-known example of the liberal critique is the Laffer curve (popularised by the American supply-side economist Arthur Laffer), which is intended to demonstrate that government revenues actually *decrease* once rates of taxation go above a certain level. The reason for this is that people will simply lose interest in working harder if they know that the fruits of their extra labors will be confiscated by the state in the form of excessively high rates of taxation. Briefly, too much taxation kills off taxes.

This critique spawned a whole school of economics whose political influence in the 1980s was enormous, inspiring a multitude of tax reforms. Britain and the USA drastically reduced income and corporate taxes; France committed itself to stabilising, and eventually reducing, the level of social security contributions; liberal governments in Germany, Sweden and the Netherlands soon followed suit.

If the argument against direct taxation made so many converts, it was because it contained more than a grain of truth – especially where European social democratic traditions were strongest. No one would deny today that British and Swedish rates of taxation had, by the late 1970s, reached such dizzying heights that they were choking the economy and proving oppressive to society in general. Some of the most dynamic and talented individuals chose to leave Britain and Sweden (the film-maker Ingmar Bergman, for one), and the phrase 'tax exile' was born. Not only were tax levels excessively high, but the measures adopted to enforce collection amounted to a veritable inquisition, creating a climate of suspicion and presumption of guilt that resembled that of a police state. Meanwhile, the business of collecting taxes grew increasingly complex and bureaucratic – in other words, costly and inefficient – and it had to be paid for out of tax revenues (naturally). As the machinery ate up more and more of the money it was collecting, taxpayers were justified in feeling cheated by an inherently wasteful system.

The high tax burden on employers, too, was clearly a disadvantage for companies striving to enhance their performances in increasingly competitive world markets. Just as some individual taxpayers chose to seek tax relief abroad, a number of firms (notably in the textiles and electronics sectors) felt impelled to move parts of their operations to foreign climes where fiscal and social policies were more favorable.

The critics, no doubt, had scored several valid points. Their mistake was to go overboard: in excoriating the compulsory contributions system, in making it the bogeyman and source of all economic evils, they focused too exclusively on the overall *levels* of direct taxation. It is a short-sighted view. There is no automatic connection between contribution levels and a country's economic performance. If proof were needed, it may be deduced from the following figures.

In the USA, taxes deducted at source amount to 30 per cent of GDP. In France they add up to 44 per cent, and in Germany, 40 per cent. The Swedish figure is 52 per cent. Most interesting of all is the case of Japan:

its 29 per cent rate, seemingly at the same level as America's, is (often wrongly) cited by liberal economists to support their argument. The figure is in fact highly misleading, for at least three reasons. First, because of demographic factors: if Japan had the same proportion of elderly people as the USA, the ratio would be 32 per cent. Secondly, most pensions are not included in the figure, as they are usually funded by private organizations rather than by the state, and thus do not appear in the public accounts. Finally, even in Japan the level of compulsory contributions has been rising steadily for the last 20 years.

France: mortgaging the future

It is apparent from the above figures that Germany's enviable economic performance has not been hampered by its relatively high level of direct taxation, while swingeing cuts in taxes and social programs have neither halted America's economic decline nor made her industries more competitive in the face of the Japanese onslaught. It is no longer possible for Americans to blame the unions, the government or 'welfare cheats' for the country's lamentable situation. Once in the vanguard of social progress, Americans now have to work under worse conditions than most of their West European counterparts. If the USA sometimes seems to be travelling away from, rather than towards, greater economic development, perhaps it is time to question the ultra-liberal theories which have been used to chart the nation's course.

The importance of money in American society is not something its citizens have ever been ashamed of; on the contrary, they are rather proud of it – which is why their declining competitiveness causes such acute embarrassment. Equally, in a land where people must be subservient to money, there is no shame in relegating social welfare to the back burner. Yet it is precisely this 'unsentimental' attitude towards social needs that is beginning to cost America dear.

This apparent contradiction is perfectly illustrated in the debate over compulsory contributions, and the failure to understand that it is not so much the total sums involved as the way they are structured that matters. In other words, more important than how much one pays is whom one pays, and by what method. Once again, all the Rhine countries have developed structures which are strikingly similar, and which could not be more different than those of the Anglo-American economies.

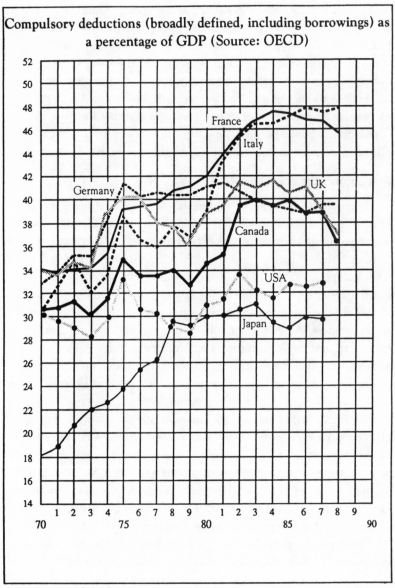

Compulsory deductions (broadly defined, including borrowings) as a percentage of GDP (Source: OECD)

SOURCE: *Chroniques de la SEDEIS*, no. 6, 15 June 1990.

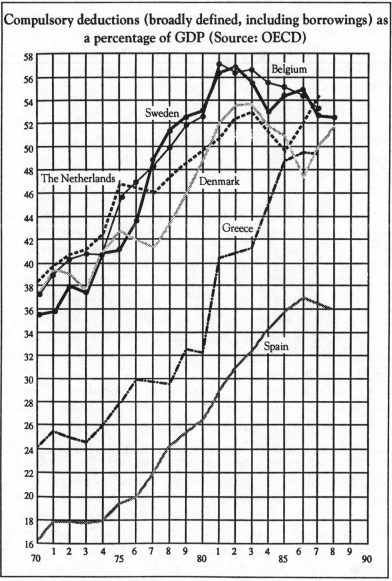

Compulsory deductions (broadly defined, including borrowings) as a percentage of GDP (Source: OECD)

SOURCE: *Chroniques de la SEDEIS*, no. 6, 15 June 1990.

In Rhine countries, for example, social security contributions invariably account for at least 35 per cent of all direct taxes, while they represent only 28 per cent of the American total. Even more significant is the fact that the employee's share (as opposed to the employer's) of social security contributions is much higher, at about 40 per cent, in Rhine countries than in the USA, where it is only 25 per cent. The tax 'bite' which reduces take-home pay is thus considerably greater in Rhine economies. By implication, the general public accepts that aid for the needy must not only be generous in order to be effective, but it must also come out of everyone's pay cheque, in a gesture of national solidarity.

The existence of a highly developed welfare system need not be a crushing economic handicap, then. It may even be an advantage, if the German example is anything to go by. State revenues go to finance a variety of programs designed to increase efficiency and competitiveness, such as training schemes, research projects and improvements to major infrastructure. There are a number of areas of 'invisible' public-sector spending (roads, postal and telephone services, railways, harbours etc.) from which industry benefits, directly or indirectly, and which are seldom given the consideration they deserve – until they fall into such disrepair (as currently in the USA) that it becomes impossible to ignore the consequences.

For all these reasons, the battle over taxes and social security contributions is certain to break out again, in the USA and the UK in particular, where the inevitable result will be new tax increases.

France, too, will have to join the fray, but it will be moving in the opposite direction. Its levels of direct taxation are the highest of all the large industrialized nations (44.6 per cent as against 40 per cent in Germany and the UK); moreover, the government's relatively successful management of its budget cannot hide the inexorable increase in spending on health and especially on state pensions. The government of France is justifiably proud of having paid back its foreign debt *in toto*, and having kept its domestic debt within reasonable bounds. But French companies have failed to make adequate provision for pension financing and have thus accumulated their own debts (off balance-sheet) of some FF 10 trillion ($1,800,000,000,000) – the equivalent of 2 years' GDP or $30,000 per inhabitant. This phenomenal sum, needed to pay out the pensions of the future, will have to be raised through compulsory contributions: a financial nightmare, in short, which threatens to compromise the efforts of French companies to remain lean and competitive.

France, in this respect, is in a category of its own, for both models of capitalism (even the neo-American, despite its general neglect of the longer term) have made provision for financing workers' pensions. Formerly a nation of savers noted for their cautious approach to spending, the French are only now waking up to the realization that they have somehow squandered their inheritance and mortgaged their own future.

If there is a lesson to be learnt from the preceding discussion of the social economy, it is that it would be unwise to dismiss the medium- and long-term importance of what might be termed the social cohesion factor. The extent to which harmony reigns and imbalances are corrected within a given society cannot be ignored: it is crucial, albeit difficult to measure precisely. Like the proverbial water in the well, social cohesion is only missed once it has evaporated; only then does it become apparent that there is an economic cost to the stresses and strains which tear at the social fabric. The ultra-liberal economists have been spectacularly blind to the unforeseen side effects of social injustice, and to the benefits of consensus and solidarity. There is no room in their supply-side calculations for unquantifiable 'details' such as the fact that, in a more homogeneous society, the average level of education will be higher, and this in turn will facilitate society's ability to cope with change and adapt to new circumstances.

There is ample evidence to support the claim that social harmony goes hand-in-hand with economic success, no matter how obstinately the new conservative thinkers persist in ignoring it. The Austrian economist Joseph Schumpeter summed it up in a famous metaphor: it is only because they have brakes that cars can go faster. And so it is with capitalism. Because the authorities and the citizenry set certain limits and intervene to correct certain faults in the machinery of market forces, capitalism can be made to perform more efficiently.

As this enquiry into the nature of capitalism has by now made clear, there is no reason to believe the new orthodoxy when it proclaims that economic progress must be accompanied by increasing social injustice.

The dichotomy which pits development against welfare, and assumes that one cannot prevail unless the other is crushed, does not stand the test of observable fact. However antithetical they may at first appear, fairness and efficiency can be reconciled; they can even act in concert for the good of the economy – and the Rhine model serves as 'living' proof that this is no dewy-eyed fantasy.

That is the good news. But there is another, far more worrying, paradox which needs to be unravelled. At the very moment when the defects of the neo-American model stand revealed for all to see, the Rhine model remains largely unknown and unappreciated. Worse, it is actually losing ground on the political and ideological battlefield.

Chapter 9
The Rhine model in retreat

The economic and social superiority of the Rhine model is manifest, and ought logically to confer a measure of political respectability, if not outright triumph. Given their successes in so many areas, the Rhine countries should be fairly resistant to outside influences, and more especially to the siren song of the USA and the superficial glitter of its casino economy. Incredibly, the reverse is true.

The Rhine economies today are increasingly falling under the spell of American politics, culture and media. In terms of ideological status and political prestige, the Rhine model is in retreat – and not only in countries which are undecided (so to speak) or share certain features with it. It is actually losing on its home ground.

America's seductive powers are such that even those societies which embody all the virtues of the Rhine model, and enjoy all its advantages, seem to be succumbing to her charms. In other words, they are in grave danger of becoming the latest victims of the neo-American illusion. A number of recent economic, financial and social trends are symptomatic of this drift, and in this chapter I will provide a few examples of them, and of their potential for undermining the foundations of the model itself.

The inequality trap

With its fundamentally egalitarian ethos, the Rhine society, as we have just seen, is noticeably more cohesive than its neo-American rival. The social consensus founded on the ideal of equality is plainly one of the cornerstones of the model's success. But in practice, the relative equality of Rhine societies is under attack. An atypical species of 'nouveau riche' – ostentatious and self-indulgent – is making its appearance. This is particularly true of Japan, where the break with traditional values could not be more dramatic.

Japan's post-war economic growth brought considerable rewards for the vast majority of its population. Most of the old, established fortunes lay in ruins by 1945; afterwards, in the rush to Americanize and learn the ways of the democratic West, education was thrown open to one and all. Gradually, a Japanese middle class came into being. The rebuilding of the Japanese economy thus incorporated a strong element of egalitarianism. This is not to say that everyone benefited equally: some did spectacularly better than others. But the new fortunes tended to be discreet, and were 'acceptable' to the culture; the hardships of the war justified the accumulation of new wealth, and the fortunate few were thought (rightly or not) to have earned their success through exceptional personal merit. Frugality and modesty continued to define the national consensus until the mid-1980s.

How times have changed! A new moneyed class of conspicuous consumers devoted to the pursuit of luxury is now on the rise. Their emergence can be traced to the extraordinary urban property boom of the 1980s, and the rapid development of speculation on the Stock Exchange. These two sectors of activity have, in recent years, generated an estimated 400 trillion yen (approximately $2.6 trillion) in windfall profits, according to the experts. Thus, a few land-owners, property developers and stockbrokers have become very rich – very quickly.

In Tokyo, Osaka and other big cities, even the owners of tiny plots of land which happened to be strategically located joined the ranks of the super-wealthy. Japanese society is increasingly split between landowners and the rest – and it is increasingly unlikely that the 70 per cent of the population who do not own land will ever do so. They may continue to save towards that goal, but the dream is fading. As it fades, one of the basic pillars of the post-war period is being undermined: home ownership was one of the key ideas the Japanese copied from the American way of life (the expression 'mai homu' – my home – has even entered the language). That this hope should be dashed is an ominous portent of social tensions to come.

The new wealth of the few is also seen by the many as somehow less legitimate than was formerly the case, if only because it has been acquired so quickly, i.e. it has not stood the test of time. A land-owner in today's Japan can make his fortune, amounting to billions of yen, almost overnight – and without selling his land! The boom in property prices means he can borrow money on favorable terms and invest it in speculative ventures, something the non-land-owner simply cannot do. The largest individual taxpayers in Japan are now thought to be property owners whose assets have increased tenfold, or even a hundredfold, over the last few years. The contrast is striking in a society whose capitalist ethos has traditionally been founded on hard work and meritorious effort. The new magnates of finance and speculation are, broadly speaking, resented by the average Japanese.

In addition to the sudden, spectacular wealth of a small minority, Japanese society is having to come to terms with new patterns of consumerism. Nothing would seem to be more alien to its age-old values than lavish self-indulgence or the flamboyant exhibitionism of the conspicuous consumer. Yet the descendants of samurai warriors, inheritors of an ascetic tradition, have been astonishingly quick to adapt to the new narcissism of moisturising creams and designer fashions – just ask any European couturier, jeweller or wine merchant for whom Japan is now a lucrative export market. The sale of diamonds increased by 58 per cent between 1987 and 1988; the luxury car trade is doubling annually (the Japanese term for the nouveau riche is 'Benz-soku': literally, 'Mercedes-Benz people').

Japanese society is thus making a headlong dash to consume that threatens to erode its traditional values; this often takes the form of an exaggerated attempt to make up for lost time. There is, for example, a hugely popular late-night television program which goes far beyond anything dreamt of by American 'tele-shopping' promoters. The Japanese variant offers its viewers such tempting merchandise as a French chateau (a snip at $1.5 million), a vintage Rolls Royce once owned by the Duchess of Kent, or a modest Fiat that used to belong to the Pope. The new Japanese élite can be compared to the thrusting English middle class of the late nineteenth century or the flamboyant Americans of 30 or 40 years ago who gambled away millions of dollars in the casinos of the Riviera. Age-old values have begun to give way to a fascination with glamor and money, fuelled by the international purchasing power of the 'almighty yen'.

More than ever, such blatant inequalities are stirring resentment among ordinary citizens who feel left out of the new consumer culture. When Japan's prestigious *Asahi Shimbun* newspaper asked in a survey, 'Do you live comfortably?', 62 per cent replied in the negative; 60 per cent went on to say that they believed Japanese society would continue to become more unfair, and dangerously so. Little wonder, then, that the 'silent majority' of Japanese are increasingly ill-disposed to accept without question the traditional pattern of life shaped by work, thrift and civic duty.

The Japanese economy cannot escape the consequences of this galloping Americanization of its culture, and notably of its young people. The snob value automatically attached to foreign luxury goods is in danger of overtaking the economic nationalism which hitherto has been the best guarantee of Japan's perennial trade surplus. Worse, it could undermine the habit of saving which, as previously noted, is one of the great strengths of the Japanese economy. The decline is already significant: as a proportion of gross disposable income, savings have dropped to a level of 16 per cent in 1989 from 24 per cent in 1970. Plainly, fewer Japanese households feel the incentive to save, particularly towards housing.

As they gradually acquire a taste for hedonism and mass consumerism, Japanese workers are likely to develop a corresponding detachment from the work ethic and their traditional devotion to the company. In Tokyo one can already overhear ironic remarks concerning the workaholic behaviour of Koreans.

These changes within Japanese society are likely to give heart to those industrialized countries most vulnerable to the seemingly unstoppable tide of Japanese exports. Many in the West would be only too happy to see in them the symptoms of their main competitor's irreversible decline.

A fractured consensus

The social consensus characteristic of the Rhine model is also in jeopardy. One by one, the priorities that underpin this consensus – the primacy of collective over individual interests, the power of trade unions and the voluntary sector, co-responsibility in company management – are proving vulnerable to new and destructive forces.

Sweden is one of the Rhine-model countries which most vividly illustrates the breakdown of collective responsibility and the rise of individualism. The cradle-to-grave welfare system is increasingly under attack. Numerous commentators have already written off the 'Swedish model' of social democracy, and even the government's own economists are on record as believing that the nation can no longer afford the high price of universal social protection. Taxation levels remain relatively high; the emigration of 'tax exiles' goes on unabated and Swedish firms continue to see investment abroad as more attractive than expansion at home. Capital is in fact pouring out of Sweden at an unprecedented rate: from less than $1 billion in 1982, Swedish investment overseas totalled about $7.5 billion by 1989. The tax system also discourages individual and household saving, to such an extent that the savings ratio is now into negative figures.

Such losses are only to be expected in any national economy where direct taxes, and more particularly social security contributions from wages, are significantly higher than in neighboring countries. The French would be well advised to reflect on the Swedish experience in this area! As the sense of community solidarity begins to weaken, so abuses of the social security system tend to become more widespread. The Swedes themselves are not joking when they say that their country holds two world records: one for good health and the other for sick leave. The latter amounts to an average of 26 days per person per year, fully paid and subject to only perfunctory checks. Absenteeism is another Swedish speciality, often reaching the unheard-of level of 20 per cent.

Swedes, then, are increasingly keen to take personal advantage of the system without giving any thought to the consequences their behaviour must inevitably have on the system's very survival. Or, in the wry observation of one Swedish economist, 'Compulsory social insurance works very well indeed – until people figure out how to make use of it'.

So many aberrations and inconsistencies inevitably sparked a backlash. In October 1989, the Social Democratic government headed by Ingvar Carlsson announced that state spending would be slashed by 15 billion crowns (nearly $2.25 billion). At the same time, measures were introduced to liberalise the economy. These included tax cuts, deregulation of the banking sector, freer movement of capital into and out of the country, and less subsidising of agriculture, among others.

The Swedish model is beset by nearly every problem in the book at the moment (although many of its difficulties go back to the early 1960s at least). The *Financial Times* of 29 October 1990 summed it up:

> Indeed, the Swedish economy began to reveal alarming signs of sclerosis. Its growth rate – which, apart from Japan's, had been the best in the Western industrialized world since the 1890s – began to falter. Poductivity became sluggish. The balance of payments fell into deficit. [. . .] Above all, wage and price inflation in a tight labor market undermined its international competitiveness.

Sweden's current plight has the signal merit of illustrating those aspects of the Reagan–Thatcher revolution which were right on target, and remain valid today. Like Labour Britain, Social Democratic Sweden has finally realized that it simply went too far in the direction of solidarity; what began with generous intentions ended up bogged down in a mire of irresponsibility and indolence that would inevitably attract all the economic demons from inflation to trade deficits – and, ultimately, a lower standard of living.

In the battle of capitalism against capitalism, the first casualty in the ranks of Rhine model will be Sweden.

Individualism and demography

Demographic problems are not, perhaps, something one would expect to find in a chapter on the retreat of the Rhine model. But if one accepts that demographic decline is always accompanied by increasing individualism, then the choice is entirely justified.

All the Rhine countries are facing a serious demographic shortfall, having failed to maintain the population replacement rate of 2.1 children per female. As a result, the working population is shrinking, and the ranks of the non-working will grow correspondingly to a proportion of about 60 per cent. It is a trend characteristic of all developed societies, but nowhere more so than in the Rhine countries.

If there is a convincing interpretation of this tendency, it surely lies in such factors as the rise of individualism, the desire to live more comfortably, and a less optimistic view of the future (the newspaper *Le*

Monde put it more bluntly in a recent article entitled 'Germany is Afraid of the Future'). In Japan, the housing crisis is just one of the social, economic and financial constraints which have conspired to lower the birth rate. There is no lack of statistical proof of the debilitating effects of an ageing population on the economy, many of which are perfectly obvious. As the working population declines in relation to the non-working population, the inevitable results are manpower shortages, social security deficits and increased expenditure on pensions.

There are other, less easily measurable, consequences too: research programs suffer for want of young scientific brainpower, the economy becomes generally less dynamic, and society as a whole becomes more inward-looking. It would seem only logical that the Rhine countries – any ageing society, in fact – threatened with a demographic crisis on this scale would actively pursue a policy of encouraging larger families. So far, this has not been the case. The authorities have been extremely reluctant to implement measures which could be widely misinterpreted and whose efficacy in promoting the birth rate is far from guaranteed.

In Germany, at least, a new variable has been introduced which is certain to alter the fundamental aspects of this problem: I am referring, of course, to the flood of immigrants from Eastern Europe already pounding at the gates.

New habits, new demands

A further example of changing perceptions and new patterns of behaviour in the Rhine countries is the general attitude towards work. Already, the shortest working week in the OECD is Germany's (still on course for a further reduction to 35 hours); in Japan, too, a shift in attitudes is under way which looks all the more remarkable because it is so sudden.

The Japanese work ethic, founded on the employee's unquestioned devotion to his company, is showing signs of fatigue. At present, the average Japanese worker takes only one week of holidays per year. But the younger generation wants more: two or even three weeks. The government actually encourages this trend, and has been trying (so far, unsuccessfully) to reduce the official work week from 44 to 42 hours. Another sign of the times is the fact that leisure industries are booming. And there is a general movement of opinion which is increasingly critical of the Japanese obsession with hard work and all its ill effects: the problems of stress, family break-up and early death linked to overwork are abundantly reported in the media. The Ministry of Health itself carried out a study of cases of sudden death which indicated that 10 per cent of all adult males who die each year literally 'worked themselves to death'. The damage can be measured in terms of sociological consequences which are no less worrying. Long working hours and chronic exhaustion may lead to suicide, divorce and alcoholism.

The 'Japanese miracle' has its limits, and the lifestyle which it demands is being openly challenged by the younger generation. As in Germany, the youth of Japan cannot reasonably be expected to share their parents' impulse to rebuild a nation ravaged and humiliated by war. Having experienced only prosperity, in full knowledge of the country's massive surpluses and all-conquering currency, they naturally wish to enjoy today the fruits of yesterday's labors. Yet this desire must inevitably have repercussions on the economic and ideological model which produced so much abundance. Japanese society is henceforth faced with the challenge of learning to accommodate individual hopes and freedoms which are essentially alien to its traditional culture.

The trade union movement and the bargaining procedures it has imposed are yet another (predictable) casualty of the diminishing sense of community solidarity now apparent in the Rhine countries. It is true that deunionisation is a worldwide trend: in America, the UK, France, Sweden, Japan and even, to some extent, Germany, trade union power is in decline as membership plummets. But for Rhine societies this phenomenon takes on a different meaning, given the traditional importance of the labor movement in helping to create, and perpetuate, the social consensus.

Deunionisation is particularly noticeable in Sweden, for example. The principal trade union, LO, has seen its influence greatly reduced as a result of reforms in the labor market whose effect has been to decentralise the collective bargaining process. Negotiations between management and workers now take place company by company, rather than on a national level. The new procedures have resulted – perhaps unexpectedly – in spiralling wage settlements, leading in turn to inflation and a further blow to Swedish competitiveness. The old discipline (of which LO was the chief guarantor) is cracking, as pay bargaining becomes more arduous and subject to threats and counter-threats in the absence of overall coordination and control. (Swedish employers are especially vulnerable to threats in these days of manpower shortages.)

The Swedish example thus proves a valuable point: declining union power and greater flexibility in the bargaining process are not necessarily synonymous with a more efficient, more competitive, industrial profile.

In addition to all this, the unique Rhine model of company organization is also under pressure. The traditional corporate command structure, in which promotion depends to a large degree on seniority (whose advantages have been pointed out in an earlier chapter), is thought to be inflexible and inhibiting. A growing number of young Japanese graduates balk at the prospect of a minimum 15 years' service before they can become managers or department heads, and another 15 years to reach senior management level. The exaggerated formality which characterises relations between staff and executives in Japanese companies is also coming in for criticism, with the result that Toyota, for example – a model Japanese firm in every respect – has eliminated one of its middle-management positions, whose Japanese title smacked of old-fashioned paternalism. In Germany, Siemens has struck a number of ranks from the corporate roll in a bid to speed up information exchange and decision-making procedures within the company. As for the system of boards of directors and supervisory committees at the highest level of management, it too is not immune from attack. Critics say the traditional arrangement at the top of the command structure is heavy-handed and prone to inertia.

The pay scale is another sore point. Plainly influenced by the neo-American model, the brightest German or Japanese graduates – some of whom may have been to American universities and colleges – are showing their impatience with a system that links salaries to seniority and qualifications. They are demanding a faster climb up the pay and promotions ladder, especially in rapidly expanding sectors and the most successful companies. Their frustrations may ultimately play into the hands of foreign firms 'head-hunting' for their offices in Frankfurt or Tokyo.

If the young managers in German or Japanese firms have rejected the slow but steady career path of their own corporate culture – the

Rhine culture – in favor of the American success story, it is because the latter is such a potent myth. Seen from afar, the USA still shines like an irresistible beacon; its influence may be deplored (or not) but it certainly cannot be denied. And it is felt at another level which may prove to be decisive in shaping the future of the Rhine model.

The siren song of finance

I have already had occasion in previous chapters to stress the advantage enjoyed by Rhine-model companies whose ownership is in the hands of a stable and loyal pool of shareholders, and who can count on bank financing. I wrote those passages with the small shareholder in mind.

Small shareholders possess the inestimable quality of feeling a certain attachment to the firms they have invested in. But they can hardly be blamed for showing an interest in a takeover bid, should one come along. It is, after all, a bid, which they can refuse or accept – and why refuse, if it proves to be the chance of a lifetime to make a substantial profit on their holdings?

That is the whole point of Rhine legislation regarding takeover bids: to address the legitimate interests of the small shareholder, so that they too may benefit from the offer of a better share price than that quoted on the exchange – something which elsewhere is a privilege reserved for major shareholders, those who hold blocks of shares.

If the end result is to discourage takeover bids in the Rhine countries, does that necessarily mean that shareholders miss out on profit-making opportunities? In an attempt to find out, I arranged for a statistical analysis to be carried out, based on the variations over a ten-year period in the spot share values as listed on the four major Rhine-model stock markets (Frankfurt, Zurich, Amsterdam and Tokyo) as well as on the London, Paris and New York exchanges. (The data were drawn from the usual stock indices, such as the Dow–Jones, the FT 100, the Nikkei etc.) The question asked was: How much would $100 invested in each of these markets on 31 December 1980 be worth 10 years later? Here are the answers:

	$
Tokyo	334.1
Amsterdam	252.4
Frankfurt	238.5
Paris	213.9
London	173.3
New York	172.2
Zurich	172.0

The figures are eloquent: despite the effervescence of Wall Street and the City during the 1980s, the Rhine exchanges win hands down (with the exception of Zurich, whose poor results since 1986 reflect Switzerland's difficulties as it faces the EC Single Market).

I do not wish to claim that these findings are absolutely conclusive, insofar as they are based on my own personal calculations rather than on a rigorous scientific method which would, for example, have to take account of the different approach to sampling from one index to another. Furthermore, although allowance was made for currency exchange-rate fluctuations, I did not consider dividend payments (much higher in Britain and the USA) or the effects of taxation in arriving at the final figures. All told, the 'edge' in favor of the Rhine exchanges may not be so clear-cut, but the result is, at the very least, a draw. Small shareholders in Japan, Germany and Holland can rest assured that they have not 'lost out'.

In the case of Japan, there can be no doubt that shareholders did very well indeed during the 1980s. The Tokyo Stock Exchange took off in spectacular fashion at the beginning of the decade, and the Nikkei index climbed to unprecedented heights. The price-earnings ratio (PER), which reflects the market price of shares relative to company earnings, has in some cases reached multiples of 60, whereas American or British stocks rarely exceed a PER of 10 or 15. The large Japanese banks have profited immensely from this escalation of market values, and in the small world of international finance names such as Nomura, Dai-Ichi, Sumitomo and Daiwa now trip off the tongues of the initiated. The latest arrivals on the Japanese financial scene are futures and options markets, copied on those of Chicago, London and Paris.

In Germany, the banks have at last begun to get involved in the new

international financial markets – reluctantly, because high-flying speculation is not part of their traditional culture. But the American example has proven too strong even for the sober German financiers to
resist; it is as if an order of monks had woken up one day to find that
their austere chapel had been turned into the Crazy Horse Saloon. In
Frankfurt, as in Tokyo, finance is plotting its revenge.

Two recent examples of this trend will serve to illustrate the breach
that has been driven through the traditional defenses of the Rhine
model of finance. Early in 1991, the leading Dutch insurance company,
Nat-Ned, made an offer of exchange of its own stock for that of the
Netherlands' third-largest bank, NMB Postbank. This would have produced a merger of unprecedented proportions for the Netherlands. The
small shareholders closed ranks and attempted to stop the bid, protest-
ing that the terms offered fell short of what might be acceptable. They
were joined in their efforts by Aegon, an insurance group which held
17 per cent of Nat-Ned shares. Yet together they were unable to stop
the merger, once the initial bid had been improved. An unremarkable
story, had it taken place on Wall Street; but on the banks of the Rhine,
it is the sign of a new and alien financial mentality.

The second case in point is the takeover by Pirelli, the Italian tyre
maker (ranked fifth in a highly concentrated world market), of its German rival Continental Gummi-Werke. Having gradually acquired 51
per cent of Continental shares, Pirelli was nevertheless powerless over
the affairs of the German company, whose articles of association
restricted any one shareholder from exercising more than 5 per cent of
voting rights. Such limitations are common practice in Germany, and
allow the board of directors to refuse unwanted merger bids – which is
exactly what Continental's board did. This time, however, the denoue-
ment was entirely unexpected: Continental shareholders held an
extraordinary general meeting and voted (by a 66 per cent majority) to
overturn the 5 per cent clause. The board of directors lost, the owners
won, and the financial history of German capitalism was changed forever. The rise of the shareholders as adversaries rather than allies of
management is bound to be a shot in the arm for the hitherto sluggish
German stock exchanges.

As finance takes off, the shareholder's higher profile is mirrored by
the faltering power of the banks. The traditional role of the 'house bank'

– one enjoying a special relationship with a company – is, according to observers of the German scene, on the wane. Firms are putting some distance between themselves and their usual bankers as they begin to respond to the advances of foreign banks and the lure of the financial markets. Banks, for their part, are no longer automatically entrusted with the AGM voting rights of shareholders whose accounts they manage; such proxies must now be granted in writing. In general, the banks' cosy relationship with their corporate clients (and the economic power it entails) is attracting more and more criticism: political parties such as the SPD and the Liberals have begun the attack by suggesting that a ceiling of 15 per cent should be put on bank ownership of capital stock in any one company.

The steady rise of the financial markets in Rhine countries also means that the monetary authorities, and governments in general, will lose some of their powers. Such is the logic of finance on an international scale: the more capital moves across borders, the less discretion is available to central banks and national treasuries in their attempts to influence the principal economic parameters (taxation, interest rates, money supply etc.).

When Helmut Kohl had to scrap a fiscal reform involving deductions at source because it had sparked a massive flight of capital from West Germany, he unwittingly gave a superb demonstration of the new political impotence. And although the Bundesbank may still, on occasion, go its own way in setting interest rates (as it did in January 1991, scuttling a Group of Seven agreement reached only 10 days earlier), it is obvious that the German and Japanese central banks no longer enjoy the complete independence which has traditionally been theirs. Interest rates in particular are increasingly subject to Eurodollar levels, which in turn depend on decisions taken in Washington by the Federal Reserve Bank. As German and Japanese monetary authorities lose their room to manoeuvre, the dependence of national economic policies on outside forces contrasts even more strikingly with the immensely powerful position which the economies of these countries occupy on the world stage.

There is another disquieting tendency which reflects the growing influence of American-style 'casino finance' on the Rhine model, and that is the dubious behaviour – if not outright fraud – of some financial operators. Germany and Japan can now 'boast' that they, too, have embezzlement and insider trading scandals. The Volkswagen affair, in which a top executive was found to be playing the stock market with company funds, is an especially revealing case. More notoriously, German firms provided Saddam Hussein with all the help he needed to produce chemical weapons; it is unlikely that any American company would have accepted the job. And what of the potential for criminal abuse of the sacrosanct secrecy of the Swiss banks? Again, it was the Americans who forced them to 'come clean' and freeze the $20 billion of Iraqi assets deposited in bank vaults in Geneva, Basel and Zurich – provoking, by the by, one of Saddam's more spectacular tantrums.

Business ethics are also under scrutiny in Tokyo these days, notably on the stock exchange, where the hand of the *yakusa* (a Japanese version of the mafia) has been detected in several recent cases of fraudulent operations. There is certainly no shortage of financial misdoings in the political arena; the Recruit scandal, it will be remembered, helped sink two Prime Ministers.

Plainly, the virus of 'easy money' has begun to insinuate itself into the heart of the Rhine model and its financial institutions. What is especially worrying is that Rhine countries have not yet built up as many 'antibodies' (rules and regulations, investigative methods etc.) with which to fight the infection, as the Anglo-American economies have done. They are, therefore, alarmingly vulnerable to a host of ills. But even these, in the final analysis, are only the secondary manifestations of a much larger, much more important force, which goes by the name of financial globalization.

Finance – it is worth repeating – is one of the two or three most powerful vectors involved in the spread of the neo-American model. I have tried to show how it helped fashion the present shape of American capitalism, and is now emerging with a vengeance in Japan and Germany. Just as a lever multiplies the force applied to it, finance is the perfect tool for adding strength to the capitalist ideology: what it does spectacularly well is to reinforce the status of the market as the most powerful economic mechanism and the ultimate arbiter of the fortunes of business and industry.

For the last decade and a half, the lever of finance has been exerting an unprecedented force on all the capitalist economies, of whatever scale. Three powerful factors – innovation, internationalization and deregulation – combine to fuel the drive towards financial globalization, making it much more than a passing phase. It is a new, but probably permanent, part of the world economic landscape.

Before taking a closer look at the forces behind it, let us first examine its origins in the series of dislocations and upheavals which have allowed finance to achieve its present dominant position.

Shocks to the system

It is not easy to pinpoint the beginning of globalization in the sphere of finance. International movement of capital is, of course, a centuries-old phenomenon: Renaissance Europe was largely financed by the Lombard banks (immortalised in the 'Lombard rate', the name given to the German prime lending rate, and Lombard Street in the City of London). Throughout the nineteenth century, the English and French were the great exporters of capital, via their colonial empires principally, but not exclusively: Russia and Turkey both borrowed heavily from the accumulated wealth of Britain and France.

British financial power remained considerable after World War I, but by then American finance was beginning to flex its muscles. The 1929 crash was to provide an eloquent illustration of just how crucial the movement of capital had become, as the channels of international finance became the means by which successive stock market failures gathered weight and speed. Finally, by the end of World War II, the international financial system seemed to have settled down into a respectable, and durable, maturity. Governments of all hues collaborated in shaping and maintaining a reasonably sound mechanism whose foremost achievement was monetary stability.

The Bretton Woods agreement inaugurated the first credible international financial and monetary system. The gold standard was partially revived by giving it an alter ego in the form of the US dollar ('as good as gold'); other currencies would be measured against the dollar within a parity grid. The system's watchdogs were put in place: the International Monetary Fund, on the one hand, would be responsible for mitigating the currency fluctuations caused by balance-of-payments difficulties, while the World Bank, on the other, helped finance economic development and reconstruction programs. The entire system hinged on the commanding position of the dollar as both universal standard and unit of international exchange. At a time when the USA was politically and economically dominant, accounting for half of world industrial production as well as 50 per cent of world gold reserves, and in the forefront of technological progress, this did not seem illogical or unsuitable. Certainly no other country was in a position to challenge American leadership in monetary and financial matters.

Although we refer to this post-war system as 'international', it nevertheless remained circumscribed by the economic requirements of individual nation states, and above all by that of the USA. Three shocks were soon to be administered to the system, inevitably destroying its fundamental logic. The first shock was the decline of American power, and with it, that of the dollar, while at the same time Japan and Europe were catching up. The Deutschmark, the Swiss franc and the yen were soon to join the dollar as recognized international currencies. The second shock arrived on 15 August 1971, the day President Nixon announced that the dollar would no longer be convertible to gold. The Bretton Woods system collapsed at a stroke, and the dollar lost 80 per cent of its value. The 1976 Jamaica accords made it official: fixed exchange rates were abandoned once and for all, and currencies would be allowed to float freely. The IMF and the World Bank had never worked as intended, having failed to secure a broad enough base upon which to build monetary discipline and keep member states in line. Bretton Woods had in fact broken down under the weight of its own contradictions: founded on the dollar as the vehicle of finance and development, it had to juggle two equally important but conflicting requirements in order to function properly. In the first place, a ready supply of cash had to be available to keep the financial machine ticking over – in other words, the US balance of payments had to be kept in the red so that there would be enough dollars abroad. Conversely, the dollar's gold convertibility had to be maintained, and for obvious reasons this meant that the US foreign deficit could not be permitted to grow beyond reasonable limits. It was an insoluble dilemma. Either the world economy would be starved of dollars, or the American deficit would expand indefinitely along with the dollar supply, leading to insolvency. Bretton Woods had to fall apart eventually; when it did, the sense of order and discipline which had prevailed since 1945 was condemned as well. Currencies would henceforth be left to float – or, more accurately, to be tossed about on the unpredictable seas of world money markets.

The abandonment of the Bretton Woods led to a profound change in the very nature of money itself. From now on, it would be perceived as a merchandise like any other: 'Money is a commodity', in the phrase made famous by Milton Friedman. A commodity, and nothing more: the formula may seem harmless enough, yet it marks a traumatic break with the past, when money was something more – a standard, an intangible symbol, an immutable point of reference. In its new incarnation money is merely a negotiable asset which can be traded on the market in the same way as wheat or beef (or companies, for that matter). The money markets have inevitably come to resemble those which deal in agricultural produce and raw materials, and the same techniques are brought to bear – trading in futures and options, swaps etc. It is fitting, and somehow inevitable, that such innovations as foreign currency options and futures contracts on interest rates should have been developed and refined in Chicago, home of both the Milton Friedman school of monetarism and of the great commodities markets, where pork bellies, orange juice and soy beans are traded in the same way. None of these innovations could have arisen in the era of money-as-totem; all became possible once its status had changed to that of a mere commodity.

The third great shock to the system took the form of a series of upheavals and imbalances on a worldwide scale: one oil crisis after another, a faltering dollar, massive trade gaps and oceans of the debt of the developing countries have, since 1973, kept the planet in a permanent state of red alert. Each tremor is registered on the economic seismograph as a sudden panicky movement of the major financial indicators – interest rates, exchange rates, share prices etc. In the first 4 months of 1980, for example, American interest rates fluctuated within a range of more than 10 percentage points.

Faced with so many uncertainties, financial dealers could hardly be blamed for trying to protect their own interests; the new forward-exchange and options markets seemed the best defense, and their rapid expansion was only logical in view of the risks involved. After all, if a French investor wishes to launch an operation in the USA, he must take every precaution against the eventuality that after 5 or 10 years the dollar may have lost half its value (something which in fact has happened – twice – in the space of 10 years). The profitability of his investment would thus be severely compromised. However, importers of American goods, running their businesses on very low profit margins, are equally vulnerable to any upward movement of the dollar. The point is that such brusque movements in the value of the US currency are now almost everyday occurrences, and so financiers are constantly shifting enormous amounts of capital from one end of the planet to the other in order to keep out of harm's way. This invisible 'merchandise' exists in order to provide cover for the risks inherent in the system which hardly anyone talks about, but whose costs everyone has to bear.

This brings us to the question of innovation, the first of the three major factors responsible for increasing financial globalization.

Innovation: giving wings to finance

The globalization of finance would never have been so thorough, or taken shape so quickly, without modern technology and new legal provisions. Information technology and telecommunications would prove to be the main weapons in the financial arsenal. Thanks to satellites, cables and computers, financial data travel freely around the globe and can be instantly processed and integrated into existing data – all at very low cost (it has been estimated that the real cost of financial transactions has been reduced by 98 per cent as a result). The 'golden boys' of finance never have to leave their desks in order to trade on virtually any market in the world; a computer terminal is all that is needed. American Treasury bonds can be traded in Paris, Peugeot shares bought and sold in Tokyo or London, the European ecu quoted in Chicago. Technology is the vehicle which allows finance to gather momentum.

There have been other innovations of a purely financial nature. Until the 1970s, finance was almost immune to the creative impulse: banks provided credit and stock exchanges dealt in shares and bonds, and that was that. But the last 15 years have seen the development of a bewildering variety of new financial products, from futures and forward-exchange contracts to options-convertible securities and note issuance facilities (NIFs), not to mention RUFs, MOFFs and other exotic acronyms.

It all adds up to a whole new financial universe of immense proportions. The Chicago futures markets, which specialize in these products, handle a volume of business that is two or three times greater than that of Wall Street. But the phenomenon is not limited to Chicago; the new finance has burgeoned everywhere in the capitalist world (whose markets are of course open to any and all foreign business). Moreover, governments have actually encouraged the trend towards internationalization of the new markets. When the French futures exchange, MATIF, was set up in 1986, the authorities knew it would attract German investors anxious to secure the kind of innovatory financial cover unavailable to them under the Rhine system. Where the Anglo-American financiers had been quick to develop and refine new techniques, the stolid world of German banking had been reluctant to abandon its slow and cautious approach to finance, and had thus fallen behind in the race to innovate. Financial globalization is, among other things, a process that frees capital from the earthly bonds of classical banking and propels it towards the exalted heights of speculation and the thrill of the stock market. As well as the new technology, the new concepts that have made globalization possible are, in the main, products of Anglo-Saxon cultures.

Internationalisation of the financial sphere is a logical consequence of its own growth, but it is also (if not principally) the result of a general trend encompassing virtually every economic activity on earth, not just finance.

Trade is the locomotive that drives internationalization, and that has been true even before the birth of capitalism. What is new is the rate of expansion of world trade since 1945: it has grown at double the rate of world production. This means that the proportion of goods leaving the country is increasing in relation to the amount remaining where they were produced. The corollary to this phenomenon is, naturally, that national economies are increasingly open to the outside world. The evidence can be seen in the import ratio (imports as a percentage of GDP), which doubled in the USA between 1970 and 1990 to reach 14 per cent, and in France jumped from 15 per cent in 1960 to 23 per cent in 1990.

The growth of world trade has a dynamic all its own whose effect is to internationalise industry and production in a two-pronged movement. On one side, the multinationals feel it is good strategy to estab-

lish themselves on the home ground of the new clients and new markets they are constantly seeking to win; on the other, there are the
companies who (sometimes reluctantly) delocalise part of their operations in order to save on labor costs. That is why, for example, the electronics industry has most of its basic components manufactured in
south-east Asia.

Commercial and industrial internationalization leads to gigantic
flows of capital across borders: trade and new investment have to be
financed, risks have to be insured, profits have to be sent home. An
increasingly international economy naturally creates a need in the
financial sector for vast amounts of 'cross-border capital' to be available
at all times. And on top of all this, the huge surpluses of German,
Japanese and OPEC capital need a home from home, ending up as
investments in capital-poor areas around the globe.

It is difficult to imagine what this international trade in the invisible commodity of capital really amounts to as it circles the planet at the
speed of light. The statistics tell us that the *daily* volume of transactions
on the foreign exchange markets of the world totals some $900 billion
– equal to France's *annual* GDP and some $200 billion more than the
total foreign currency reserves of the world's central banks. Capital
leaps over borders, oceans and deserts in the time it takes to type in a
computer command. It is constantly on the move, seeking investments
in every market on the planet, and it has even conquered time itself.
When the Tokyo exchanges close, computer trading moves on to London just as the British markets open, then proceeds to New York and
thence back to Japan a few hours later, to begin all over again. If they
are to cope with non-stop trading, financial operators (especially
banks) have no choice but to develop their international networks,
concentrating on the three main poles of attraction (the USA, Japan
and Europe). Thus Nomura, one of the large Japanese commercial
banks, took the decision to transfer its market operations command
center to London. Plainly, the money trade has already created its own
'Single World Market'. The individual exchanges are little more than
frail craft on the financial ocean, buffeted by the variable winds of capital as it moves ceaselessly across the globe.

Deregulation

Deregulation is the last, but not the least, of the factors contributing to financial globalization. The effects of regulation on movements of capital are well known: in the 1960s, for example, American banks migrated en masse to London in order to escape restrictive legislation at home (and thus sowed the seeds of the Eurodollar market). Conversely, deregulation is the signal that opens the doors to international markets and brings capital flooding in. When the USA rescinded the infamous Q rule, which restricted the return on sight deposits, the banks chalked up a tenfold increase in business in the race to sign up new customers. The creation of unit trusts in France, in 1978, is a similar success story: today they manage funds amounting to some FF 1.5 trillion (more than $270 billion).

America and Britain led the way in deregulating their financial markets; other countries were quick to imitate them, knowing that failure to do so would only benefit their competitors. The plethora of rules and restrictions governing securities and commodities trading were everywhere relaxed or simply abolished. The French Treasury, obsessed with the power and influence of the City of London, instituted a comprehensive deregulation of the Paris exchanges in order not to lose business to the great rival across the Channel.

The financial sector thus has an inherent tendency to expand, on at least two accounts. First, its activities inevitably extend beyond national boundaries. The framework of the nation state is too narrow, too parochial to accommodate the impetus of world finance. Individual states and their often arbitrary borders can hardly resist this built-in logic of internationalization. In the words of Nobel Prize-winning economist Maurice Allais, 'The world has become one vast casino whose gambling tables are scattered from one end of the globe to the other'.

The second reason has to do with the ideology of the 'pure' market, inseparable from the logic of finance itself. It is in the nature of the beast, so to speak, to seek out markets offering the least resistance, the fewest rules, and the greatest opportunities for initiative and innovation – but also presenting the highest risks (whether of dishonest dealings or of outright crashes).

On both accounts, then, financial globalization is the principal means by which the ultra-liberal model is disseminated throughout the world. Its power is such that even the best-organized economies – the Rhine economies – are unable to fight back effectively. Added to its media appeal and historic successes, the neo-American model has thus managed to infiltrate its Rhine counterpart by means of a Trojan horse filled with financiers and brokers.

Chapter 10
The American hare
versus the Rhine tortoise

At this point, it is essential to examine more closely a central paradox in the analysis. Of the two models of capitalism, it is the Rhine variant which is plainly more efficient than the neo-American, whether considered from the economic point of view or from the social angle. Yet there can be no doubt that the neo-American model maintains both a psychological and political edge over its rival, and has done so since the beginning of the 1980s. It enjoys this position of 'moral superiority' on Rhine territory itself – in Germany, Sweden and even Japan – and throughout much of the southern hemisphere, notably in Latin America (where, to be fair, American-inspired ideas have shaped the economic policies and management techniques successfully applied by the up-and-coming economies of Chile and Mexico).

In the struggle for influence which pits one capitalist model against the other, one is eerily reminded of Gresham's Law, the 400-year-old dictum which says that bad money will drive out good. It is a strange contrast indeed: the neo-American model consolidates its psychological advantage while at the same time offering abundant proof of its economic shortcomings. Conversely, the demonstrable qualities of the Rhine model fail to grip the imagination, in spite of the increasing public concern for the economy. On the face of it, this makes a nonsense of the market principle itself; it is as if car buyers were flocking to purchase a model whose flashy exterior concealed a third-rate, clapped-out engine.

Imagine for a moment that a survey could be carried out in the less-developed countries, in which the following question was asked: 'Given the choice, where would you rather live: in North America or western Europe?' Now, you and I may know that immigrants (legal ones, anyway) are in general better off – or less badly off – in Europe. Wages are at least as high as in the USA, there is adequate provision for social security, and in Rhine countries the right to decent housing is guaranteed, in stark contrast to the USA. No matter: the overwhelming majority, particularly the young, would opt for America. The fact that Europe is something of an unknown quantity in Latin America and Asia may go some way towards explaining this – nowhere is the USA more popular than in communist China! – but even in Africa and eastern Europe, most people would still spontaneously pick North America as their preferred destination. Canada would win hands down over Scandinavia, for example. Why should this (still) be the case?

There is a larger question which must be asked, and that is the extent to which the economic behaviour of groups and individuals is

SOURCE: *Valeurs actuelles*, 27 August–2 September 1990, no. 2804, p. 32. (Reproduced with permission.)

rationally motivated. Those who assume that the economy obeys no other logic than self-interest, or even community or national interest, are mistaken. The illusion of a system in which all economic activity results from a careful weighing-up of the pros and cons of a given decision, such that the sum of competing individual interests is evened out by the invisible hand of the market, is exactly that: an illusion. *Homo economicus*, the ideal producer/consumer whose choices are systematically arrived at through a dispassionate, almost mathematical, process of calculation, simply does not exist outside the theoretician's imagination. In the real world of real economies, the irrational is strongly represented. Passions, passing fads and improbable fantasies play a far greater part in the economy than any textbook on the subject dares suggest. Politicians, on the other hand, have to be more realistic: governments, if democratically chosen, are certainly in no position to ignore the preferences – however 'unreasonable' – of the electorate. In economics, as in everything else, it is not enough for an idea to be intrinsically worthy or valid. It must also be politically marketable.

It is clear that Rhine capitalism, quietly competent and judiciously even-handed, has failed to make much of an impression on world opinion. It is in fact so utterly devoid of glamor and panache that, in media terms, it is a 'turn-off' and its economic success a non-story. In this it resembles the EC, whose painstaking construction languished for many years in almost total obscurity until the Single Market and Maastricht came along to galvanise public opinion and attract the attention of the media.

And so the Rhine tortoise wins the race, but nobody notices – the press corps is far too busy interviewing the American hare. The neo-American model has style, if not substance; it possesses star quality. Moreover, it comes complete with a legendary past.

The greatest show on Earth

American capitalism has all the ingredients of a good Western. It promises to be rough and ready, filled with danger and excitement and suspense. There is something for everyone: the thrill of the chase, the narrow escape, the good guys shooting it out with the bad guys. As in the circus, the threat of real harm makes the audience applaud all the more at the end. 'Casino capitalism' also has its menagerie of fearsome beasts: sharks, hawks, tigers and dragons. The Rhine bestiary, consisting mainly of domesticated animals of wholly predictable behaviour, is a mere petting-zoo by comparison.

Life in the Rhine countries holds out little promise of excitement, though it may be very active. It conjures up a grey image of monotonous routine which holds strictly no interest for the producers of Hollywood blockbusters and their audiences. An evening at the Crazy Horse Saloon will inevitably make for more compulsive viewing than a day in the life of a Benedictine monastery. And no one is likely to convince teenagers to switch from jeans to lederhosen.

Capitalism in the American mode could be mistaken for a creation of Hollywood. Reagan himself could stand as a paradigm of this symbiotic relationship between the new conservatism and show business, but there are equally obvious clues in the vocabulary of business and finance which emerged during his 'reign'. It was surely no accident that the inventor of junk bonds, Michael Milken (now behind bars), was nicknamed 'The King' in financial circles. The King, of course, was Elvis Presley, the first worldwide pop idol. In a fascinating article in the *American Journal of Sociology* (January 1986), P. M. Hirsch points out that popular culture is the source of much of the imagery used in the language of takeovers, from piracy and Westerns (ambushes, heroes and villains etc.) to romances and fairy tales (Sleeping Beauty, for example), as well as sports and games. The often warlike terminology could fill a whole dictionary. It is readily apparent that 'bear hugs', 'golden handcuffs', corporate warlords, dealmakers and shark watchers all belong to the world of adventure stories and cartoons, not to mention video games. Indeed, the point at which fiction blends into fact and the game becomes reality is increasingly hard to spot; as the American sociologist John Madrick noted some years ago, takeovers are Wall Street's equivalent of parlour games, and the players are no more in touch with economic and industrial realities than children engrossed in a game of Monopoly.

America's capitalist extravaganza thus combines the spine-tingling thrill of the jungle – the fight to survive against all odds – with the playful, heart-warming scenario of romantic comedy and its inevitable happy end. Easy money, after all, *is* a dream come true. How much more attractive than the plodding prosperity of the Rhine countries! Talk of 'striking it rich' seems fundamentally irrelevant in the Rhine context, just as it is the very essence of American capitalism, Las Vegas style. The media's favorite new scenario – The Fastest Deal in the West – was not dreamt up in Zurich or Frankfurt, but in New York and Chicago. Nevertheless, even the good grey burghers of Zurich and Frankfurt are beginning to wonder what it feels like to win the jackpot with one spin of the roulette wheel. To be comfortably well-off in Germany or Switzerland does not necessarily mean that one is immune to the lure of the casino economy: small investors, too, have dreams – not, perhaps, of power and fame, but of just once making a 'killing' by betting on the right horse. The new generation of Swiss, Japanese and German managers is particularly vulnerable to the virus of 'fame and finance'. Never having experienced the privations – or the glory – of war, they may actually come to find a substitute for the thrill of combat in the power games of neo-American model; this is not by any means the most far-fetched explanation for the sudden explosion of Japanese interest in the Kabuto-Cho (Stock Exchange). It is the remedy for the ennui of economic stability and predictable prosperity. The frenzied activity of the Kabuto-Cho gets the blood pumping; its excitement is contagious. Yet 'Stock Market Mania' ultimately feeds on itself – it is little more than the froth on the tide of economic reality, fulfilling a role which elsewhere is assigned to theater or sports and games.

Media success and the success of the media

Despite its failures, despite debts and deficits, ailing industries and social inequalities that cry out for attention, American capitalism – *the* capitalism, as far as most people know – is a planetary superstar. Whether vilified by its few remaining enemies or deified by its defenders, it has a mythical quality which the media do not hesitate to exploit. Like their audiences, the media too find it all very exciting: flamboyant gamblers and financial acrobats, white knights and black knights, high drama and high risk – not to mention high incomes – are the stuff media dreams are made of. Economists ignore this phenomenon at their peril, for it is by no means a harmless by-product of casino capitalism; on the contrary, it is one of the most powerful means of (quite literally) broadcasting and amplifying the new values.

The media now play a major role in economic life, one aspect of which has already been touched on: the up-and-coming financier or the head of a recently formed company in search of funds via the stock exchange simply cannot do without publicity. It is worth recalling that the communications sector really took off in the 1980s; and in the age of communications, it is no longer enough to be a success – you must be seen (or at least seem) to be a success.

Entrepreneurs no longer have the option of merely running their businesses well. They have become personalities in a drama, and they must live up to the script or disappoint an audience of millions. More than just a personal satisfaction, being a winner – and a highly visible one – is part of the image-making which is essential for doing business in a media-saturated environment. The raider who comes back from the hunt with his corporate trophy, the company gladiator who survives the ordeal of the Wall Street arena confer an aura of prestige on their firm which is as important as its turnover or its market share. Against such photogenic competition, there is little chance that the media spotlight will linger long on the restrained, somewhat austere figure of a German senior executive, or on the discreet charms of a Zurich banker.

The media have their own laws, one of which is that the show must go on – until audience shares decide otherwise. The celebrities it creates are expected to do their part in keeping the show alive. The economy-as-spectacle works both ways, and the complicity of those in front of the cameras with those behind them is one of the secrets of its success. But the mutual reinforcement which this suggests can have disastrous side effects, as the high-profile Chief Executive Officers, market raiders and young Turks of finance all vie for media coverage. Like Hollywood stars, they may become prisoners of their image. How many high-risk strategies, how many outrageous schemes have been hatched with the unstated aim of earning media approval? The casino economy plays on the image of itself which it actively promotes, but over which it no longer has control.

When the neo-American model crossed the Atlantic, 'showbiz economy' naturally came with it. Like it or not, European entrepreneurs soon understood the importance of a high media profile, and learnt to their cost the enormous consequences a poor showing on television or a slip of the tongue in front of the microphone could have.

SOURCE: Plantu, *Un vague souvenir*, Le Monde Éditions, 1990, p. 21. (Reproduced with permission.)

They are, by now, quite resigned to being part of the galaxy of celebrities, along with sports heroes and pop stars; they know that the show will go on, and that they have been cast in it. Companies, too, have had to play along or suffer the Wildean ignomiy of 'not being talked about'. With varying fortunes, they have hired 'communications consultants' to polish and promote the company image. The in-house position of 'Communications Manager' was virtually unknown in France before 1980; now it is the job most coveted by the thrusting young men and women of the 'media generation'.

Fame begets fortune

What does it mean to be a capitalist? What is the aspiring capitalist's goal in life? For the new generation, the obvious answer is, very simply, to get rich.

The answer was not so obvious in former times. A great many of France's most distinguished industrialists apparently 'forgot' to make their personal fortunes; rather, they put all their efforts into ensuring the success of their firms. In Germany, such behaviour – unthinkable in the USA – is the rule, not the exception.

Given that a company's fortunes, in the American model, are organically linked to its chief executive's own wealth, it is imperative for the entrepreneur to get rich, and fast. Fortunately, there is a proven formula for doing so, according to which 'it is cheaper to buy than to build'. The implications of this philosophy have already been explored in earlier chapters; its usefulness here is in drawing a distinction between the two permissible strategies an entrepreneur can adopt.

The first is to invent a product, a service or a concept, and then sell it on the open market. The inventor may eschew the media spotlight in this case, but it is not in his interest to do so if he hopes to reach the widest possible audience of potential buyers. He is well advised to use the media to 'sell himself' and, thereby, sell his invention.

The second method is to raise money on the financial markets, something established institutions can do without attracting publicity. But, as we have already seen, the lone individual who chooses this 'smart' strategy must make a name for himself in order to attract investment money to his scheme. If he is to succeed in selling the hope of windfall profits to a myriad of investors, he does not have the option of remaining anonymous: self-publicity is the oxygen which breathes life into his endeavor.

The new logic of high finance thus reverses the proposition that fortune begets fame. In the topsy-turvy world of 'showbiz economy', fame and prestige must come first; only then do the millions start to pour in. The same applies to moral values and behaviour: formerly, these preceded, and justified, subsequent fame and fortune. Now that prestige and celebrity have taken over as the prime consideration, they serve to vindicate whatever behaviour may follow.

This headlong rush to secure publicity and media celebrity can be seen as the logical extension of an economy which, as it modernizes and innovates, has necessarily become an 'information economy'. American capitalism is miles ahead of its rival in this field; all the elements are in place to ensure that its winning image will dominate the media from one end of the planet to the other. From Djakarta to Rio de Janeiro and from Cairo to Cracow, vast audiences are fed a steady diet of American mini-series and Hollywood epics; every modern cultural artefact from advertisements to comic books the world over is made in (or modelled on) America. And now that Marxism is in its terminal phase, the universities too are wide open. It would no doubt come as a shock to the Brazilian lecturer, the Egyptian intellectual or the Nigerian don to find out that there is more than one kind of market economy, to be shown the proof that Rhine capitalism does not follow the same rules he has seen acted out in last night's sub-titled episode of Dallas – and that its results are, on the whole, more impressive.

Money and the media

In the sphere of public relations, the Rhine model, unable to communicate effectively, has left the field entirely to its neo-American competitor – who in turn finds itself boxed in by the requirements of the same media from which it simultaneously derives enormous strength. Taking this analysis one step further, it is clear that the media themselves are increasingly subject to the casino mentality and the obsessive pursuit of short-term profit.

Journalists themselves are often among the first to deplore the oppressive influence of money on their trade. The need to demonstrate immediate profitability has created a palpable malaise among media professionals, who view with alarm the tendency to jettison what should be the basic aim of journalism in a capitalist economy: to sell information to readers and viewers. Now, it seems, the professional code has been rewritten. Information has become a merchandise like any other, and the new goal is to sell readers and viewers to the advertisers, something we French are all too familiar with, given that France has probably gone further down this path than even the USA.

The English-speaking countries boast a long tradition of journalistic independence, in the sense that journalists have organized themselves effectively within interprofessional bodies and can therefore often keep a rein on their employers. In this they are supported by their readership, who are relatively well educated, particularly those who follow the economic and financial press. Journalism of the Anglo-Saxon school has thus been able (so far) to stave off the kind of incestuous relationship between the media and finance that has developed in France, notably since the largest television channel was privatized.

Among the many books and articles which, in just the past year or two, have examined the question of economic manipulation of the French media – not to mention manipulation of the economy via the media – I will cite two which make the point most succinctly. In a long article detailing the threat to journalism posed by big money, the writer on economics Jean-François Rouge describes the 'active and passive corruption' which he says is now rife in the French press: 'Since 1944 the principal threats to press freedom in France have come mainly from the political sphere. That is where the strongest defenses and the greatest vigilance have always been necessary. Traditionally, the corrupting influence of money has been kept to a tolerable minimum, at a level which was at least compatible with the basic independence of the press, and of the most important national titles in particular. But it is a delicate balance of forces, and recent behaviour suggests it is in danger of being upset.'

In February 1991, Alain Cotta, one of the top French economists and a long-standing champion of the market economy, published a chilling analysis of recent developments in the capitalist world (*Le Capitalisme dans tous ses états*, 1991, Fayard). Much of this study is concerned with three increasingly important, and worrying, trends: the role of 'media capitalism', the growing influence of finance, and corruption. He writes:

> The rise of corruption cannot be dissociated from that of the media and finance. Given that the overnight acquisition of a fortune, far greater than any which can be had through a whole lifetime of hard work, may result from the possession of privileged information (notably in cases of mergers and takeovers), the temptation to buy and sell such information becomes irresistible. The broker's commission thus attracts corruption as surely as the thunderhead calls forth the storm.

It was not so long ago that the well-paid public servants of the developed economies could be relied on to treat any attempt at bribery with contempt; 'baksheesh' was a foreign word and an affliction of the developing world. But now that the West has begun deregulating the economy – and deregulation is another magnet for corruption, as Cotta goes on to demonstrate – and with the role of the state reduced to a bare minimum, corruption is being rehabilitated, even glorified. It may, after all, be just one more form of entrepreneurship, and a highly successful one at that!

If anyone still has doubts that corruption is both lucrative and widespread, a few statistics concerning the drugs economy – an example of 'pure' corruption, so to speak – should suffice to dispel them. The value of the cocaine seized by the Mexican police in the 3 years to January 1991 amounted to some $150 billion, twice Mexico's foreign debt. That, of course, is only what was seized. Meanwhile, the Federal Reserve Bank, which like any central bank controls the printing of money, was looking into the extraordinarily strong demand for bank notes. It found to its surprise (and embarrassment) that 90 per cent of all the notes it was printing were not being circulated in the USA; rather, they were going overseas, where they were needed for use by a variety of parallel economies – but mainly by the drugs trade, whose aversion to bank accounts is self-explanatory. The drugs business is many things, but it is not small or even medium-sized: it is a macroeconomic giant.

When the media glorify those who make their fortunes with ease, overnight and virtually without lifting a finger, is it any wonder that others will choose the path of corruption or the drugs trade in order to achieve the same dream? Similarly, once the media have fallen prey to the law of instant profit (the last strongholds of public television services, modelled on the BBC, are likely to be the Rhine countries), their reporting of business and economic matters will inevitably become a hostage to the power-hungry schemes and rampant paranoia of the financial superstars, the prima donna billionaires who believe themselves to be above the law. In the final stages of delirium, the monsters created by the self-perpetuating hype of fame and fortune come to deny time itself. As Cotta puts it: 'Television entertainment, to achieve perfection, must refute the passage of time and focus entirely on the present moment. It is one way of banishing the limitations of the real world, the greatest of which is death. The television series may appear to mimic linear time, but it actually negates the principle that all things must pass by giving the impression that nothing ever stops.' The present is unending, so never mind the future. Why wait? Profit now!

Profit now

The intellectual scene in the 1980s was astonishingly receptive to this particular aspect of the neo-American model. It was a decade which began under the sign of ideological breakdown, a time when the star of individualistic hedonism was on the rise. Gilles Lipovetsky has dubbed it 'the age of emptiness', one whose world view 'has been emptied of everything but the quest to satisfy the ego, to serve the interests of the self, to experience the ecstasy of personal liberation, to indulge sexuality and the cult of the body'. The time was also ripe for 'massive private investment and, as a result, deactivation of the public sphere' (*L'Ere du vide*: Gallimard, 1986).

The neo-American model injected a powerful but simple idea into this atmosphere of exaggeratedly blasé individualism, an idea whose incantatory spell would prove as reassuring as the old Marxist catechism: Profit now. This may be variously restated as 'self-interest is the only legitimate interest' or as the systematic preference for the short term and a corresponding mistrust of any plan requiring collective action. The logical absolutism of this neo-American creed, its covert cynicism, even its corrupting effect on the media are all eerily reminiscent of the communist dragon which it has just slain.

Eminently 'broadcastable', the message of 'Profit now' is in 'synch' with the times. It is simple to grasp, and possesses the absolute clarity of purpose which is balm of Gilead to the distress and confusion of an epoch robbed of traditional values. In its glorification of personal success, its exaltation of the winner, it serves the cult of individualism; in assigning top priority to the short term and justifying the addiction to credit and debt, it meshes perfectly with the climate of hedonism. In times of moral and ideological drift, people will tend to cling to the present in order to ward off an uncertain future; exhortations to save up for rainy days, to plan ahead, simply fall on deaf ears. The result is the law of the jungle, i.e. that which remains after all other 'laws' governing collective behaviour have been rendered suspect. In a peculiar way, it is also a return to base reality once the flights of ideological fancy have come crashing down.

That the religion of 'Profit now' was wildly successful in the 1980s can be seen in the number of temples devoted to its worship. The decade saw an astonishing proliferation of business schools, where initiates were called upon to read from sacred texts with intriguing titles such as *The Price of Excellence*; excellence in pursuit of what goal, you may well ask. Profit, of course, is the goal; but do not then presume to enquire whether profit is to be pursued other than for its own sake, for you will be cast out of the temple. None may doubt the first article of the new faith, which is that profit is an end in itself. To question this is to be guilty of heresy. In the new religion, any enquiry into 'philosophical' matters has been resolutely set aside in order to concentrate on techniques, ways and means, methodology, 'how to' but never 'why'. The new synthesis of American capitalism thus comes down to a perfectly circular, self-contained logic: profit is for the present and the present is for profit. This is more than superficially related to the kind of sophistry which elevates a given economic system into the guiding principle of a whole society, whereby 'whatever succeeds is efficient; whatever is efficient is right; whatever succeeds is therefore right'.

There are, nevertheless, encouraging signs of a certain reaction against the cynicism of the trendy values of the 1980s. The heady days of executives revelling in their own ruthless efficiency are beginning to recede, as 'business ethics' comes back into fashion. Today's 'with-it' manager recognizes that a purely utilitarian approach may have its limits. The fact that this latest trend, too, originated in America is both good and bad news for France; good news, because any concept stamped 'Made in America' is sure to be snapped up by the French, and bad news, because Americans, unlike the French and other Latin peoples in general, actually take ethics very seriously.

The charms of Venus and the virtues of Juno

America's change of mood may become more pronounced over the next few years; prevailing conditions nevertheless continue to give the neo-American model a formidable advantage, in almost every field, over its opposite number. Whether viewed from the perspective of the trade unions and other faltering institutions, of the company-as-community, or of the Stock Exchange and other booming financial markets, the Rhine model seems constantly to be swimming against the tide. Its concern for the longer term would seem to be wholly incompatible with the unstoppable drive to consume, while the predictable career path it stakes out for managers and workers looks increasingly old-fashioned to those who yearn for heroism and adventure, and who reject as 'nannying' the tradition of social protection and social security.

Rhine capitalism suffers from an image problem: it looks out of date, it breeds neither dreams nor excitement, it is not fun. In the language of the media consultants, it is not a 'sexy' concept. If the neo-American system has all the seductive charms of Venus, then the Rhine version is clothed in the ordinary virtues of Juno. And just as Juno has never had her Botticelli, so the extraordinary socioeconomic success of Germany has no widely respected advocate in the universities or on the hustings.

The fault cannot be assigned exclusively to a low media profile or a momentarily unfashionable set of values. Deep down, the Rhine variant of capitalism has its source in two great currents of thought, one of which is largely unknown and the other in disrepute.

The role played by the mainly Roman Catholic CDU and the mainly Protestant SPD in shaping the German social market economy points to the influence of Christian social doctrine on the Rhine model, but, amazingly, almost nobody seems to know this. Such ignorance is all the more astonishing as Catholic social doctrine since Pope John XXIII has finally recognized, not just the legitimacy, but the positive creative potential of private enterprise. The moral authority of the Church has been strengthened by this recognition. It is worth noting that in Japan, too, the community-building role of the company is a profound reflection of Confucian philosophical values. Perhaps the West will see a rise in the influence of a newly energetic 'social Christianity' – heretofore confined mainly to the Rhine countries – now that the post-communist era has wiped the ideological slate clean.

The influence of Christianity has been overlooked while the social democratic component draws all the critical fire. Social democracy, that vast and multi-faceted European movement of which the Scandinavian countries (especially Sweden) are the best examples, bears more than a passing resemblance to the *Sozialmarktwirtschaft*, the social market economy; and it may be argued that the Rhine model which I have described in this book is a modernized and updated version of social democracy, seen from a new perspective. What is certain is that social democracy has tumbled in the public esteem, having sacrificed much of its vitality in the last 20 years or so to become a complacent and bureaucratic incarnation of the labor movement. Asked how many people were working in his plant, a Swedish factory supervisor can truthfully reply, 'About half of them'. The Swedish system is in deep waters: its rates of taxation, inflation and investment are simply not up to the challenge of European competition.

Swedes woke up to this grim reality towards the end of the 1980s, and are now attempting to put their economic house in order, in much the same way as other European socialists before them – Italy's Bettino Craxi, Spain's Felipe Gonzalez, Mario Soares in Portugal and François Mitterand in France – went about their respective U-turns. Whether Scandinavian social democracy can pull out of its present tail-spin may depend on how well it manages to come to terms with the worldwide collapse of state socialism. The prognosis is, to say the least, uncertain.

Socialism dismantled

What François Furet has called 'the enigma of communism's disintegration' is not something I wish to dwell on in these pages. We have, in any case, only begun to measure the effects of this extraordinary, unpredictable ideological earthquake. One of its consequences, as I stated at the beginning of this study, has been to leave capitalism alone to face itself; this book might never have been written had it not been for the demise of communism and of East–West confrontation.

It is not simply that a liberal system has triumphed over a state-run system. It is as if a tidal wave has swept over the continents, causing the planet itself to list dangerously to one side; in the aftermath, it appears that a whole body of ideas, an entire corpus of study, analysis, sensibilities and reflexes has been washed away by the flood waters. And it is not just Stalinism or bureaucratic Soviet communism that have gone overboard, but almost anything connected with the socialist ideal or bearing the imprint of social reform, however faintly. This wholesale abandonment is both unfair and unwise. History will ultimately be the judge of how much can, or should, be salvaged from the cataclysm, but for the moment, the dismantling of socialism and of the wider social dimension is total, uncritical and uncompromising.

The shock waves released by the collapse of communism are still echoing, with amplification, within the hollow shell of every East European state – so much so that even words in common use have been thoroughly discredited and inspire revulsion: words like 'party' or 'collective' or even 'workers' can no longer be pronounced without a grimace. Thus the new political parties in the East call themselves forums, alliances or unions, anything but parties; newspapers now studiously avoid any mention of yesterday's topics (workers, plans, strategic objectives etc.), all of which have been consigned to oblivion along with the hated system.

We have not yet reached this point in the West, at least with respect to vocabulary; but in the realm of ideas, the consequences of communism's downfall may prove to be equally devastating. Notions of social justice and social democracy, aspirations towards group action or collective discipline, institutions such as trade unions, national economic plans and direct taxation – all are now branded with the mark of disapproval, insidiously prefaced by a minus sign. Not quite discredited, perhaps, in the strongest sense of the word, but suspect, not to be trusted. A great void has opened up in Western political culture, too, on its left and center–left flanks.

European politics has suffered the equivalent of a stroke, in which one side of the brain is left disabled. It is the reverse of what happened in France after 1944: the right's collusion with the Vichy regime meant that an entire political, cultural and even literary sensibility was to remain under a cloud of opprobrium for many years. The left was handed its *de facto* monopoly on culture and higher education more or less by default. Today it is the left, perhaps even the center, whose universe has suddenly collapsed into the black hole of historical censure. And not only in France: the center of political gravity throughout Europe has shifted towards conservatism, whether openly proclaimed as such or not.

The neo-American model – which has no inhibitions when it comes to proclaiming its credentials as an ultra-conservative exponent of 'pure' capitalism – is the obvious beneficiary of the left's sudden paralysis. Just as obviously, the Rhine model, with its overt social agenda, cannot escape being tarred with the same brush as its Scandinavian cousin, social democracy.

In the coming ideological beauty contest, it is easy to see who will score more points. The neo-American model proudly presents itself as a hard-headed professional, undisguised and untroubled by sentiment or second thoughts. Its main rival comes across as complicated, opaque – if not obscure – and cloaked in too many overlapping folds of social considerations, financial constraints, cherished traditions and good intentions. It is a bit 'soft' in the middle, and fails to dazzle. Yet the day is not far off when the divide between the haves and the have-nots, so readily apparent in America today, will split East European societies down the middle. The dislocation will be violent in the extreme; perhaps only then will there be a serious revival of interest in this form of 'capitalism with a human face' (there is already a glimmer of curiosity in Poland) which I have here designated as the Rhine model.

The psychological, political and media success of American capitalism is not as paradoxical as it first appears, given so many contributory factors and advantages. What is deeply troubling, on the other hand, is the fate which may befall those who, seduced by the image, import it wholesale with no regard to its possible secondary effects. When it crosses the Atlantic to infiltrate the Rhine countries, seducing the UK and France along the way, the American model does not bring its own antidotes with it. The USA possesses its personal pharmacopoeia of remedies and corrective measures designed to curb the excesses of the 'law of the jungle': a meticulous legalism, morality inspired by religious faith, a civic sense underpinned by voluntaryism, and so forth. The cultural foundations of Europe and the emerging countries of the South are entirely different. They do not have the same checks and counter-weights; they cannot apply the same brakes that the USA keeps in reserve.

The 'export brand' of American capitalism, which Europe is so eager to imbibe in its current enthusiasm for ultra-liberal economics, may prove to be a far coarser brew than the original, a drastic remedy of the sort that must be administered with extreme caution and an adequate supply of back-up procedures to counter violent reactions. It now looks as if the frail figure of Eastern Europe is going to be the first, and most vulnerable, candidate for this experimental – and dangerous – treatment.

Long live the multinationals!

Everything, then, points to the inevitable victory of the less efficient neo-American model over its less glamorous Rhine cousin – everything, that is, except for one very important element: the phenomenon of multinational corporations. Again, the paradox seems at first unbelievable. What could possibly be more American than American Express or Coca-Cola, what more blatantly patterned on the American model than Colgate, McDonald's, Ford, IBM or Citicorp? Yet a closer examination reveals that the giant American multinationals are hardly typical of the neo-American model, in two basic respects.

First, multinationals are essentially the products of internal growth, based on an industrial plan which in turn is driven by technological or commercial innovation. They are thus firmly wedded to the longer term, and have never given in to the temptation to abandon it. It was the multinationals who invented corporate planning; it was their success which put corporate planning on the business school curriculum.

The other atypical characteristic of such corporations has to do with employment and labor relations. The need to implant itself overseas and recruit staff of widely varying cultural backgrounds means that the multinational must offer a coherent corporate culture and marketing concept; it must, in other words, train its employees and encourage their loyalty through an attractive career structure. This cannot be done overnight, and it cannot be left to the rough-and-tumble of the open labor market.

However paradoxical, the fact is undeniable: the big American multinational corporations are more closely related to the Rhine model than to the neo-American one. And in the case of the European multinationals (e.g. Bayer, ABB, Nestlé, L'Oréal, Schlumberger, Shell), the Rhine component is even more pronounced.

The case of Shell is especially interesting. On the face of it, the hybrid nature of its financial base – 40 per cent British and 60 per cent Dutch – should constitute a handicap: theoretically, the balance is too delicate to be durable. Yet its balance-sheet shows that Shell is the greatest generator of corporate profits in the world. This is in large measure thanks to superb economic forecasting. Shell's economists were probably alone in predicting, long before it came to pass, the oil crisis of the 1970s; moreover, they were able to convince management to develop a corporate strategy that would take their forecasts into account. At another level, Shell has always distinguished itself from its European brethren in insisting on ethical standards which are both extremely rigorous and well accepted by its employees.

The multinational corporations mentioned above have in common at least two characteristics which point to the possibility of some future synthesis of the conflicting models of capitalism.

In the first place, all of these long-established and powerful firms seem to have defied the law of 'corporate biology' which usually applies, to wit: the older and larger an organization is, the higher the risk that it will fall prey to the double threat of bureaucratic inertia (because upper-echelon management tends to proliferate beyond reason) and poor employee motivation (because everyone knows the company is 'fat and rich').

Why should the big multinationals be any different from other organizations? It is principally because they are listed on the Stock Exchange; however powerful, they are nevertheless dependent on the financial market – the hardest of taskmasters, the most ruthless of industrial fitness trainers. Whereas the Rhine model is inclined to underestimate the invigorating action of the financial markets, the European multinationals and their successes are a kind of homage to their beneficial effects. Moreover, with success and power comes the need to invest more, and thus to seek increases of capital on the stock market; this presupposes that the firm's shareholders are happy ones.

Yet the second reason for the resilience of the multinationals is that their dependence on the financial market does not mean they are entirely subject to its whims: with share capital widely distributed, no one shareholder can ever dominate the others. Such corporations are simply too big to fall victim to an outside raid or a hostile takeover. As long as they remain profitable and dividends go on rising, this protection is theoretically unassailable.

And so, bending to the prevailing winds of the market but unperturbed by sudden strong gusts or momentary lulls, the multinationals can (and must) devote all their efforts to the long-term development of their respective industrial and global strategies. In so doing, they create a web of élite staff who work together across oceans and continents; the more multicultural they become, the better their claim to be true multinationals.

For all these reasons, the multinationals, whether of American or European origin, can be said to have achieved an elegant, best-of-both-worlds synthesis which manages to avoid the protectionist temptations of the Rhine model and the dangers of the neo-American addiction to finance.

Chapter 11
The second German lesson

The first 'lesson' Germany teaches us, that top economic performance can be wedded to social solidarity through the social market economy (Chapters 6 and 7), has failed to reach a substantial audience. During the 1980s, in fact, West Germany was routinely taken to task over its day-to-day economic policies or its responses to specific events; the wider context was ignored. The critics, it seemed, could not see the forest for the trees.

The events of 1990 silenced most of these protests. The world looked on dumbfounded as Helmut Kohl grasped the nettle of reunification and accepted what is perhaps the greatest economic and social challenge ever to face a modern capitalist state. In taking up the challenge, the German incarnation of the Rhine model has embarked on an uncharted course that may well serve as an example to all of Europe, if not the world.

The scapegoat of Euro-stagnation

The bombast and bright lights of the Reagan–Thatcher decade kept the German model firmly out of the spotlight. Its image was that of an outdated piece of heavy machinery whose complexities might hold some interest for antiquarians, but whose upkeep was proving an unnecessary burden on West Germany's European partners.

Germany in the 1980s was held responsible for the snail's pace of European economic growth, which since the first oil crisis of 1974 had languished well below the levels everyone had grown accustomed to during the 30-year post-war boom. European growth rates had more or less been cut by half, whereas the effects on America and Japan were much less dramatic: of course they experienced a slowdown, but in no way comparable to the European débâcle. Furthermore, the employment picture remained encouraging (except in the immediate aftermath of both major oil crises) in both Japan and the USA – the latter even chalking up record successes in job creation.

Europe began to wonder if its economy would ever recover. Euro-stagnation led to Euro-pessimism, a period of gloom and intense self-doubt embracing all possible scapegoats: an ageing population, the high cost of social cover, an apathetic workforce and a complacent business élite etc. Germany was specifically accused of fostering these unhealthy trends because, said the critics, it was refusing to play its 'rightful' part as the locomotive of the European Community. The Germans were simply being selfish: a 2 per cent annual growth rate was quite sufficient to ensure their own prosperity, and never mind the rest.

It is true that demographic factors in Germany made rapid economic growth a less pressing priority. Sharing with Sweden the distinction of having the highest proportion of over-65s in the West – a proportion predicted to reach 25 per cent of the total population by the year 2030 – Germany knew that there would be fewer jobs to create, less infrastructure to build (crèches, schools, universities, housing etc.), fewer needs to be met. Why, then, should the country strive to maintain a high growth rate?

France, at the time, was still coping with the effects of the baby-boom. Growth was urgently required, in the form of new jobs and new public investment, in order to wean the baby-boomers on to the joys of consumerism, now that they had got the radical student politics of May 1968 out of their system.

A disciplined currency

German adherence to financial and monetary orthodoxy was another source of intense irritation to a number of European detractors, who saw it as further proof that the economic slowdown had been engineered in Bonn. No one is unaware of Germany's abhorrence of inflation as the economic evil which brought the nation to its knees in the 1930s, ultimately paving the way for Nazism. The reforms of 1948 thus wrote into the Bundesbank charter the requirement, on the part of the financial authorities, to maintain the stability of the mark; more recently, the experiment of the late 1970s was still fresh in every mind: the Germans had finally acquiesced to their partners' insistence that they play the role of European economic locomotive, and as a result had again found themselves in the red.

West Germany, then, was intent on creating the 'virtuous circle' of a strong currency, as described in Chapter 7: a strategy which requires short-term economic growth to be put on hold, while overall financial stability is given priority. That means limiting government expenditure to reduce state debt, and raising interest rates when necessary. It is a Spartan discipline which nevertheless pays handsome rewards, once inflation is under control and the currency stabilised, in the form of medium-term economic growth.

Germany's impatient partners blamed this strategy on her demographic weakness. The residual Keynesianism of the other European governments (which one could even detect in Britain, under the cloak of Mrs. Thatcher's pseudo-monetarism) meant that a certain monetary laxness was still accepted as the inevitable accompaniment to strong economic growth. Because they were themselves under considerable demographic pressure to create jobs for their relatively younger populations, they assumed Germany was acting from similar motives.

Then came the European Monetary System, and German-style management of the currency became an irresistible force within the Community. Once capital was allowed to circulate freely within the EC, separate and divergent national monetary policies became untenable. No country within the Exchange Rate Mechanism could afford to stray very far for very long from the general trend in interest rates, as any unilateral lowering of rates would simply prompt investors to take their money where it would earn more – abroad, in other words – and the country's currency would lose its appeal (and value) as a result. Thus, whichever country had the strongest currency and the healthiest economy would inevitably set the standard, in terms of monetary policy, for everyone else. Within the EMS, that country is, of course, Germany. Its financial rigour has spread, via interest rates and the Bundesbank, to all the members of the system – whether they like it or not.

This 'contagion' was not, at first, welcomed by those who assumed that Germany's financial orthodoxy was a pretext for building up huge trade surpluses or even attempting to 'take over' Europe on the strength of its monetary superiority. But many of those same critics soon saw the benefit of EMS discipline as their economies improved. The change has been most noticeable in the traditionally high-inflation Latin countries (France, Italy, Spain and Portugal) where socialist governments were among the first converts. Who could have predicted that the robust strength of the French franc would be credited (by no less an authority than the English-speaking press) to the steadfastness of a socialist minister, Pierre Bérégovoy?

At a more general level, Germany's critics (in particular those fascinated by the neo-American model) condemned the rigidity and inertia of its industrial and financial structures, so pale in comparison with the feverish activity of Chicago and Wall Street. Germany's financial markets were too narrowly based, too inhibited, they said; its big corporations were penned in by overly timid policies of capital management; the social market economy was an anachronism and mainly to blame for slow growth. Some went so far as to predict that German industries and the economy itself had already entered a phase of permanent decline. I have my own personal (and embarrassing) memory of this school of thought. It so happens that I am the director of the CEPII (Centre d'études prospectives et d'informations internationales), a Paris-based institute whose record on economic forecasting, thanks to the quality of its staff and of my predecessors, is widely respected (notably in the USA). But in October 1981, an article appeared in the journal of the CEPII whose central premise now seems perfectly ludicrous: it was entitled 'The Deindustrialisation at the Heart of the German Model'.

All in all, the portrait painted of the Germans in the 1980s showed them as a selfish nation of wealthy pensioners living off the accumulated wealth of their surpluses and investments. A caricature, undeniably; but it is equally undeniable that by 1985 German per capita consumption was the highest in Europe, at $8000 per year; that Germans were, at the same time, saving at an increased rate – unlike virtually everyone else in the world; that the terms of trade continued to be massively favorable, with each year bringing another record surplus (DM 130 billion in 1988). Germany was replete with its own success. To be German was, in a word, to be comfortable.

Then reunification struck, like a bolt of lightning.

The shock of reunification

Just as surprising as the fall of the Berlin Wall was the speed and energy with which the Federal Republic responded to the political and economic challenge it posed. Even before it became inevitable, reunification had all the makings of a Pandora's box of difficulties and dangers, a real 'can of worms'. There were dozens of reasons to proceed with caution.

In purely domestic terms, once the patriotic euphoria had subsided, West Germans began to fear the high cost of taking in their Eastern compatriots. What would happen to their generous social security system, their hard-earned standard of living? The arrival of 700 000 refugees from the East had already put them on their guard.

Politically, the consequences looked equally unpredictable and, for Chancellor Kohl and his party in particular, highly destabilising. The Christian Democrats looked embarrassingly vulnerable, in electoral terms, under any new unified structure; according to all the opinion polls it was their rivals, the SPD, who would most benefit from reunification. There was even a point, during the summer of 1990, when reunification was more popular in France than in the former Federal Republic.

International opinion was in fact a major consideration. Germany could hardly ignore the deep anxieties which her European partners would naturally feel when confronted with this new giant of 80 million inhabitants, now the dominant member of the Community.

The Yalta Conference, in dividing Europe – and above all Germany – had established the basis for a delicate equilibrium which had lasted for 45 years. The existence of the two Germanys guaranteed the military status quo, with the two superpowers able to maintain the 'balance of terror' in a continual build-up of nuclear weapons (officially described by each side as the attempt to achieve parity with the other). Medium-range missiles (Pershings on the one hand, SS-20s on the other) brought the doctrine of nuclear dissuasion onto European soil itself; not to put too fine a point on it, this meant that Europeans could now destroy themselves on their home ground. As for conventional warfare, NATO and Warsaw Pact armies were being trained for a future conflict in central Europe. Each side had its troops, tanks, jets and artillery lined up in sufficient quantity to suggest that the clash would be of titanic proportions; this, too, was part of the logic of dissuasion.

Germans on both sides of the East–West divide naturally felt concerned, if not directly targeted: any future battle would ineluctably be fought on German territory, and both German armies were on the front lines. It is little wonder that the pacifist movement became such a force to reckon with in West Germany; in some respects the national yearning for peace could be seen as the equivalent, in military terms, of the economic 'selfishness' decried by its European partners.

Now reunification was about to change all that. The old balance of forces, the power blocs, strategies, the configuration of armies and arsenals would have to be reconsidered. Reunification was a problem – perhaps a threat. What kind of foreign policy would a united Germany pursue? Firmly committed to the West via capitalism, was it not also irresistibly drawn to the East, as Willy Brandt's Ostpolitik had demonstrated in the early seventies?

Germany's EC partners were no less concerned over the economic consequences of reunification. As the memory of an earlier 'Gross Deutschland' sent shivers through the Brussels bureaucracy, the new challenge inspired a variety of responses: the British dreamt of a new Entente Cordiale while simultaneously hoping to strengthen the 'special relationship' with the USA; the French began to feel a certain nostalgia for past policies incorporating a Franco-Russian alliance.

The cost of reunification – variously estimated at between DM 600 billion and twice that – seemed enormous, even for Germany; but that was only one obstacle. There would be macroeconomic consequences: reunification would have to be financed on the markets, already stretched by a decline in savings and a general increase in capital requirements. Interest rates would inevitably be subject to upward pressure as a result. Foreign capital would then, just as inevitably, be drawn to the German financial market rather than to other, less prestigious or less predictable investments.

But another alarming possibility was that the German economy would overheat, stimulated by rising consumer demand in the former GDR, and lead to inflation. There is certainly no lack of inflationary pressures in the world economy – American deficits, the volume of cash in circulation, and high levels of industrial capacity in actual use, to name but three of the most important. My own view is that the

developed economies are no longer at risk from high, long-lasting inflation (above 10 per cent), and that this has been the case since the mid-
1980s. The reason is essentially that the effects of such inflation, trans-
mitted round the globe in real time thanks to computerised markets,
would be so horrendous for any nation's businesses and their ability to
compete that countermeasures would be taken without delay. Not
everyone shares this view, and many believed reunification was the
spark that would ignite the powder keg, sending prices sky-high.

On the social front, an endless stream of questions would have to be
answered. The disparities between the two halves of the new Germany
were daunting: gross income per capita in the Federal Republic was
three times higher than in the GDR (an explosive factor in itself), and
prices were notoriously dissimilar. In the old GDR, some basic goods
and services (bread, potatoes, rents, transport) were five times cheaper
than in the West, while consumer durables (televisions, refrigerators,
personal computers) were vastly more expensive. The former East Germans would presumably find it so difficult to take care of basic necessi-
ties that, in the end, they would be no nearer to entering the Valhalla
of the consumer society. How much patience and restraint could they
be expected to show?

There were still other inauspicious omens, less easily quantifiable –
but no less real – with respect to the cultural and behavioural differences that 40 years of separation had produced. Surveys carried out in
1990 showed that a united Germany was far from being of one mind on
a host of issues. Only 7 per cent of adults in the West, for example,
described themselves as atheists, as against 66 per cent in the former
GDR. A whole raft of terms and concepts familiar to every 'Wessi'
(West German) were simply unknown to the average 'Ossi' (East German), as advertising agencies were soon to discover.

The cumulative effect of so many disparities and potential dangers is
impressive, and would have been more than enough to discourage, if
not paralyse, most countries. The Germans nevertheless pressed forward with great energy, in spite of the many voices which counselled
prudence. With the benefit of hindsight, however, the go-slow
approach, had it prevailed, could so easily have gone wrong – if only
because reunification depended on Moscow's approval. It was essential
to make the process irreversible before some new twist in the Soviet

power structure could throw up new obstacles. The coup d'état against Mikhail Gorbachev in the summer of 1991 might, after all, have ended differently. . . Germany was certainly right to proceed with all deliberate haste.

Helmut the bold

It was Chancellor Helmut Kohl's decision to act speedily. His boldness – verging on audacity – took everyone by surprise, and made it possible for Bonn to overcome every obstacle in short order.

The very first barrier was lifted almost immediately: Kohl made it clear that a united Germany would continue to be a full member of NATO. The Soviet government, caught unawares, was in no position to offer even token resistance, especially as the 'sweetener' offered by Bonn was tempting: Germany would pay for the Red Army to be removed from the ex-GDR. A detailed and orderly withdrawal was agreed, and Germany could consider that 12 billion marks was not too high a price to pay for a 'liberation' so peacefully obtained. The Deutschmark thus prevailed over the military might of the Kremlin.

European doubts were also quelled in short order, not least because Germany's partners were given no time in which to mobilise resistance, if there was to be any. Bonn was organizing history; the others could only react. All the skills of German diplomacy were put to the task of solemnly reaffirming the country's total commitment to the Community, and the spectre of a return to the bad old days of 'Greater Germany', which had initially provoked a flood of (sometimes rabid) speculation and commentary – notably in France – was soon laid to rest.

When it came time to test the domestic electoral waters, Kohl and the Christian Democrats, in coalition with the Liberals, won an unambiguous vote of approval on both sides of what was once the Iron Curtain. Reunification was not to be the political manna Kohl's opponents had confidently expected.

The Chancellor's boldness, rewarded with a comfortable government majority, has been matched by an unprecedented effort on the part of the authorities to meet the financial challenge. The stakes are certainly high: the burden to be borne over a 5-year period by the public finances (i.e. the budgets of the federal government, the Länder and the social security agencies) could not amount to less than DM 600 billion. Of this, DM 115 billion is to come from a 'German Unity Fund' – the equivalent of annual overseas investment by West German firms, or of nearly half the total of household savings. The sacrifice being demanded of the German taxpayer is considerable; but the only alternative – massive borrowing – is unpalatable in the extreme, given the dangers involved (a rise in the annual national debt to DM 100 billion, upward pressure on interest rates, flight of capital etc.).

During the election campaign, Helmut Kohl hinted that it might be possible to raise the necessary funds without increasing taxes. In so doing, he was obeying the first commandment of the new American capitalism, more at home in California than on the shores of the Rhine, which states: thou shalt not raise taxes. The power of contagion is such that even in Germany, even in the midst of a great patriotic leap of solidarity and unselfishness, Kohl had to defer to the visceral anti-tax reflex of the man in the street. By early 1991, however, he was asking Parliament to approve the inevitable tax hikes.

It was estimated that the year 1991 would see a West-to-East transfer of funds from the public purse amounting to some DM 150 billion (over $75 billion). This is about what the French spend on health, and three times what they pay in income tax, every year.

It is not only the sums which boggle the mind. What is most extraordinary is that, in the midst of a global widening of the 'equality gap' such as the world has not seen since the nineteenth century, and at a time when 'cut-throat capitalism' is at its zenith, there is still one nation where the priority of priorities remains the reduction of inequalities among its citizens – whatever the cost.

Reunification will not be financed entirely by state funds, of course. The private sector is heavily involved, thanks mainly to cooperation agreements between West German firms of all sizes and their counterparts in the East. Such cooperation is essential, for the industries of the GDR were unprepared for the harsh realities of the free market, and many have gone under. The government agency responsible for privatizing them, the Treuhandanstalt, made a total of DM 55 billion available in guaranteed loans during 1990 – in the full knowledge that at least half this debt may never be recovered. Plainly, the 'upgrading' of the new private sector in the East is going to require a huge injection of investment by West German firms.

SOURCE: Plantu, *C'est la lutte finale*, La Découverte/Le Monde, 1990, p. 135.
(Reproduced with permission.)

Mezzogiorno or Fifth Dragon?

This unprecedented financial effort by the Federal Republic to bail its
long-lost Eastern sibling out of bankruptcy shows an admirably bold
and hugely generous spirit; it is not a perfectly disinterested gesture,
however. Germans know that this is exactly the kind of investment
that pays off in the medium-to-long term. Eventually, the absorption of
the five Eastern Länder into the FRG will bring economic rewards. The
world, too, knows this and still sees Germany as a pillar of growth in an
otherwise stagnant global economy. This is not to suggest that nothing
can go wrong; reunification may yet prove a tougher nut to crack than
anyone could predict. But it would be reasonable to expect that one of
two possible scenarios (as envisaged by CEPII analysts) will unfold over
the next 5 years:

1. In the optimistic 'Fifth Dragon' scenario (an allusion to the four
   'dragons' of the booming Asian economy), the former GDR gener-
   ates growth, and spectacularly so. This hypothesis is based on three
   premises: first, that salaries will rise to no more than 75 per cent of
   West German levels by 1995 (in 1990, they stood at only 30 per
   cent, but by 1991 had already reached 50 per cent). Next, there
   would have to be DM 110 billion of new investment every year until
   1995. And finally, foreign goods would enter the market at a rate of
   40 per cent, and 'Ossi' emigration to the West would have to
   decrease from a high of 360 000 in 1990 to 50 000 by 1995.

   If all these conditions were met, the economic results of reunification would be truly impressive: the country as a whole would
   record an average growth of 3.7 per cent per annum over 6 years
   (1990–95), the inflation rate would remain stable, and the balance
   of payments would still show a surplus, amounting to 2.7 per cent of
   GDP. Crucially, the gulf between the two Germanys would begin to
   close, with unemployment in the former GDR brought down to 11.8
   per cent and the deficit in its current account at only 1.2 per cent of
   GDP.

   In this scenario, Germany is not the only beneficiary: all the
   countries of the OECD ought to derive some advantage, whether in
   terms of growth or inflation, budget deficits or balance of payments,
   from the newly invigorated German dynamo. The signs are there: in
   the first quarter of 1991, for example, sales of French cars to Germany
   grew by 40 per cent, while at home they had dropped by 20 per cent.

   The 'Fifth Dragon' scenario is founded on patience and foresight;
   its premise is that sagacity will prevail.

2. The 'Mezzogiorno' scenario takes its name from the southern half of
   Italy, where years of government action have signally failed to bring
   the region up to the level of the North. In this forecast, salaries in
   the former GDR rise much faster, reaching 90 per cent of 'Wessi'
   levels by 1995. This is the essential point, for it means that impatience, not sagacity, will prevail. As an immediate consequence,
   investment will be much lower, at only DM 90 billion per year on
   average; and immigration to the West will remain high (at an average 200 000 persons per year).

The economic returns would be significantly lower than in the 'Five Dragons' scenario. GDP growth would be only 3.5 per cent per annum, and unemployment would reach 9.8 per cent (East and West combined). The pace of inflation would quicken, and the famous trade surplus would represent a relatively meagre 1.2 per cent of GDP. The most disturbing aspect, though, would be the persisting gap between the two halves of the nation: unemployment in the Eastern Länder alone would reach 20.8 per cent by 1995, and the current accounts deficit would amount to a whopping 16.1 per cent of GDP.

In the words of the CEPII research team, the picture is one of progressive deindustrialization of the former GDR as it becomes an economic desert in comparison to its lush Western neighbor.

There are two lessons to be learnt from these contrasting scenarios. In the first place, the former West Germany has everything to gain from the strongest possible solidarity on behalf of the East, even if it means huge sacrifices in the short term. The 'Fifth Dragon' scenario implies a larger commitment of public resources and general belt-tightening on both sides, but it ultimately brings more substantial benefits. Secondly, and more importantly, the 'Mezzogiorno' forecast shows what could happen if salaries in the East rise too sharply. Wage restraint is the *sine qua non* of a gradual reduction in unemployment and a return to robust economic growth.

This second lesson, as the French found out between 1981 and 1984, is a painful one. The deluded belief that the best way to reduce unemployment was to work less and earn more gradually gave way to the realization that steadily rising wages and salaries only look good on paper if, in real terms, purchasing power is being eroded and jobs are being lost. This constitutes a major advance in public perceptions of economic reality, bringing with it a salutary recognition of the role of the company, a vastly improved economic performance and – for the first time in French history – a national consensus on the merits of capitalism. It is just such an awakening (but on a far greater scale) that is now required of the former citizens of East Germany and of other central European nations. Helmut Kohl never stopped reminding his compatriots of this during the 1990 election campaign. How many heard his message that 'the road to prosperity will be long and hard' over the jubilant cries of 'One Germany, One Fatherland'? Already, there are troubling signs that impatience and frustration are mounting: widespread unemployment has sparked demonstrations and protests in the East, and the metalworkers' union, IG Metall, has won for their 'Ossi' members 100 per cent wage parity with their counterparts in the West by 1994. Such deviation from sensible restraint may yet produce a Mezzogiorno on the eastern flank of the Rhine model.

Why Herr Poehl had to go

On 26 March 1991, the then President of the Bundesbank, Herr Otto Poehl, speaking in Brussels, declared that the Inter-German Monetary Union (IGMU) was 'a perfect example of what ought not to be done in the European Community'. He upbraided the government in Bonn for having 'introduced the Deutschmark into the former East Germany overnight, with hardly any preparation and no means of subsequent rectification, but worst of all at an unsatisfactory rate of conversion. The consequences are disastrous'.

What is in fact disastrous is that this adjective should have been used at all, especially by the head of a central bank (and not just any central bank, but the legendary 'BuBa'). One cannot blame Herr Poehl for having made every effort to persuade Bonn not to resort to borrowing in order to help finance reunification; such was his duty. But having failed, he was surely not entitled to take his revenge so publicly and so sweepingly as to condemn European Monetary Union (EMU) in the same breath. His words immediately caused the mark to fall, but that is secondary; more seriously, they betrayed a shocking eagerness to play down Helmut Kohl's achievement, to forget that the speed and determination of his response was absolutely right – for who can say that anything less might not have ended with the Iron Curtain making a return appearance in the middle of Berlin?

There is an element of wounded pride in Poehl's remarks which can be traced back to the argument over the rate of convertibility to be applied to the Deutschmark vis-à-vis the Ostmark (the GDR currency). Poehl lost this argument, too. He had proposed a rate of 1:3, or at the most 1:2, which was technically sound, because it was based on the productivity ratio between the two Germanys – comparable to that between West Germany and Portugal. Kohl, however, opted for parity. One Ostmark would be exchanged for one Deutschmark.

The consequences of this decision might have seemed disastrous in the short term: unemployment and factory closures rose precipitously, while the enthusiasm of a few months before gave way to gloom. But what would the outcome have been if Poehl's advice had been followed instead? The rise in East German incomes would have been much less dramatic, and unemployment would not have climbed so quickly. But the huge disadvantage to Poehl's scheme was the mass immigration that would ineluctably have taken place. As Kohl remarked, 'If the mark had not come to Leipzig, Leipzig would have come to the mark'. In 1990, up to 150 000 'Ossis' were making the journey to the West; but by Spring 1991, the wave had slowed to a trickle – only a few hundred each day.

It was, from the start, a particularly thorny dilemma: either the Easterners stayed put, and waited out the inevitable – but temporary – period of unemployment, or they left, reducing East Germany to an industrial and economic ghost town for years to come. When Poehl condemned the former path as 'disastrous', he was feigning ignorance of the latter. Kohl's decision does entail hardship and sacrifice, but it is plainly the lesser of two evils.

Poehl's outburst was motivated by more than just spite, however. For decades, German monetary authorities have tirelessly preached the doctrine of convergence, according to which no monetary union should be attempted between two states before their political and economic positions have grown sufficiently alike. Obviously, no two situations could have been less convergent than those of East and West Germany; it was thus inevitable – and essential – in the eyes of the Bundesbank that IGMU should be pronounced a disaster. Any other outcome would result in a galling loss of face, not only within Germany, but within Europe and its institutions. The wider issue of European Monetary Union, and the prior convergence that the Bundesbank has always insisted (and staked its reputation) upon, was uppermost in Herr Poehl's mind when he warned that IGMU was a model of 'what ought not to be done'. Yet, here too, Poehl was feigning ignorance of the facts, for all the evidence of the past decade has shown that monetary union, even in the attenuated form of the EMS, actually promotes economic convergence. To deny this is to imply that Portugal, Greece, probably Spain as well – perhaps even Italy – will have to be excluded from any future European Monetary Union.

If that is so, then what hope is there for Hungary, Poland, Czechoslovakia and the other countries of Eastern Europe? Their successful transition to the market economy is increasingly tied to European progress towards economic and political union; and if European union does not come to them, they will come to us.

Otto Poehl resigned soon after his intemperate remarks. The jury is still out on the question of whether German reunification will be a success, or if (as Helmut Kohl's present political difficulties and the impatience of IG Metall seem to suggest) the 'Mezzogiorno' scenario is nearer the mark. But my personal view is that, notwithstanding Herr Poehl's prediction of disaster, the German experience has already proved to be a salutary illustration of what ought to be done in Europe, if only Europe could grasp the nettle of real union as boldly as Helmut Kohl did. That is the second German lesson for our times.

What Europe could achieve

There is a saying which sums up a government's pledge to its own parliamentary majority: 'Give us good finances and we will give you good politics.' Helmut Kohl may go down in history as the embodiment of this principle. For more than 40 years, Germany has been the citadel of financial orthodoxy, yet Kohl had the courage to insist on instantaneous monetary union between the two Germanys. Against the advice of the experts, despite the internationalization of the economy (which reduced his room for manoeuvre) and the risk of alienating the voters, despite the combined forces of vested interests of every description – in spite of all this, a politician widely dismissed as timid and unimaginative pulled off a stroke of genius. For once, the federal power in Bonn was able to impose its political will on the Länder and their representatives who run the Bundesbank.

It is a truth too easily forgotten that economic strictures must occasionally be relaxed in order to accommodate political necessity. The corollary to this principle is also too often ignored: that is, the primacy of the political sphere is conditional on the prior success of the economic and financial sphere. In other words, political necessity must not be used as an alibi; politics can free itself of financial constraints only when the economic base is already strong. If Germany had not already built up its hoard of trade surpluses, or if its currency were not so strong and its industries not so dynamic, Bonn could never have brought off its extraordinary buyout of the GDR – one merger that has every chance of proving beneficial to all concerned.

A further lesson to be digested from recent German history is that bold, imaginative action in the economic sphere is not necessarily synonymous with inequality, social injustice or marginalisation; and that such action combines well with solidarity, which need not be synonymous with bureaucracy, inertia and heavy-handed interventionism.

Two essential characteristics of the Rhine model have made possible this reunification without tears, and it is not for the first time that they appear in these pages – but in this context they take on special significance. First, of course, is the long-term vision of the nation's interest. Germans on both sides of the former divide understand that today's sacrifices are an investment that will pay off handsomely in the future. However ill-tempered they may occasionally feel in the short run, however unpleasant some of the immediate consequences may be – and there will be deficits, social problems and, yes, higher taxes – they know that if they stick together now, their patience will be rewarded.

The second Rhine factor is the priority assigned to the common good over individual interests. This is the bedrock on which the long-term vision is founded. If given free reign in the case of reunification, individual interests in West Germany would have imposed a cautious, go-slow approach, with as little commitment of public and private funds as possible. Chancellor Kohl would never have taken the plunge had he listened to the advice of the taxpayers or unemployed of his country. And what if he had listened to the financial markets? Reunification was beyond all doubt a gamble they would never have accepted, given the choice: much too uncertain, with absurdly high stakes. It is undeniable that the financial risks were – are – considerable. The sums required are gigantic, and no one can say for certain that the shock waves of so much borrowing and spending can be absorbed without doing too much damage to the system.

What is certain is that such shocks can be more easily absorbed by a system whose financial institutions are fundamentally sound. The financial markets, had they been the dominant force (as in the neo-American model), would have proved too volatile, too nervous and unpredictable to absorb the shock of reunification. A stable and powerful banking system, with close ties to business and industry, is in a far better position to adapt relatively smoothly to the new financial requirements. The collective interest is already part of the vocabulary of such solid structures, founded on the patient accumulation of assets over many years; conversely, it stands little chance of being heeded by thousands of independent financial dealers, each driven by the need to produce instant results and influenced, moreover, by a host of ephemeral criteria – of which the most important is the high opinion which some dealers have of the opinions of a few others.

The 'German lesson' is sure to inspire more than a few provocative thoughts on the subject of Eastern Europe. Just as the Germans have taken on the formidable task of rescuing a third of their own nation from the dustbin of history, Europe is now called upon to devise a strategy for reclaiming its own center from the abyss of 50 years of communism.

Before examining this new perspective, however, it is worth looking at the mistakes now being made in the former East Germany, mistakes whose consequences could be even worse than those predicted by the Mezzogiorno scenario. Essentially, they come down to policies on wages and welfare benefits: the former are rising much faster than productivity, while the latter are so generous that many unemployed 'Ossis' now earn more than they once did as workers. Yet public dissatisfaction is increasing with the realization that living standards and future prospects in the East remain well below those of the West.

How much longer can the East continue to sink into torpor and acrimony, despite all the financial sacrifices made by the West? That will depend on the pace of investment in production, which will come mainly from West Germany. The point is that, whatever its pace, it will be German. The East European context is entirely different: in countries like Poland and Hungary, national investment in production will be almost negligible – the resources simply do not exist. Only substantial *foreign* investment can provide the necessary boost towards a fully fledged market economy. Again, it is the pace that matters. At present, no doubt, it is arriving too slowly; but there is a risk, should it speed up too quickly, that foreigners would be perceived as having 'taken over' the national economy. The result could be an exacerbation of already volatile populist and nationalist tendencies – and further deterioration of the economy.

Logically, the European Community should be seeking to strike a balance between the overabundance of aid available to East Germany and the paucity of resources currently on offer to the rest of Central Europe. Yet this is to beg the question, for the EC is not yet in any position to decide on, much less carry out, a coherent policy on the matter.

On the face of it, the EC can take heart from the fact that West Germany, with a population of 58 million, could undertake to 'rescue' 17 million East Germans, for the proportions are identical with respect to the Community, whose twelve member states have a population of 340 million, and the 100 million inhabitants of the four major Central European countries – East Germany, Poland, Czechoslovakia and Hungary. But the latter three are already beginning to discover that the events of 1989, far from ushering in a golden age of prosperity, were only the first steps in a long journey through the wilderness – a wilderness dangerously populated by false prophets and demagogues. Unlike the 'Ossis', the Poles, Hungarians, Czechs and Slovaks will not be on the receiving end of generous, long-term financial assistance, despite all the efforts of the newly created European Bank of Reconstruction and Development, because – unlike Germany – the EC is not a political federation, not even a fully operational single market: more a free-trade zone, with few common policy areas apart from agriculture and the EMS.

If the twelve countries of the EC were to pool, not just 1 per cent or 2 per cent of their resources, but 10 per cent or even 15 per cent (as all federations in the free world do), they would take a giant leap forward in the direction of the Rhine model, towards solidarity and mutually reinforcing wealth creation. And that is not all: they would be able to find the means to make the new economic deserts of Eastern Europe bloom again. Not in precisely the same terms as German reunification, of course; they ought to aim for something along the lines of the Marshall Plan, the twentieth century's most impressive testimonial to the idea that one country's efforts to assist others can, in the end, prove indirectly rewarding to the donor.

It is an idea whose discovery we owe to the United States of America. That there is, at present, no United States of Europe is a great pity. The failure to create European union will cost us dear – eventually – because of what is about to happen in Hungary, Poland, Czechoslovakia and elsewhere. The longer we in the EC resist the notion of the United States of Europe, the more we are helping turn Eastern and Central Europe into what Vaclav Havel has called 'a zone of despair, instability and chaos, posing no less a threat to Western Europe than the Warsaw Pact's armored divisions once did'.

Chapter 12
France at the crossroads
of Europe

When the Gulf War broke out, Europeans absorbed every detail on their television screens, avidly following a drama that seemed to concern them as much, if not more, than anyone else. And they made an astonishing discovery: as events unfolded, Europe was nowhere. America, with a population of 250 million, had immediately sent 550 000 soldiers to the Gulf, while the 340 million people of the European Community had only mustered 45 000 men, under various flags, to put under American command.

It was a shock to realize that there was no European army: Europe had been discussed for so long that, in France as well as elsewhere, people had subconsciously formed the vague idea that Europe was a fact. Now, instead of European unity, they saw Britain marching in step with America, France following militarily while trying to take the initiative diplomatically, Germany barred by its constitution from sending a single soldier, and the Latin countries divided, with a number of anti-American demonstrations in Spain, for example.

This disunity, this powerlessness and ignorance merely underline how urgent it is for the European Community to choose its own model of capitalism. If it fails to do so, market forces will make the choice. This has already begun – badly.

We have noted how, beyond its superficial unity, present-day capitalism is divided into two profoundly distinct currents. Most European countries are closer to the Rhine model than to the neo-American model. But we have seen how the Rhine model is steadily retreating.

This can be seen particularly clearly in the development of the

European construction industry. Having been almost at a standstill for about 10 years, from the first oil crisis to the Fontainebleau summit of European Community leaders in 1984, the industry has started up again magnificently in the approach to the single market. But what will this market consist of? It is striking that though the French have keenly supported the project, its content has been largely inspired by Thatcherite concepts. Although the Germans have approved the steps towards economic and monetary union, their main concern has been to avoid damaging the stability of the German mark.

Now we have our backs to the wall. In the ongoing effort to define economic and monetary union on the one hand, and political union on the other, European leaders will have to decide between the radically opposing ideas revealed in two remarkable speeches delivered in Bruges. Should Europe be nothing more than a large market, as Margaret Thatcher argued in 1988, or should it be a social market economy, which would imply genuine federal power, as Jacques Delors urged the following year? That is the fundamental dilemma that is crucial to the destiny of the 340 million inhabitants of the European Community countries, and, indirectly, to that of the people of Central Europe and North Africa.

But among the 12 European Community countries, there is none for which the choice is as important as it is for France.

France's break with the tradition of Colbert

It is hard to know where to place France in the great struggle between the two forms of capitalism. That is what Professor Prodi, one of the world's shrewdest observers of French affairs, said in a particularly penetrating analysis published in the journal *Il Molino* (No. 1, 1991). The article by the former president of the IRI, the state holding company set up to rebuild Italy's heavy industry, was called 'Between Two Models'. It was an apposite title since Professor Prodi was discussing two distinct models of capitalism defined according to criteria very close to those used in this book. He wrote:

> France is one country that has never entirely opted for one model or the other. Its Stock Exchange and financial markets have traditionally played a modest role. The size of the Paris Bourse compared to that of London is plain and unquestionable proof of

that. On the other hand, France has not seen the creation of banking groups or of forms of ownership like those found in Germany. In France, state-owned corporations have always played a deciding role, and this applies both to industrial companies and to those involved in banking or insurance. Although the significance of developments in the eighties may not be clear, they are still worth looking at closely. In 1986, pressed by Jacques Chirac, the prime minister, Edouard Balladur, the finance minister, prepared a plan for the large-scale privatization of state-owned companies. Under this plan, 27 groups employing 500,000 people were to move into the private sector. As a result of the change of government that followed, the plan was only partly put into practice.

Nevertheless, eight large groups were transferred from the public to the private sector, and for the most part they were of enormous importance. They included Saint-Gobain, Paribas, CGE, Havas, Société Générale and Suez.

The immediate motives of this new French policy might suggest a movement towards the Anglo-Saxon model, in which priority is given to expanding the stock exchange by creating several million new shareholders. However, the importance given to this goal has been steadily reduced, because many of the new small shareholders have quickly sold their shares to make an immediate profit. The way in which these privatizations have been achieved, on the other hand, has paved the way for a movement towards the forms of ownership that are found in Germany. In all the privatized corporations there is a hard core which holds on to the power, even though it has only 25 per cent of the shares. Deals, made possible by an advanced information network, have progressively rationalised share ownership, such that some large financial and industrial groups are now forming in France. In terms of their ownership and their connections, these groups tend towards the Germanic rather than the Anglo-Saxon model, even though they are far less compact and watertight than those in Germany.

Moreover, France still has a large number of publicly-owned corporations which do not fit into either the Anglo-Saxon or the

Germanic system, even though in recent years the strategy of the French public corporations – particularly regarding the acquisition of companies in other countries – is inspired more by Germanic than by Anglo-Saxon logic.

In fact, these acquisitions have provoked strong reactions in Britain and elsewhere within the European Community because they have been interpreted not as the fruit of a commercial strategy, but as the instrument of a national strategy.

Why then does France, which for half a century has been so keen to promote its own model – the elusive 'third way' between capitalism and communism – now present such a blurred profile? There are two main reasons. The first is that the French have finally broken with a tradition which goes back to the mercantilist policies of Jean-Baptiste Colbert, Louis XIV's chief minister, in order to enter fully into the European and international economy; the second is that in making this transition they have borrowed as heavily from the Anglo-American model as from the German–Japanese one.

In the French tradition of social Colbertism, it is the state that directs the economy in order to fulfil political ambitions and achieve social progress. This tradition is now rapidly losing ground. The proof of this is the fast decline of the standing of the civil servant in French society – yesterday honored and envied, today often held in low esteem – and the simultaneous ascent of the celebrity capitalist. On the first point, it is worth noting that in Japan two people of similar age and qualifications can expect to earn about the same, even if one works in the private sector and the other in the public sector. Also, teachers are better paid than other public employees because their job, in this Confucian country where learning is a virtue, is seen as a noble one. For the Japanese, teaching is a life-long vocation, not a job. The social standing given to teachers is a guarantee that children will be well taught.

Nevertheless France is still characterised by an omnipresent central state. On the political level, despite decentralisation, government from the center, which dates back to the Jacobins, is still the norm. There is nothing like the federal-type organizations which dominate in Germany, America and Switzerland and which act at local level. In France, the state remains at the forefront. In Germany, for example, much of the industrial aid on offer is distributed by the Länder, or regional governments. The board of the Bundesbank is in any case made up mainly of Länder representatives who take little notice of the great movements of international finance and even less of the opinions of Bonn.

As for the economy, it is a mistake to think that in 1991 France is still the classic planned economy, merely because it has important nationalised industries. In fact, there is a sharp distinction between public monopolies such as the electricity and gas industries, the railways and the national savings association, on the one hand, and national corporations, both industrial and financial, on the other, which trade internationally and which, for 15 years at least, have been run according to the principles of open competition.

In technology, however, the public sector has retained its dominance over most of the research organizations (such as those dealing with nuclear energy and fuels, medical and scientific research etc.). The situation is quite different in both the Anglo-American and Rhine models, where it is mainly private companies and universities that carry out research, though they often do so with public money.

More than any other capitalist country, France has long had a powerful state at the heart of society, a state that has always taken the economy under its wing: protecting and planning on the one hand, but on the other investing and creating in the spirit of Saint Simon, the social philosopher who promoted the development of industry and science.

The opposition between the two models of capitalism is reflected in two equally distinct models of trade unionism. The Anglo-American trade unions have always rejected the notion of social partnership, refusing to participate in company decision-making or to accept co-responsibility. They maintain this refusal by confining themselves to issues of pay and conditions, as in the USA, or by acting as a political force, as in Britain, where trade unions support the Labour Party and combat capitalism from the outside, in an approach that owes as much to anarchism as to interventionism.

In contrast, trade unions in the Rhine countries (which have strongly influenced those of Japan) have opted for integration with the employers. They collaborate in order to compete: in these countries, each trade unionist is like a member of a football team, whose main motivation is the wish to help the team win.

French trade unionism has been influenced too much by Marxism and the ideology of class struggle to belong to either camp. Caught between the pincers of a Colbertist state and a broadly Marxist workforce, French capitalism has long wavered between authoritarianism and mob rule. The results of the latter can be seen in the figures on wage inflation and the devaluations of the franc. The authoritarian strain manifests itself particularly in the absolute monarchy within companies: the all-powerful managing director is not a German idea, but a very French one. While the Rhine countries constantly demonstrate that collective management is more efficient, France still puts its faith in Napoleon's belief that one mediocre general can command an army better than two outstanding ones.

All of which helps to explain why market forces and free enterprise have for so long been distrusted in France, and why profit was until very recently seen as a cardinal sin. It is hard to believe now that in *The American Challenge*, which appeared in 1967 – 5 years into Georges Pompidou's conservative government – Jean-Jacques Servan-Schreiber was moved to protest that 'all that is private – private enterprise, private property, private initiative – having been associated once and for all with Evil, everything that is public is seen as Good'.

The socialist government must take the credit for having cured France – deliberately or otherwise – of its inhibitions and for having reasserted the basic values of a market economy.

It remains the case, however, that for more than 30 years France has remained radically estranged from the two models of capitalism, each of which ascribes crucial importance to these values. In the case of America, that is self-evident. As for Germany, it must be remembered that the *Sozialmarktwirtschaft* is above all a market economy, in which the State merely makes up for the market's most glaring deficiencies without either intervening directly or distorting free competition.

Another distinguishing feature of the French economy is the financial system, and the way in which companies are controlled. In this area French capitalism differs from both the neo-American and the Rhine models. The Stock Exchange in France has nothing like the importance that it has in the USA. General de Gaulle used to say: 'French politics is not decided on the trading floor.' Indeed company financing was largely done by the banks and by the treasury and its associated bodies. The percentage of company cash movements that went through the banks was 90 per cent throughout the 1960s, the 1970s and right up to 1985. Despite that, capitalism in France is significantly different from German 'bank capitalism', which depends upon the links between banks and industry. No financial institution in France can boast anything like the influence of the Bundesbank. There are still a number of very powerful capitalist families in France; not, perhaps, on the same scale as in Italy, where two-thirds of the share capital listed on the Milan Stock Exchange involves family companies, but the importance of family capitalism is still manifest in such first-rate French companies as Michelin, Peugeot, Pinault, DMC, Dassault, CGIP etc.

French capitalism, which remains hard to classify, has for a long time given the impression that it is trying to find its way, or even battling against the current within Europe. At the beginning of the 1980s, after the left came to power, it went through an interventionist phase. Then in 1983 it did a U-turn and took the Anglo-American route with the zeal of the converted – a zeal which did not weaken, but rather the opposite, during the 'cohabitation' period of 1986–88, when the country had a conservative prime minister and a socialist president.

France's double conversion

But what sort of conversion was it exactly? It is hard to say. Monetary policy was borrowed from Germany and everything else from Britain.

By 1991 it could be confidently predicted that the French rate of inflation would be about the same as Germany's. Ten years previously, there had been a persistent 10-point difference. The improvement is the result of a steady and exemplary effort begun by Jacques Delors, continued by Edouard Balladur, and for which Pierre Bérégovoy will certainly claim most of the credit. Behind this policy of the strong franc (to which everyone now pays homage) there have been innumerable decisions, starting with the abolition of price controls for services as well as products, and ending with the introduction of free movement of capital on July 1st 1990. I remember, about 2 years before this, telling an important Paris banker that the decision had just been taken to abolish exchange controls on that date. He was incredulous, saying it would be impossible for the French franc to resist the outward flow of capital that would immediately be triggered.

It is to the influence of Britain – and, it must be said, to the rivalry with the City of London – that the extraordinary financial deregulation process must be attributed. It began in 1984 with the removal of barriers separating the interbank, securities and mortgage markets, the ending of the stockbrokers' monopoly on trading, the strengthening of the Stock Exchange regulatory commission (which has acquired a full set of very sharp teeth), and finally, the development of the financial futures market, which has overtaken its London counterpart by attracting considerable foreign business, notably from Germany.

The volume of business on the stock exchange has increased by a factor of 25 in just 7 years (from FF 124 billion in 1980 to nearly FF 3.1 trillion in 1987), and the rate of turnover of the most active shares has multiplied 50 times in the same period. In the company that I run, for example, the level of stock rotation went from 12 per cent to 123 per cent between 1980 and 1987. Ten years ago, securities management consisted of receiving the coupons and waiting for the payment date. Financial engineering has become so sophisticated that in the AGF Group, for example, a capital share changes hands every few minutes.

The new rich and the new poor

The new rich are those involved in the financial sector as it strives to emulate its British rival. The new poor are at the other end of society, as the extremes of wealth drift inexorably apart, American-style.

At the end of the 30-year post-war boom, inequalities had visibly narrowed in France. Two figures illustrate this trend. The first measures the gap in income between the poorest 10 per cent of the French population and the richest: in 1970, the latter group earned 3.12 times more than the former. This was an all-time low. The second figure measures the concentration of national wealth. The richest 10 per cent held 65 per cent in 1960 and only 54 per cent in 1985. Again, the reduction in inequality was significant.

Since 1984, however, we have witnessed a reversal of this trend. The income gap was back up to 3.2 per cent by 1988. As for the wealthy, thanks to the surge in property and share prices, they have seen their capital grow much faster than ordinary earned income.

In this respect France is a long way behind the USA, where the

Department of Commerce calculated that between 1980 and 1989, company directors' pay increased by 260 per cent, while that of employees rose by only 50 per cent.

These figures reveal profound social changes. For example, there is an American-inspired tendency to decide each employee's pay individually, and to enforce what is called 'greater flexibility'. Companies are ensuring that they apply principles of neo-liberalism to the workforce just as they are applied to other production factors. An employee's annual pay will thus reflect his individual efficiency, or what economists call marginal productivity.

That is not simply a change in methods. It is the expression of a logical process of growing inequality which results from supposedly 'natural' laws. The rich need no longer feel ashamed of their wealth.

SOURCE: Plantu, *Des fourmis dans les jambes*, La Découverte/Le Monde, 1989, p. 99. (Reproduced with permission.)

Where they once shunned any hint of ostentation, they now display it with an immodesty that the French used to consider shockingly vulgar when they witnessed it in Americans. And this wealth increasingly rubs shoulders with a new poverty of the kind that is flourishing in the USA. France, too, now has its zones of urban blight, dumping-grounds populated by a growing army of the unemployed, those whose benefit has run out, young people seeking their first job, and immigrants – illegal or otherwise. As in America, there are sporadic charitable efforts which step in where the state has failed: soup kitchens – something the French thought had vanished forever – reappeared during the 1980s, at the same time as the expressions 'polarized society' and 'the new poor' became common. Inevitably, a Minister of State was appointed to direct the massive task of improving conditions in deprived urban areas.

The open sore of run-down, crime-ridden neighborhoods in America is an obvious result of the state's enforced impoverishment and its abdication of social responsibility. In France too, now that social Colbertism has been put to flight, the question arises: surely the most eminent among these 'new poor' is the state itself?

The evidence for this is not just the peeling paint and broken-down lifts, but rather the French aversion for public service. Not long ago, to take on public office was a noble thing, and recruitment by means of competitive examinations made it an option widely available to ordinary people. Today public servants are held in low esteem. Ridiculed and demoralised, they are, above all, badly paid. Nobility has been conferred on dealers, on winners, on whoever can make a killing ('killing' having become something positive and desirable). These sought-after 'killings' are an obvious sign of how strongly American values have taken root in France.

Even the French postal service is no longer very efficient. It is much worse in the USA, where private mail is one of the fastest growing industries. The owner of the leading company in this field recently went to Switzerland intending to buy a second home. He came back disgusted, saying: 'Switzerland is not the place for me: the public postal service there is the best in the world.'

The choice between the neo-American model and the Rhine model is no abstraction: it will even determine how our mail is delivered!

France needs the Rhine model

Let us go back to basics. The role of the company is now so important, and at times controversial – particularly in France – that it is time to put before the public, and the appropriate authorities, a proposed 'declaration of the rights and duties of companies' like that which Jacques de Fouchier, President emeritus of Paribas, and Alexandre de Juniac have already outlined for the European Parliament.

The Rhine model responds quite well to this search for balance between companies' rights and their duties. It embodies, on the one hand, capitalism which can provide social security, and on the other, a system in which the company is seen not just as a heap of capital but as a group of people. This is exactly what France badly needs.

Undoubtedly, the reason we have heard so much over the years about problems with social security, hospitals and pensions is that France, unlike the other developed countries, has barely started dealing with them; and yet we have just discussed how another problem, equally daunting for democratic governments, has been dealt with – the management of a strong currency. Another reason why these problems have attracted so much attention is that the steady advance of the neo-American model, whose public acceptance depends largely on tax cuts, inevitably means a weakening of the protection provided by the social security system. France has been unwilling to consent to this. In another chapter, we will see what would happen if it were suddenly decided that the French would pay no more tax than the Americans.

Apart from the need to maintain social cover, France needs the Rhine model to strengthen the capacity and financial stability of its companies. Following the Anglo-American example, the restructuring of industry has recently gathered speed, with mergers and takeovers becoming bigger and more frequent. In 1986 they amounted to FF 61 billion, in 1987 to FF 165 billion, and nearly doubling in the following year to FF 306 billion.

Only a tiny proportion of these operations resulted from takeover bids, to which the French (like the Germans and Japanese) are allergic. It is perhaps in France that the term 'takeover bid' has the most negative connotation, being automatically associated with the law of the jungle. Restrictions on takeover bids are explicitly aimed at protecting the interests of minority shareholders against so-called dawn raiders. This is no doubt partly the result of the media attention lavished on two bids in particular, that of Suez for Compagnie Industrielle in 1989 and the Paribas bid for Compagnie de Navigation Mixte in 1990.

Takeovers, whether of French firms by foreign companies or vice versa, have virtually never been followed by asset stripping. On the whole, their objectives have been genuinely constructive, aiming for the kind of industrial restructuring that is necessary in the run-up to the Single European Market.

In this regard the industrial company that has succeeded most brilliantly is probably the Schneider group. In 1982 it was a non-specialized company largely dependent on state orders and subsidies, and it posted a deficit of FF 350 million on a stock market value of FF 250 million.

In less than 10 years, Schneider dispensed with its loss-making divisions and began to concentrate its activities on electricity, becoming the world's number one distributor and the leader in electrical automation, ahead of such companies as Westinghouse, General Electric, Siemens and Mitsubishi. By 1990 its stock market value had increased sixtyfold.

This extraordinary turnabout was only possible thanks to more than 50 acquisitions, which were all agreed amicably, except in the case of Télémécanique. In 1988, Schneider launched a particularly controversial bid for Télémécanique, an outstanding company that was cited as an example of participation by workers in both management and funding. I confess that at the time I was sorry things had to be done so speedily. If it had been happening in Germany or Switzerland, the business would have been handled more gently, with bankers as intermediaries. But in the end this restructuring was imposed in Télémécanique's own interest: the company is now in a much stronger position in the world market than it was at that time.

In the spring of 1991 Schneider launched another remarkable takeover bid on the American company Square D, which was shielded by particularly protectionist statutes in force in the state of Delaware. These gave the intended victim a whole cupboard full of poison pills with which to defend its independence. Also, to comply with anti-trust laws, Schneider had to send to the USA more than a ton of documents, all of them translated into English. Yet throughout the bid most share-holders were in favor of the buyer. Schneider raised its initial offer, and since everything in America has a price, the president of Square D shamelessly announced that he had struck a good deal.

Europe's version of the Japanese zaibatsu

If France wants to move towards a system that combines the perfor-mance and social solidarity of the Rhine model, it must take account of the new paradox that goes against our received wisdom: the power of banks and insurance companies has become indispensable to any attempt to wed economic efficiency to social justice. Roger Fauroux said simply, 'I am in favor of the German model, because their finance is at the service of industry'.

France has a deficiency that is rarely acknowledged: it lacks depend-able, stable shareholders. For shareholders to give their loyalty, it has to be in their interests to do so. At the moment it is not, because the tax advantages of mutual funds, which are judged on their short-term per-formance, have the effect of moving the small investor's money about – which in turn tends to favor takeover bids. To give small investors and fund managers a renewed desire to support sound, long-term strategies, the old long-term savings accounts would have to be revived. These would be confined to shares in European Community companies; a shareholder would be able to buy and sell shares on account without paying capital gains tax, provided the total investment on the account was not reduced. In the same way the shareholder would be exempt (within a limit that would have to be fixed) from paying wealth surtax. This would give the investor the same advantage currently enjoyed by the head of a company who owns more than 25 per cent of the shares and need not declare this as capital for purposes of surtax.

As far as companies are concerned, it would be sensible to follow Germany's example by increasing taxation on undistributed profits, and by taxing dividends paid on paper more than dividends paid in cash. Such policies have been shown to stabilise shareholding and to curb the market forces that encourage immediate profit-taking.

All this would allow the great financial institutions to raise more funds in order to invest them, at their own risk, in the form of capital or long-term loans, as they do in Japan and Germany.

That is why Jean-Yves Haberer, president of the Credit Lyonnais bank, has become an advocate of the German-style multi-purpose 'universal' bank. It is striking that in the great debate going on in the USA on the banking reform plan drawn up by the Treasury in 1991, the main question is whether this reform should be along German and Japanese lines. The argument that stands out in this affair is the one put forward by the opponents of any such innovation: given that in the USA bank deposits are guaranteed by the federal government, a universal bank system would increase the risks run by the federal insurance scheme, which is already on the verge of collapse.

France's national business institute published a study in January 1991 entitled 'Strategies for capital and share ownership' which came to the implicit, though quite clear, conclusion that France needs to move towards the Rhine model in order to strengthen its worryingly vulnerable capitalist structure. Since 1990, the fashion for takeover bids has given way to one for marriages of convenience and internal reorganization. Nevertheless, the weakness of company share capital and the volatility of institutional investment, dominated by unit trusts and investment pools, has the effect of making share ownership as unstable as it is in America. The 40 or so well-qualified people who contributed to this study stated: 'The publication of monthly performance tables has the same effect on unit trust managers as the publication of quarterly results has on managers of American companies: they impose a short-sighted attitude, which in France leads to a fast rotation of portfolios. Unit trusts are gradually replacing individual small shareholders, who until recently would keep their blue chip stocks for a lifetime before passing them on to their children.'

The institute demanded the usual tax incentives to stabilise share ownership and went on, remarkably, to propose that France should completely copy the Rhine model. It advocated company laws requiring supervisory boards and tribunals, in order to ensure a balance between the power of shareholders and that of management; it also called for statutory limitations on voting rights for single shareholders and on the use of dual votes, although it noted that these two proposals go against the fifth Brussels directive (of Anglo-American inspiration).

In that case, some might say, France must be wary of Europe and of the European Commission's ideas, but that is the opposite of the truth.

Although a number of the technical standpoints taken by the Commission on industrial and financial matters are inspired more by the Anglo-American model than by the Rhine model, that is simply because Brussels was never given the chance to plan a social market economy under the authority of a European federal organization. Rather, it was asked to devise a Single Market for goods and services which, unless it is accompanied by a strengthening of the network of European financial institutions, will inevitably become a market controlled by companies.

In such a market, the company is seen as an item of merchandise. That is why France is veering towards the Anglo-American model, even though its political tradition, its social aspirations and the demands of its financial make-up should be nudging it towards the Rhine model. Why is it going in the opposite direction to the one it wants to go, and should go? Simply because these matters are now way beyond the scope of a single state, and one state cannot hope to deal with them. As soon as the economy of the developed world began to cross borders at high speed, the individual state was out of the game, whatever its politics.

It is almost futile to look to the state for improved social policies. There is virtually nothing the state can do. If the aim is to harness capitalism without impairing its efficiency, it is no longer to the nation state that we must look, but to Europe. And Europe must produce both powerful financial structures – its own answer to the Japanese family-run corporations called zaibatsu – and political institutions for which the European Coal and Steel Community (ECSC) is the model that is too often forgotten.

The ECSC, a European prototype for the Rhine model

The life and works of the economist Jean Monnet explain a great deal about the recent evolution of the Anglo-American model and the dominant influence it has had on the European Community.

The small-time brandy merchant who became a great banker was a man who shared the values of Roosevelt, Truman and Kennedy. He was firmly in favor of a market economy and did more than anyone to get France away from protectionism and into international free trade. On a personal level, he was capitalist enough to refuse any payment from the state when he was appointed head of the planning ministry, so that he could be sure of remaining completely independent. Nevertheless he had a specifically Rhine conception of the market economy. He could not conceive of one that was not a social market economy.

What he accomplished at the planning ministry is proof of this – particularly his setting up in 1952 of the ECSC, precursor of the European Community, with its 'High Authority' (a name that gives pause for thought).

Initially the idea was to create a common market with completely free trading in the two products that armed Europe during the war: coal and steel.

At the same time, though, it was necessary to modernize Europe's iron ore and coal mines, which were less and less able to compete with overseas suppliers. Because modernisation would inevitably reduce the workforce, a grave social problem was clearly on the horizon. To resolve it, Jean Monnet got the six founding countries of the ECSC to agree on the need for an institution that today sounds almost mythical: the 'High Authority'. This authority was granted wide statutory and fiscal powers with a double aim: to encourage investments in increased productivity and to finance a pro-active social policy.

What could be more contrary to the philosophy of Ronald Reagan and Margaret Thatcher than a European tax and a European 'High Authority' to decide the fate of mines and steelworks?

It is a particularly interesting topic now that the American and British steel industries are in deep trouble, while the French giant Sacilor has been beating world records for productivity and profits.

These powers – and the very idea of a 'High Authority' – alarmed governments, who feared that some of their sovereignty would be lost to European institutions. That is why the Treaty of Rome, signed in 1957, gave far fewer powers to Community institutions. The Commission in Brussels, so often accused of wielding too much power, is actually a very toned-down version of the 'High Authority'. In particular, it has practically no responsibility or power over industrial policy – indeed, even the phrase itself has been banned. The Commission's vice-president, Martin Bangemann (former West German Minister for the Economy), provoked an uproar when he used it in a document on the crisis affecting the European electronics industry – a crisis we are sure to hear a great deal more of, incidentally. By the year 2000 electronics will be the most important global industry and will constitute 10 per cent of the gross domestic product of Japan, for example. Yet the present crisis in European electronics was foreseen at least 25 years ago. The European Council of Ministers had been warned as early as 1965 by one of its vice-presidents that this sector was particularly vulnerable, and that its decline was an absolute certainty in the absence of concerted action by the Community. His warning was in vain: the Common Market did not concern itself with industrial crises. So it was left to Japan to take up Mr. Colonna's ideas: MITI launched its celebrated robotics program, which put Japan ahead of the world in the field of electronics. The USA is doing the same in other ways: the Pentagon's military research budget is equal to the total spent on research and development in Japan.

In Europe, meanwhile, progress towards the Single Market continues, but there is no institution able to raise European competitiveness in the great technologies of the future. There is a choice of routes now: one leads to a genuine Europe and the other leads to a collection of nations that happen to be neighbors. The latter route is the one that most member states have chosen, despite the Commission's warnings. It has led to the grave situation in which the last three European electrical component manufacturers, Philips, SGS Thomson and Siemens, find themselves. The proof lies in the fact that ICL in Britain has fallen prey to the Japanese, Olivetti in Italy to the Americans, and in France Bull had no option but to accept an infusion of capital from NEC of Japan.

Because of the European Community's failure to follow the ECSC's example, each of these companies has carried on down the wrong turning at the European crossroads, playing the role of national leader right up to the moment when there was no alternative to becoming American or Japanese.

A community, or twelve competing tax havens?

The general agreement among member states to prevent the Community from playing a proper European role in technology and industry is only the most visible aspect of the Community's movement towards the Thatcherite model.

To put that into perspective, it is worth looking at the conclusions of a report produced for the Commission in 1987 by a group of experts led by Tomaso Padoa Schiopa, head of the Bank of Italy. The content of the report is perfectly clear and boils down to these words: efficiency, stability and fairness.

Economic efficiency, as this book has constantly pointed out, results from market mechanisms. It is thanks to the Common Market and the planned Single Market that the countries of Western Europe should between now and the year 2000 overtake the living standards of America – provided exchange rates remain normal.

Monetary stability, thanks to the single European Monetary System (EMS), will contribute to this growth, particularly if it results in a genuine economic and monetary union in which none of the 12 member states will initially be compelled to join. The Bundesbank must stop trotting out the argument that convergence of economic and monetary policies is an essential pre-condition for union: it is just as well that German unification did not have to wait for the systems of East and West Germany to converge.

Fairness, or social justice, remains. This has only a limited connection with monetary stability: certainly, inflation further impoverishes the poor and adds to the wealth of the rich, but beating inflation is not enough to prevent inequality from growing. On the contrary, it is a basic principle that market forces draw their efficiency from these very inequalities.

In order to combat them, government must supplement private and charitable initiatives by redistributing resources. This is becoming more and more difficult for two reasons. We have seen how states are being sidelined, not by the Common Market, but by the globalization of the economy, which in the short term means that a country's ability to compete economically depends on the reduction of its public expenditure and ultimately on the impoverishment of the state. Yet there is really nothing at the European level to take the place of states which have been bypassed by globalised capitalism and turned into provinces. And it is this institutional void that is dragging the EC from the crossroads towards a Thatcherite destination.

The most significant example of this, and the one that concerns us all, is the way taxation has evolved in Europe.

What is the European tradition? Since the beginning of this century it has essentially been that the poor should pay less and the rich more. That is the principle of progressive taxation which gradually spread from the Scandinavian countries towards the Latin countries.

Mrs. Thatcher's idea of taxation is quite the opposite of this. The most spectacular illustration of the Thatcherite approach was her reform of local government taxation. In Britain, as in other European countries, this tax was not a progressive tax, in that it did not depend on income. However, everyone paid according to the rentable value of their home, so that the rich, who generally had good houses, paid more than the poor who were not so well housed. Mrs. Thatcher announced that this was unfair because the poor did not take up a smaller share of public expenditure than the rich – quite the opposite, in fact – ergo, they should pay at least as much. The poll tax was introduced, with everyone from the duke to the chauffeur paying the same. The subsequent popular revolt forced Mrs. Thatcher's successors to act quickly in abolishing the hated tax, so that such an excessive affront to the majority of the population might be forgotten as soon as possible.

That is a well-known story. But what is less well known is that it is being repeated on a much wider scale all over the European Community and in a more critical area than local government taxation: that of capital gains and capital earnings.

If you are French, living in France and the owner of French bonds, the issuer gives the tax authority the details of the coupons you have received, on which you have to pay a tax of 17 per cent (above a certain threshold). If, however, you own foreign stock, the coupons will not be declared by the issuer. Certainly, despite the ending of exchange controls, you should declare them yourself – but if you do not, the risk you are taking is infinitesimal. That is why in February 1989 the Commission proposed to introduce a 15 per cent deduction at source on all stock bought by European Community residents. A report by the research group CEPII, published in 1991 and entitled 'Towards a European Tax System', said: 'The Federal Republic of Germany, which had agreed (in a spirit of European solidarity) to make deductions at source from January 1989, stopped doing so the following June, following massive outflows of capital, often into Luxemburg. This failure sounded the death knell for the Commission's project and zero deductions are gradually becoming the norm.'

Who benefits from these zero deductions? Those who own stocks and bonds – the most privileged section of the population. Other things being equal, if the rich pay less, it follows that the poor must pay more – as was the case with Mrs. Thatcher's poll tax. Most European governments find that unfair, but majorities count for little in the European Community because, in financial matters, the rule of unanimity applies, supposedly as a safeguard of national sovereignty. In other words, nothing can be decided without Luxemburg's agreement, and it is because of Luxemburg that the other 11 states have set off down the road to being a tax haven. Margaret Thatcher is no longer in power, but she can be proud of the influence she still exerts over taxation in the European Community. Her legacy amounts to a kind of generalised poll tax on the thing that matters most in capitalism: capital itself.

This is but one of many indications that the Single Market, unless it leads rapidly to true political union, will turn Europe into a sort of American subsystem, with a lot less state and a lot more market, an outcome that would delight Margaret Thatcher and distress Jacques Delors. At the crossroads of Europe in 1992, it is difficult to imagine two ideas further apart than theirs. A crucial part of France's future depends on the choice that must be made between them.

Ronald Reagan and Margaret Thatcher built their popularity largely on the promise to cut taxes. At the national level they succeeded only partially; the European Community may actually go one step further than either Reagan or Thatcher in instituting a 'competition of rules' (rather than the rule of competition) whereby, on the face of it, the state that can operate most cheaply and make the fewest demands will have the advantage.

Chapter 13
Conclusion

Having dissected a problem from top to bottom, the author of any economic study is tempted to conclude with a barrage of advice. It is so easy to put forward a few recipes for reform, just vague enough to be unarguable, and appeal to everyone's better instincts to 'do the right thing' in future. In my previous works I have so often denounced this facile approach (the one that begins, 'All we have to do is. . .') that I am not about to start indulging in it now. I am too confident of the persuasive power of the facts and the force of reason alone to feel any need for a final flourish of rhetorical eloquence. The facts in this book, it seems to me, speak for themselves. Capitalism has vanquished its only comparable rival: that is obvious; its undisputed authority makes it dangerous: that, too, is plain to see. The existence of two differing, and opposing, models of capitalism has been demonstrated beyond reasonable doubt, and the ascendancy of the less efficient, more aggressive of the two variants is, I believe, a clear and present danger. My principal objective in writing this book has been to point out just how dangerous it has become.

In seeking to present my case, however, I do not wish to overstate it by ignoring certain facts that may not quite fit the overall picture. It would be wrong to pretend that the past decade or so has not brought its share of good news as well as bad. After all, the collapse of communism is a triumph for democracy; the all-conquering market and the rise of economic interdependence and world trade has certainly meant greater prosperity for millions of people. Perhaps never before has the global economy provided so generously for so many. The retreat of centralised planning, bureaucratic meddling and the empty ideological slogans of state socialism has truly given wings to individual initiative and creativity – even in Reagan's America and Thatcher's Britain. No, the 'new conservative revolution' has not been all bad, far from it. The balance-sheet of our era will undoubtedly show that greater individual freedom and mobility, a more dynamic entrepreneurial spirit and a keener sense of competitiveness are all precious assets, not liabilities. The American dream that continues to fascinate whole populations in all parts of the world, the magnetic pull of a Western lifestyle for millions of men and women in the East and the South – these cannot entirely be put down to mass hallucination or a well-orchestrated 'media event'. There is no reason to think that the Hungarians and Albanians who look longingly to Chicago and New York are wholly deluded; if Lech Walesa goes from his royal audience at Buckingham Palace to a meeting with Margaret Thatcher, it is not because he is a simpleton. For us, the advances and advantages of the last 10 years can be difficult to gauge, because they have come to us more gradually, almost naturally.

The preceding remarks are not meant to be incidental; they are fundamental to an understanding of capitalism today. But they are not enough. For, despite its recent successes, its undisputed victories, its solid record of achievement, capitalism is well and truly in peril of being blown off course. Its current drift into dangerous waters is what this book attempts to describe; moreover, I hope to have shown that this is not merely a temporary loss of bearings but is part of a larger pattern in the world economy – a pattern which reveals a fundamental break with the history to date of the industrialized world. It is a momentous change, and I doubt that we have yet grasped its full import.

The three ages of capitalism

In order to explain myself more fully, I will take the risk of simplifying the picture at this point. My view is that capitalism, in its relations with the state, has gone through a three-staged metamorphosis over the last two centuries. We have just recently entered – almost without realising it – the third phase.

1791: Capitalism against the state

The first stage is dated from 1791 in homage to a French law passed in that year. The Le Chapelier law was perhaps the most important piece of economic legislation to come out of the French Revolution: it abolished the old corporatist guilds and syndicates, and freed trade and industry from the grip of the monarchist state. For the next hundred years, progress was continuous and spectacular. The state was made subordinate to the rule of law; a genuine civil service took shape, and official corruption became the exception rather than rule; above all, the prerogatives of the state were rolled back as market forces began to prevail. The state returned to its primary role as the agent of law enforcement, responsible for keeping the 'dangerous classes' (i.e. the new industrial proletariat) in order, and in their place. It was the age of a new 'exploitation of man by man', of the insidious decline of the peasantry and traditional rural life, of working-class oppression and the appalling hardships of the industrial revolution.

By 1848, all of these ills were glaring enough to be exposed and denounced by Karl Marx in a brief pamphlet entitled The Communist Manifesto. And by 1891 the religious establishment had entered the fray: Protestant and (especially) Roman Catholic thinkers had set themselves the task of proposing a Christian alternative – cooperation between capital and labor – to the Marxist remedy of class struggle. In that year, Leo XIII published the encyclical *Rerum Novarum*. Its call for the state to ensure the just treatment of workers was to prove enormously influential in the moulding of twentieth century capitalism, and it still has a prophetic ring about it today.

1891: Capitalism disciplined by the state

In this second phase, a multiplicity of reforms were undertaken, all of which had the same goal: to correct the excesses of unregulated capitalism, to temper the more violent side of its nature. The state became the advocate of the poor and the only sure defense against the seemingly arbitrary and unfair workings of the free market. Governments everywhere – often goaded into action by labor movements – applied themselves to the task of humanising and moderating the 'raw' form of capitalism. Laws and decrees were issued, working conditions were regulated, wage bargaining was encouraged, taxation was increased and made more redistributive. America was slow to join the rush to legislate on 'working-class issues', which did not burn quite so fiercely there until the Great Depression of the 1930s; thereafter, from Roosevelt to Carter (via Kennedy and Johnson, notably), the USA kept pace with the European drive to discipline capitalism (although it did not go so far as to create a post-war welfare state).

During most of this hundred-year phase which saw the rise of the state, capitalism was not so much evolving at its own pace as reacting to – lest we forget – competition; its communist rival had assigned itself the high moral and ethical ground, and claimed to have cornered the market on hope and a brighter future. It takes a concerted effort now to recall just how strong the pressure exerted by communism once was. Thirty years ago, François Perroux, one of France's most subtle economists, wrote that 'capitalism has been so disfigured by attack and so insidiously brought into disrepute that, for many if not most people, it is the enemy of all mankind. Those who wish to go on criticising it may do so without fear, for they are merely preaching to the converted; those who dare to defend it are instantly banished from the court of received opinion and must do their preaching in the wilderness' (*Le Capitalisme*, F. Perroux, 'Que sais-je?', 1962).

1991: Capitalism instead of the state

For the last 10 years or so, the tendency has reversed. Having tried so hard to mould the economy and regulate its behaviour, the state was in danger of suffocating it. Too much discipline was paralysing the market, and ordinary people simply got fed up with the Kafkaesque bureaucracy that seemed to dog their every step. Mrs. Thatcher was helped to power by the 'Winter of Discontent' (1978–79), when a series of public sector strikes (notably by the ambulance drivers) brought the Labour government into thorough disrepute. Priorities had changed.

The state was no longer seen as a protector or organizer but as a parasite, a strait-jacket, a dead weight on the economy. This third phase of capitalism, initiated by Mrs. Thatcher's triumph in 1979, came into full bloom with Ronald Reagan's 1980 election victory – but it has taken us more than a decade to realize that neither event was a quirk of domestic politics or a routine change of government. This time, a whole new ideology of capitalism had come to power.

Its essential principles are well known and can be summed up in a few words: the market is good, the state is bad; social welfare provision,

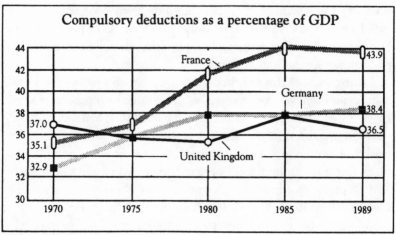

SOURCE: OCDE.

once a sign of progress, is blamed for encouraging laziness; taxation, once an indispensable means for reconciling economic development and social justice, is accused (not without reason) of discouraging talent and initiative. The powers and privileges of the state must therefore be reduced, by cutting taxes and social insurance contributions and by deregulating business and industry – only then will society recover its creative energy. Where the nineteenth century saw capitalism challenge the state, but with no thought of replacing it in such areas as health, education or the media (because hospitals, schools and newspapers were already in the private sector), the late twentieth century now proposes to substitute market forces for the state. And so it shall be: in the majority of developed countries, more and more services, from broadcasting to rubbish collection and from the water supply to the post office, are being transferred from the public to the private sector.

Before 1991, it was still possible to suppose that the 'conservative revolution' might be a temporary break, a passing phase, one more fashion among many. Many Europeans took this view, and mocked Reaganism and Thatcherism to their heart's content. The latter is, indeed, undergoing something of a (perhaps cosmetic) transformation in the hands of John Major, notably in the case of the poll tax. But on the other side of the Atlantic, Reaganism is solidly ensconced in its position of authority.

The Gulf War, the 'genius' of General Schwarzkopf and the triumphant homecoming of the troops (followed by a rise in the dollar) seem to have banished the last shadow of America's doubts about itself. More than ever, the USA believes its own form of capitalism to be the best system in the world; and it is not alone in this belief. This is a crucial point. It is because not only Americans but virtually everybody else as well is convinced of the success of the conservative revolution, and is busily trying to emulate it, that a fundamental historical turning-point has been reached.

One glance at the ex-communist countries makes the point with added irony. No one there has ever heard of the social market economy or the Rhine model. The Poles, for example, lost no time in setting up the Warsaw Stock Exchange (in the former premises of the Communist Party), and Lech Walesa trumpets the ultra-liberal doctrine of the Chicago school from one end of Europe to the other – but they have yet to create a banking system worthy of the name.

Then look at the developing world: prior to the advent of Reaganism, it was taken for granted that any significant progress towards development would have to involve vigorous governmental action, following the example of Japan and South Korea. But the great success stories of the past decade, such as Chile, Mexico and Thailand, are all devotees of deregulation and privatisation. And there is certainly no denying that whereas the Rhine model works supremely well in Europe, transposing it (in its social democratic variant) to the developing world can be a hazardous exercise. Too often it has been the alibi for the proliferation of ruinous public expenditure and government manipulation of the economy, both of which are a powerful stimulant to corruption. Some pruning of public spending and government deficits, some cutting back on taxation, some privatising and deregulating may actually work wonders, however difficult it may seem at the time.

Now, turning to Europe, we are about to enter the Single Market – essentially a Reaganite construct – whose double-barrelled leitmotiv could be 'maximum competition, minimum state intervention'. The social consequences of the Single Market are certain to be profound and long-lasting, for in the absence of any political union to accompany (and discipline) it, each of the twelve member countries, of whatever political stripe, will feel increasing pressure to boost its economic competitiveness. They will do so, inevitably, by withdrawing resources from the state and, following the Reagan recipe, taxing the rich rather less and the poor rather more. This is already under way. In a few years, moreover, the new managers and directors of European companies will be those same students who today, in every university and business school, are being taught that all of this is the lesson of the past and the way of the future.

For 100 years or so, the forces of democracy and the nation state had gradually caged and tamed capitalism, and now the tables have turned. Divided and disunited, the nation states and their puny borders can offer no real resistance to the globalised capitalist economy. In 1991, this much is obvious. Capitalism intends to tame the state; eventually, it hopes to do without it altogether.

Capitalism's third stage has been characterised by prosperity and a new energy, as we have seen. But it has also brought distress, and even despair, to some sections of society. The new conservatives would have us believe that all the measures introduced over the past 100 years to provide social cover were in fact anti-economic aberrations; they would ask us to accept that the industrialized nations must now become jungles of dog-eat-dog competition and naked greed if they are to be fit for the twenty-first century. No sector will be spared, and no one will be 'nannied', in this harsh new world. Incredibly, there is almost no argument over this assertion! It has somehow already taken root and displaced 'passé' notions of solidarity and social justice. The Rhine model, whose virtues and superior performance I have tried to portray in these pages, holds no allure in 1991. It has no more status than some unmarried cousin from the provinces in dowdy attire, laden down with old-fashioned moral scruples and 'afflicted' with the laughable virtues of prudence, patience and compassion. Should the visitor be mugged in the mean streets of New Dodge City, no Boy Scouts will come to the rescue: they, too, are down at the Crazy Horse Saloon whooping it up.

If there is one thing, finally, that infuriates me as I conclude this study, it is this outrageous paradox. I have often mulled over the question of what I, or anyone, can do to alert my fellow humans to the dangers at hand. No doubt it is pointless to appeal to higher principles by sermonising. There is an aphorism of Lao-Tzu, however, which strikes me as apposite in this case: Every problem on earth must ultimately come down to something as simple as 'frying a little fish'. I shall thus place my trust in the virtues of education, and assume that, in a democracy, my fellow citizens can and will exercise their intelligence – once they are in possession of the facts. How, then, to get the facts across?

Perhaps it would help to imagine what our lives would be like, in concrete terms, if the present drift of capitalism in Europe were allowed to continue and develop into full-blown Reaganism. The hypothesis is far from fanciful; Europe is Americanizing in more ways than financially and economically. The current runs deep, as revealed by a survey carried out by the consumer research center CREDOC in 1990. The results of this enquiry into the main changes in recent French behaviour, lifestyle and attitudes were published at the height of the Gulf crisis and thus barely earned a mention in the mass media. A pity, because CREDOC identified four fundamental changes:

1. Attitudes to money are now guilt-free: this, in France, is a decisive break with Catholic tradition, and brings us nearer to the Anglo-American world.
2. Individualism has triumphed: what CREDOC calls 'everyman for himself' is matched by a spectacular decline in group participation (trade unions, clubs, associations of every variety).
3. Social attitudes have hardened – notably in the workplace – and new factors of stress (linked to competition, fear of unemployment etc.) are on the rise.
4. Behaviour is becoming uniform: in particular, the gulf between Parisians and provincials is narrowing, thanks to the now-dominant influence of television.

There is much more to be said about these four conclusions, but what must be obvious is that together they point to a profound Americanization of French society. If our habits and thoughts have already been so thoroughly and so insidiously transformed, can the economy be very far behind?

An offer we can refuse

In order to convey what it would mean to the ordinary citizen if France were to adopt the neo-American model, let us imagine that the tax system were to be recast in the Reagan mould. Taxes, after all, are the foundation on which the state's power and wealth must rest. Without fiscal resources, the state can hardly pretend to regulate the market or protect the needy.

Say, then, that the rate of direct taxation in France, currently standing at 44.6 per cent of personal earnings, were to be reduced to the 30 per cent rate applicable in the USA. However one calculates it, this would be money withheld from the government and its many branches, and put back into our pockets. I estimate that on a yearly basis it would amount to FF 920 billion in all, or FF 16 400 per person. In other words, a family of four would find that they were better off by some FF 65 600 per year – the equivalent of the annual guaranteed minimum wage. It would seem to be an offer we could not refuse.

But would we really be better off? This tax windfall would have to be compensated for, sooner or later, by shifting the burden of a whole range of expenses from the community at large to the individual. A few examples follow.

Social welfare programs would naturally be the first to suffer. No longer would 80 per cent of the cost of drugs and treatments be automatically refunded; universal free access to hospitals and the most advanced medical techniques would become a thing of the past. Health would become a regular household expense, like rent and food. Accident victims would have to accept that emergency care could be withheld until their personal finances have been investigated, as in America. As for old-age pensions, the basic benefit might remain intact, but almost all supplementary pension schemes would be adversely affected since these, too, come out of compulsory contributions.

Education would have to change beyond recognition, since universal free schooling from kindergarten to university would be out of the question. Children would receive the schooling their parents could pay for, full stop. Higher education would become prohibitively expensive, as in the USA, and would become the privilege of the wealthy, plus a handful of scholarship winners.

Public transport would likewise come to resemble the American system, or lack thereof. The car would definitively supplant an increasingly outdated, uncomfortable and badly maintained public transport network, with a consequent worsening of traffic congestion, parking costs, pollution etc.

The quality of community facilities and the national infrastructure could not possibly be maintained at present levels. Governments strapped for cash do not assign a high priority to parks and wildlife areas, secondary roads and bridges, railway stations and airports. Never mind the aesthetic dimension, which would obviously suffer; the overall quality of such amenities would deteriorate, in spite of the fact that a first-rate infrastructure has been shown, in study after study, to be an important factor in determining the competitiveness of business and industry.

Social inequalities would deepen and become more dangerous for society as a whole. The wealthy would be wealthier, but the poor would not only be poorer, they would also be much more numerous. It is difficult to assess exactly what the consequences would be in terms of social disorder – violence, crime, drugs etc. – but they, too, would increase in number.

To give the neo-American model its due, the one area where some improvement might be noticed is in employment. France has, since the 1970s, been lamentably unsuccessful in putting the unemployed back to work, whereas Reagan was able to reduce American unemployment almost by half by reducing state benefits – thus forcing many people to accept unskilled and poorly paid jobs (notably in the booming security and property-protection business). The question of whether it is preferable for individuals to be in badly paid work or on the dole is at least debatable.

The list of examples could go on almost indefinitely, but the point is surely obvious: the change from one type of capitalism to another cannot be made without a host of other changes also ensuing, not all of them welcome or expected. The distinguishing feature of the neo-American model is that it deliberately sacrifices the future for the present; yet, in each of the areas examined above, quality and well-being are strictly tied to investment in the future. It is a wise society that understands the 'productive delay' of such investment.

We Europeans are, more than anyone else on the planet, faced with the question of which sacrifices we shall make, and for which gains. The European Community is the main battleground on which the conflict of capitalism against capitalism will be fought. Without presuming to see into the future, I maintain that we cannot have it both ways:

1. Either Europeans will fail to understand what is really at stake, and so will not press their leaders to make the imaginative leap towards true political union: in which case, the Single Market will begin to fray and disintegrate before it has begun; the possibility of unity will recede ever further under a cloud of permanent Euro-pessimism; the slide towards the neo-American model will accelerate as the zones of decay and deprivation already staked out on the periphery of our cities continue to swell; and we will be increasingly importuned by those in the old 'Third World' (the South) and the new (Eastern Europe and the former Soviet Union) who seek to enter our own, inner 'Third World' of American-style urban blight on the outskirts of Manchester or Lyons or Naples.
2. Or we will actually begin to build the United States of Europe: in which case, we will have all the means at our disposal to choose the best possible socioeconomic system, that which has already proven its mettle within one part of the continent and which will become the 'European model' of capitalism.

The United States of Europe can do better than the United States of America, if we put our minds to it. It is entirely up to us, each of us; after all, tomorrow will be decided today.